SO-CRS-778

LAVENTHOL & HORWATH

SMALL BUSINESS TAX PLANNING GUIDE

**Other Laventhol & Horwath Books
from Avon Books**

LAVENTHOL & HORWATH SMALL BUSINESS
TAX PREPARATION BOOK—1989 EDITION
by Albert B. Ellentuck

Avon Books are available at special quantity discounts for bulk purchases for sales promotions, premiums, fund raising or educational use. Special books, or book excerpts, can also be created to fit specific needs.

For details write or telephone the office of the Director of Special Markets, Avon Books, Dept. FP, 105 Madison Avenue, New York, New York 10016, 212-481-5653.

LAVENTHOL & HORWATH

SMALL BUSINESS TAX PLANNING GUIDE

Albert B. Ellentuck

AVON BOOKS ◆ NEW YORK

The author has attempted to ensure that all information in this book is accurate. However, errors can occur, rules and regulations regarding tax and other matters do vary from location to location and are changed from time to time. The final 1988 income tax forms and schedules and the updated official instructions had not yet been released by the Internal Revenue Service when this book was prepared. Therefore, the author and publisher disclaim responsibility for the complete accuracy of the text. And as is always mere common sense, the reader is cautioned to consult a qualified accountant or attorney regarding accounting or legal problems.

LAVENTHOL & HORWATH SMALL BUSINESS TAX PLANNING GUIDE is an original publication of Avon Books. This work has never before appeared in book form.

AVON BOOKS
A division of
The Hearst Corporation
105 Madison Avenue
New York, New York 10016

Copyright © 1988 by Laventhol & Horwath
Published by arrangement with Laventhol & Horwath and the author
Library of Congress Catalog Card Number: 88-92097
ISBN: 0-380-75618-8

All rights reserved, which includes the right to reproduce this book or portions thereof in any form whatsoever except as provided by the U.S. Copyright Law. For information address Helen Rees Literary Agency, 308 Commonwealth Avenue, Boston, Massachusetts 02116.

First Avon Books Trade Printing: December 1988

AVON TRADEMARK REG. U.S. PAT. OFF. AND IN OTHER COUNTRIES, MARCA REGISTRADA, HECHO EN U.S.A.

Printed in the U.S.A.

K-R 10 9 8 7 6 5 4 3 2 1

Acknowledgments

Special thanks to Marvin Greenberg, a partner in our San Diego office, and to the writers and editors at Wordworks. Thanks also to our very able editor, Linda Cunningham, and to Helen Rees, our friend and adviser.

The taxpayer—that's someone who works
for the federal government but doesn't have to take
a civil service examination.
—Ronald Reagan

CONTENTS

Chapter 1
FORGET THE CRYSTAL BALL
Tax Planning in Uncertain Times
1

Chapter 2
A FIRM FOUNDATION
Choosing the Right Form of Organization
for Your Business
5

Chapter 3
GOING IT ALONE
Why a Sole Proprietorship Could Be Right for You
13

Chapter 4
SIDE BY SIDE
Unlocking the Secrets of Partnerships
26

Chapter 5
TO INC. OR NOT TO INC.
So You Want to Be a Corporation
35

Chapter 6
WHAT'S IN A NAME?
S Corporation S Marvelous
50

ix

Chapter 7
THE NUMBERS GAME
Cashing In on Cash and Accrual Accounting
58

Chapter 8
THE PAPER CHASE
Understanding LIFO and FIFO
68

Chapter 9
SAFETY IN NUMBERS
Locking In Depreciation Deductions
73

Chapter 10
THE PROMISED LAND
How to Use Business Real Estate As a Tax Shelter
84

Chapter 11
HOME SWEET HOME
A Home Office Is Where the Deductions Are
90

Chapter 12
DRIVING FOR DOLLARS
The New Rules for Writing Off Business Cars
99

Chapter 13
MANY HAPPY RETURNS
Capturing Attractive Travel and Entertainment Deductions
107

Chapter 14
**THE MANNER OF GIVING IS WORTH
MORE THAN THE GIFT**
The Right Way to Write Off Business Gifts
123

Chapter 15
ADDING IT UP
How to Make Fringe Benefits Pay
129

Chapter 16
A HOUSE DIVIDED
Splitting Income to Slash Taxes
152

Chapter 17
WE'RE IN THE MONEY
Smart Retirement Planning
156

Chapter 18
NO FEAR OF FILING
Year-End Tax Planning
164

Chapter 19
I SPY
How the IRS Catches Unreported Income
169

Chapter 20
INFERNAL REVENUE SERVICE
Surviving an Audit
176

Bonus
**COMPLETE CHECKLIST OF OFFICIAL
IRS TAX INFORMATION**
185

INDEX
233

Chapter 1

FORGET THE CRYSTAL BALL

Tax Planning in Uncertain Times

Every accountant has a favorite story about income taxes, and I'm no exception. Mine goes something like this.

One day, back in the 1920s, an official-looking envelope was delivered to the London home of Joseph Conrad, the distinguished novelist and short story writer.

When it arrived, Conrad tossed it onto his desk, where it remained, unopened, for several weeks. In time, the British government dispatched a messenger to Conrad's home.

Why, the messenger inquired with some annoyance, hadn't Conrad responded to the British government's offer of knighthood? The answer, it turned out, was quite simple.

"I had been afraid to open it," Conrad replied. "I thought it was a tax notice."

Like Conrad, most of us—even if we have absolutely nothing to worry about—fear the clutches of the Internal Revenue Service.

Our concern, by and large, stems from ignorance: we don't know precisely what we're up against—and that's the way the IRS wants it. If we're trembling in our boots, the agency figures, we'll stay honest. In reality, though, fear only causes us not to claim the deductions to which we're genuinely entitled.

And the government never intended it that way.

As the noted jurist Learned Hand pointed out: "There is nothing sinister in so arranging one's affairs as to keep taxes as low as possible. Everyone does so, rich or poor. And all do right, for nobody owes any public duty to pay more than the law demands."

WHY PLAN AHEAD?

There's only one way to guarantee that you pay no more in

1

taxes than you should: you must engage in some solid, nuts-and-bolts tax planning.

You may do the work yourself or pay someone to do it for you. But whether or not you enlist the aid of an outsider, you should understand the basic provisions of the tax code. Just as you would not turn over the management of your money to another person, you should not blindly allow someone else to take complete charge of your taxpaying responsibilities.

Know the basics of the tax system. It's in your own best interest.

KNOWLEDGE IS POWER

"Easy enough for you to say," I can hear you grumble.

And it's true that no less a person than Albert Einstein once noted that "the hardest thing in the world to understand is the income tax."

But fear not. The difficulty most of us have in comprehending the U.S. tax system is more a problem of style than substance. The government loves to couch its dictates in official-sounding gobbledygook. Moreover, while the IRS happily imparts the basics, it's less likely to provide you with information about available—and perfectly legal—tax breaks.

That's where this volume comes in. *Laventhol & Horwath Small Business Tax Planning Guide* is a complete up-to-date handbook of business tax planning. It explains in plain English how to slash—legally and honestly—your tax liability. And, unlike other tax planning books, it is written specifically for you—the small business owner or professional.

WHO WE ARE

Laventhol & Horwath was founded in 1915. By 1928, we were a national firm with a growing reputation as the small and midsize businessperson's accountant.

With more than fifty offices and thousands of business clients nationwide, Laventhol & Horwath today ranks among the country's largest and most respected accounting firms. We are also among the fastest growing of the big CPA partnerships.

Since 1981, our revenues have more than quadrupled. So we know—from firsthand experience—what it means to run a dynamic business.

These days, our clients include some of the biggest names in corporate America, but our specialty remains small and midsize companies and individual professionals. Each year, we prepare in excess of 75,000 income tax returns for businesses that range from fast-track entrepreneurial companies to one-person shops.

AUTHOR! AUTHOR!
I'm a senior tax partner at Laventhol & Horwath.

I've just completed a ten-year stint as national tax partner, which means I was in charge of the firm's entire range of tax planning and preparation services.

I have also served as tax division chairman of the American Institute of Certified Public Accountants, a national professional organization.

By education and training, I'm both an accountant and an attorney. (I hold an accounting degree from New York University and a law degree from Harvard Law School.)

But here's something else you should know about me.

Before joining Laventhol & Horwath, I worked for the IRS for a full six years in several of its corporate income tax divisions. So I know the agency from the inside.

HOW TO USE THIS BOOK
We've designed this book to make it easy to use and easy to understand. First, we tell you what you need to know to build a solid base for sound tax planning. Then we clarify—with examples and actual cases—the vital sections of the tax code, so you can map out your own dollar-saving tax strategies. You'll learn, for example, the ins and outs of travel and entertainment deductions, the right way to plan for retirement, and the latest word on fringe benefits.

Scattered throughout each chapter are a number of special features. In "TaxTips" we provide specific strategies for paring down your tax bill. In "TaxTraps" we alert you to little-known rules and regulations that may, if you aren't careful, cost you hundreds of dollars in extra taxes. In "FYI" we offer intriguing and useful nuggets of information. We also tell you which tax forms you must file to report, say, income from a partnership.

At the end of each chapter is a section called "For More Information." Here, we list publications—available free from the IRS—that are relevant to each chapter. Copies are easy to obtain. All you have to do is write the IRS Forms Distribution Center for your state at the address shown in the chart printed in the last chapter. Use these same addresses to obtain tax forms.

Also in "For More Information" are listings for Tele-Tax, a telephone service that provides taped information on about 150 subjects. Taxpayers using a push-button telephone can call Tele-Tax twenty-four hours a day, seven days a week. Those with a rotary (dial) phone can use the service during normal business hours. Instructions on how to use Tele-Tax, as well as a list of required phone numbers, may also be found in the last chapter.

BACK TO THE FUTURE

One last word: many businesspeople and professionals think that it's futile to learn anything about the tax system. Why? "As soon as I figure out one set of rules," they say, "the entire code will be turned upside-down again. So why bother?"

The reason is simple. The changes Congress has adopted to date have done no more than fine-tune the tax system. Even with the so-called major reform of the Tax Reform Act of 1986, the basic structure of the U.S. Tax Code remains the same.

Take the laws governing depreciation. Despite the "reforms" in this area, little more than the length of time you take to write off equipment has changed. The principle underlying the concept of depreciation—that the equipment you buy is "consumed" or used up over the period you own it—still holds true. And that's only one example out of hundreds.

So, while it's as certain as—yes, death and taxes—that our lawmakers will continue to tinker with the tax code, that's no reason to ignore tax planning. You can master the basics with the certainty that these fundamentals won't change dramatically from one year to the next. Once you've mastered the basics, you'll find yourself at year's end with a lot more money in your pocket—not Uncle Sam's.

Believe me. Forewarned, as far as taxes are concerned, is indeed forearmed. The small investment in time you make now in reading this book will be repaid amply at filing time in hundreds—perhaps even thousands—of dollars in tax savings.

So let's get started.

Chapter 2

A FIRM FOUNDATION

Choosing the Right Form of Organization for Your Business

The first step in tax planning—for small business owners and professionals, at least—is to select the right form of organization for your enterprise.

The choice is up to you. But a word of warning: you'll end up paying radically different amounts of income tax depending on the form you select. And your odds of being audited by the IRS will change, too.

Of course, before you settle on a form of organization, you need to know some fundamental distinctions. To begin with, it doesn't matter whether you operate a tiny cheese shop, run a huge textile mill, or moonlight as a magician. Your business must take one of four forms. You must organize your enterprise as a sole proprietorship, a partnership, a corporation, or an S corporation.

SOLE PROPRIETORSHIP

With a sole (or individual) proprietorship, one person owns the enterprise. In fact, in the eyes of the IRS, the owner *is* the business.

You may pick a fancy name for your proprietorship—Worldwide Financial Advisers, say, or Marketing Consultants of America. You may even use the word "company" in your title and have employees. But when profits and losses come in, they are still recorded on your personal income tax return. You pay no separate, federal business income tax.

The liabilities of a business organized as a sole proprietorship are the liabilities of its owner, so personal assets may be seized to satisfy business debts.

We all know—or have heard of—people who went into business for themselves, then lost everything when their enterprises went belly up. Chances are, these individuals operated their companies as sole proprietorships or partnerships.

―――――――――――――――――――― **FYI** ――――――――――――――――――――

Proprietorships are by far the most common form of business organization. They dominate both the retail industry and agriculture.

All told, some 5 million enterprises—or more than 50 percent of the country's businesses—operate as sole proprietorships. They post annual sales in excess of $500 billion, a figure that equals a little more than 7.1 percent of all U.S. business receipts.

PARTNERSHIP

My favorite definition of a partnership comes from Jim Fisk and Robert Barron, authors of the tongue-in-cheek reference, *Buzzwords—The Official MBA Dictionary.* A partnership, they pun, is a "merchant vessel prone to collision with other ships in bad weather, especially friendships."

The IRS definition is, as one might expect, somewhat less colorful. A partnership, Uncle Sam maintains, is simply two or more people who agree, either verbally or in writing, to carry on a business. Each person contributes money, labor, or skill to the enterprise and expects to share in its profits and losses.

Profits and losses from a partnership are distributed pro rata among the partners, unless the partnership agreement specifies that the income or losses be divided some other way. Income from a partnership is treated just like income from a proprietorship. That is, it is reported on the partners' personal income tax returns.

But a partnership, because it involves more people, is necessarily far more complicated than a proprietorship. Adding to its complexity is the fact that a partnership can include two types of partners—general and limited.

General partners are personally liable for all company debts—just as if they were sole proprietors. If a partnership goes bust, these general partners may have to sell their houses, cars, and other personal assets to satisfy their company's creditors.

Limited partners, on the other hand, enjoy virtually complete protection from liability. They are seldom held personally responsible for any debts of the business beyond the amount that they have invested or—and this is the sticky part—promised to invest.

_____ **CASE IN POINT** _____

Say you purchase an interest in a research-and-development limited partnership and agree to kick in $35,000 phased in over three years. In year one, you contribute $10,000, and, in year two, $15,000. Then, with virtually no warning, the company goes belly up.

Here's how your losses add up: You're out the $25,000 you invested to date. But you also must fork over the $10,000 you promised to invest in year three—for a total loss of $35,000. The money goes to satisfy the partnership's creditors.

_____ **FYI** _____

Partnerships, the IRS says, are the third most popular form of business organization, behind sole proprietorships and corporations.

U.S. partnerships number more than 1.7 million and equal about 17 percent of the nation's business enterprises. Their sales top $271 billion each year—a number that accounts for some 3.8 percent of the country's total business receipts.

CORPORATION

A corporation, cynic Ambrose Bierce once noted, is "an ingenious device for obtaining individual profit without individual responsibility."

He wasn't far off the mark.

Under the law, owners of corporations are absolved from any personal responsibility for the liabilities of their companies. A corporation is, in fact, completely separate from its owners: it figures its own deductions, files its own returns, and pays its own taxes.

It—like you and me—is a bona fide taxpayer.

Money is taken out of a corporation only in the form of salaries and dividends. Salaries are deducted by the corporation as ordinary business expenses. Dividends are not, and, as a result, they are taxed twice—once at the corporate level as corporate earnings, then again as personal income when the money is paid out to shareholders.

Since a corporation is established under the various laws of each state, the procedures for creating this form of organization vary enormously, as do the costs.

_____ FYI _____

At present, some 2.6 million corporations are operating in this country. They account for only 26 percent of all U.S. businesses. However, they dominate America's economic landscape in one key respect: their revenues—more than $6.1 trillion annually—add up to 86 percent of all business sales.

S CORPORATION

Owners of S corporations have the best of both worlds. They pay taxes like proprietors and partners. That is, they generally pay no separate, federal business income tax. But their owners enjoy the protection of an ordinary corporation and bear virtually no personal responsibility for the liabilities of their businesses.

_____ FYI _____

S corporations number nearly 737,000 and account for less than 1 percent of American businesses. Their sales exceed $210 billion a year or about 3 percent of the country's total business receipts. They are the least common form of organization.

ALL MIXED UP

You may also divide your business into logical segments and adopt a different form of organization for each.

_____ CASE IN POINT _____

Say you own a small realty company. You devote half your time to selling houses and half to managing the rental properties you own.

You decide to incorporate your sales operation. The reason? You want to protect yourself from liability should a customer file suit against you for, say, misrepresentation.

At the same time, you decide to continue to operate your rental business as a sole proprietorship. Why? You want to capture real estate tax breaks on your personal income tax return.

IT'S BETTER TO KNOW SOME OF THE QUESTIONS THAN ALL OF THE ANSWERS

After learning the basics comes the tricky part—choosing the correct form of organization for your enterprise. Alas, with few exceptions, there is no single recommended business form. You must base your selection on your individual circumstances. And, as those circumstances change, you must reexamine your choice of organization with both business and tax issues clearly in mind.

In the next four chapters, we'll take a hard look at each form of organization by analyzing the fourteen key issues that every businessperson should examine before making a selection. Following is a list of these issues, along with some important questions to ask yourself. Read through the questions carefully, then jot down your answers.

As you'll discover, your responses to these questions will determine, in large measure, which form of organization is right for you.

Capital
- Is your business capitalized with funds from outside investors?
- If so, how much management control do these investors now exercise?
- How much do you want them to exercise?
- Are you planning to go public?

Complexity
- Is it important to you that paperwork be kept to a minimum?

Control
- Do you need complete freedom to make your own decisions?
- At what point do you consider you have too little control?

Cost
- Can you afford the added costs that you may incur if you choose a complicated form of organization?

Flexibility
- Do you now take money out of your business at will?
- Would limiting this ability to draw on your company accounts present problems for you?

Liability
- Is it critical for you to protect your personal resources from debts or other claims against your company?

Life
- Do you want a form of organization that will make it easy for you to pass on your company to your heirs?

Losses
- Is your business losing money?
- Do you have other income that you could offset by claiming business losses on your personal tax return?

Ownership
- How many owners does your company have?
- Does ownership of your company change frequently?
- Do you want to transfer ownership of your business to your employees or family members?
- Are you planning to merge with another company?
- Is an acquisition in the offing?

Perks
- List the fringe benefits that you now provide to yourself. Which of these benefits do you write off on your tax return?
- Is it important that you provide yourself with the maximum number of deductible fringe benefits possible?

Privacy
- When seeking capital for your business, do you usually reveal the extent of your personal assets to bankers and potential investors?
- Does this invasion of privacy present a problem for you?

Shelter
- Does your company pay out most of its earnings to you?
- Does your company need to hold onto a portion of its profits to finance growth?
- Do you want—or need—to shelter a portion of your income in your business?

Taxes
- If your business is organized as a proprietorship or a partnership, what is your marginal tax rate?
- If your business is incorporated, what is your company's marginal tax rate? (You'll find tax tables that list marginal rates at the back of this book.)
- Does your company receive passive income, such as rents, royalties, and interest?
- How much Social Security tax do you now pay?

Year
- Does your fiscal year mirror the calendar year?

With your answers in mind, you're ready to take a closer look at the forms of organization. First, though, time out for an important piece of information.

Predictably, one of the questions our clients ask us most often is, "What are my chances of being audited by the IRS?" The answer, as you might expect, depends on the form of organization you choose as well as the amount of money you earn.

The following table contains the latest statistics from the IRS. The numbers are taken from the 1986 annual report of the IRS Commissioner.

Your Odds of Being Audited

Type	Audited
Sole Proprietorships	
Less than $25,000 in income	1.33%
$25,000 to $100,000	2.24
$100,000 or more	4.68
Partnerships	1.00
Corporations	
Less than $50,000 in assets	0.75
$50,000 to $100,000	1.49
$100,000 to $250,000	1.46
$250,000 to $500,000	1.34
$500,000 to $1 million	1.88
$1 million to $5 million	4.71
$5 million to $10 million	12.81
$10 million to $50 million	23.87
$50 million to $100 million	47.55
$100 million to $250 million	71.13
More than $250 million	78.05
S Corporations	1.08

FOR MORE INFORMATION
See these IRS publications:

- *Tax Information on Partnerships* (Number 541)
- *Tax Information on Corporations* (Number 542)
- *Tax Information on S Corporations* (Number 589)
- *Your Federal Income Tax* (Number 17)
- *Tax Guide for Small Business* (Number 334)

- *Farmers' Tax Guide* (Number 225)
- *Tax Guide for Commercial Fishermen* (Number 595)
- *Tax Information for Direct Sellers* (Number 911)

Try these IRS Tele-Tax tapes:

- *Business Income* (Number 136)
- *Sole Proprietorship Income* (Number 137)
- *Rental Income and Expenses* (Number 143)
- *Farming or Fishing Income* (Number 202)
- *Small Business Tax Workshops—Tax Help for the New Businessperson* (Number 102)

Chapter 3

GOING IT ALONE

Why a Sole Proprietorship Could Be Right for You

Let's go straight to the heart of the matter. How do sole proprietorships stack up against other forms of business organization? Our analysis—arranged alphabetically by the fourteen major issues we outlined in the previous chapter—follows.

CAPITAL

J. B. Fuqua, founder of Fuqua Industries Inc., a giant Atlanta conglomerate, maintains that there are two keys to unlocking entrepreneurial success—OPB and OPM.

OPB stands for "Other People's Brains."

OPM stands for "Other People's Money."

If you plan to use OPM to capitalize your small company, we advise you to steer clear of the proprietorship form of organization.

A sole proprietorship is, as its name suggests, a one-man or one-woman show. By definition, its ownership may not be shared with outside investors. As a result, sole proprietors must capitalize their small businesses with borrowed funds or with their own savings.

COMPLEXITY

The sole proprietorship form is so popular, in part, because you need do nothing to create one. In fact, many people operate as proprietorships by default.

Here's why: The minute you accept money for, say, setting up the books for a friend's business, you are—in the eyes of the government—operating a proprietorship.

─────────────── **CASE IN POINT** ───────────────

You're employed as a salesperson for a large oil company, and a neighbor asks you to write a marketing plan for his new auto parts business.

You agree and receive a $3,000 fee. You deposit the money in the bank. You may not know it, but from that moment on, you are the proprietor of your own business.

And you must fill out and file an additional form—Schedule C, "Profit (or Loss) From Business or Profession" and Schedule SE, "Self-Employment Tax"—with your income tax return.

CONTROL

Some people want to be in complete control of their business enterprises. If you're one of them, the sole proprietorship form could be right for you.

With proprietorships, business owners have absolute authority. Their ability to make decisions is checked neither by partnership agreements nor by state laws governing corporations.

─────────────── **CASE IN POINT** ───────────────

As the owner of a small printing company, you, along with a competitor, are offered an equity interest in a promising new regional magazine. In exchange, you must print the publication at cost for two years.

You operate as a sole proprietorship. Your competitor is a corporation with more than a dozen shareholders.

Even though your company is much smaller, you have the upper hand over your rival. As a proprietor, you call your own shots. So you quickly tell the magazine's owners to count you in. After all, the owners have an impeccable track record.

Meanwhile the president of the other printing company is left spinning his wheels. He needs the approval of his board before he can enter into an agreement, and two of his four board members are out of town on business. He can only watch in frustration while you lock up a lucrative deal.

COST

Running your business as a proprietorship helps keep overhead low. Proprietorships generally require less paperwork than partnerships or corporations.

For example, you don't need to do two separate tax returns—one for you and one for your corporation—so you save yourself extra accountant's fees. (Since you must, however, prepare a Schedule C form, your return will be more complicated than an employee's.) You also avoid the costs associated with incorporation. Legal bills for setting up a corporation can run $100 to $750 or more. In addition, there are hefty filing fees to pay.

TAXTIP

Many sole proprietors pay their business expenses with checks written on personal bank accounts. Our advice: Maintain a separate account for your company. This separate account will make it easier to keep tabs on business income and expenses and to substantiate deductions if the IRS audits your return.

FLEXIBILITY

A sole proprietorship gives you complete flexibility to operate your business as you see fit. You don't need permission from partners or shareholders to expand or go into another line of business.

Another plus of the proprietorship form: you may draw money from your business bank accounts any time you need cash.

With a regular corporation, it's a different story. Under the law, money may be withdrawn by a corporation's owners only in the form of salaries and dividends.

LIABILITY

Clearly, the biggest drawback to operating as a sole proprietor is that you are 100 percent responsible for the liabilities of your business. Your personal assets may be seized to satisfy business debts—bank loans, accounts payable, and so on—or legal claims against you.

Our advice: If you're in a risky business, such as chemical distribution or hazardous waste disposal, operate as a corporation or an S corporation, not as a sole proprietorship.

LIFE

A sole proprietorship ceases to exist when its owner dies. So you may not leave your business—as an entity—to your heirs. You may bequeath only company assets to them. But that's good news.

Here's why: When you die, your assets are appraised for estate-tax purposes at their fair-market values. If your heirs sell these assets later on, they are taxed on profits from the sale. These profits are calculated by subtracting the value of each asset at the time it was inherited from its selling price.

The plus? When your heirs sell, they are not taxed on the amount an asset appreciated during your lifetime—only on the difference between its value at your death and the selling price.

LOSSES

If you operate your business as a sole proprietorship and fail to make money, your losses are fully deductible on your personal tax return.

Also, you may use losses in one year to offset income in prior and subsequent years. Under the rules, your loss may be carried backward three years and forward fifteen years. Most taxpayers carry losses backward first, then carry any remaining losses forward. If you carry losses forward first, you lose the right to carry them back.

Remember, though, business losses that are carried backward or forward are offset by income you receive from other sources in the year the loss occurs.

_____ **CASE IN POINT** _____

Say your sole proprietorship reports a $50,000 loss in 1989. But, on your personal tax return, you also record $13,000 in dividend income.

From this dividend income, you subtract your personal tax deductions—$7,000 in state and local property taxes, mortgage interest expenses, and so on. The result: You have taxable income from other sources of $6,000.

Under the rules, you may carry forward or backward only a $44,000 loss (that is, your $50,000 business loss less your $6,000 in taxable income from other sources).

Of course, if your income from other sources matches or exceeds your business loss, you may not carry forward or backward any of the loss. But you still win, because you use your business loss to offset income you receive from other sources during the current year.

Another cautionary note: You must be prepared to show that you were legitimately attempting to make money. Losses you incur pursuing hobbies are not deductible.

And, believe me, the IRS watches out for people who constantly report taking a bath as operators of tiny farms, for instance, or as breeders of show dogs.

The agency decides whether your enterprise is a bona fide business—or a tax dodge—under section 183 of the Internal Revenue Code. Known as the "hobby-loss rules," section 183 considers a business profit-oriented if it reports taxable earnings in three of any five consecutive years.

In the case of breeding, training, showing, or racing horses, the Internal Revenue Code requires that a profit be made in any two of seven consecutive years.

The regulations list nine factors that must be weighed in determining whether or not an individual or company is engaged in an activity for profit. The IRS must consider:

- The manner in which you conduct your business

You should—obviously—operate your business in a business-like way. And that includes maintaining a complete set of books.

- Your finances and other sources of income

If you are a high-bracket taxpayer and claim large losses, the IRS may suspect that you are engaged in an activity solely to capture tax write-offs—especially if the activity is of a recreational nature.

- Your expertise

If you know little about the activity in which you are engaged and don't seek outside counsel, the IRS may question your profit motive.

- The time you devote to the business

The more hours you spend on your business, the easier it is to establish that you were trying to make a profit.

- The expectation that the assets used in your business will appreciate in value

Say you purchase a small apartment building. With interest and depreciation deductions, you report a loss for the year. But the property is appreciating at some 15 percent annually, so you expect to make a killing when you unload it.

In this instance, you'd pass the test.

- Your success in other similar activities

If you've made money in much the same kind of venture in the past, your business is more likely to be viewed as profit-making.

- Your history of profits and losses

You're inviting trouble from Uncle Sam if you claim business losses year after year.

Don't worry if your business is drowning in red ink during its initial or start-up phase. Such losses are expected. However, the IRS may question your profit motive if you continue to operate in the red long past the time when similar businesses have turned a profit.

There is a way around this rule—if your losses are due to circumstances beyond your control, such as drought, fire, theft, or depressed market conditions.

- The amount of earnings you report

You're in hot water if you report only a small occasional profit from an activity that generates big losses.

- The element of recreation involved

If you devote only your off-hours to the activity and it is of a recreational nature—such as fly-fishing—watch out. (The rules contained in section 183 of the code apply not only to sole proprietorships but to partnerships, corporations, and S corporations as well.)

————————————— **TAXTRAP** —————————————

The losses you claim on your personal tax return are limited by the government's "at-risk" rules. These regulations allow you to write off losses only to the extent that your losses do not exceed your "total at-risk investment."

Here's how the IRS defines an at-risk investment:

- Cash you have contributed to your company
- Plus money you have borrowed for your business—but only those funds for which you are personally liable
- Plus your basis in property and equipment that you have contributed to your business

Your basis—and this is a fundamental concept in the tax law—is the original cost of property or equipment purchased for your company less any depreciation you have claimed.

————————————— **CASE IN POINT** —————————————

Say you pay $45,000 for three delivery vans. You make a

down payment of $2,000 out of your own pocket and finance the remaining $43,000 at a local bank.

The loan is a nonrecourse one, meaning it is secured only by the vans. If you're unable to make your payments, the bank may seize your vehicles—but nothing else.

Under the rules, then, you are at risk only for the $2,000 down payment. You are not at risk for the remaining $43,000, because you are not obligated to repay the loan.

The one exception to the at-risk rules: In the case of real estate investments financed by someone other than the seller, you may write off losses that are greater than the amount you have at risk.

—————————————— **FYI** ——————————————

It is not unusual for a new company to post a loss. It is also not unusual for a business awash in red ink to rebound—in a very big way.

A few examples to consider:
- R. H. Macy's first three department stores went belly up.
- Coca-Cola sold only 400 bottles of its soft drink during its initial year of operation.
- Henry Ford filed for bankruptcy twice before he opened his third automobile business—Ford Motor Co.
- King Gillette sold a mere 51 razors and 168 blades in 1903, the year he invented the safety razor.
- Paul Galvin failed twice with his storage-battery business before he established Motorola.

OWNERSHIP

A proprietorship is the property of only one person. Its ownership cannot be shared with anyone—and that includes a proprietor's employees and children.

As we've seen, bequeathing a sole proprietorship as an entity is impossible. Selling one can also be complicated.

—————————————— **CASE IN POINT** ——————————————

You decide to sell your fourteen-year-old sporting goods store—Sam's Place. But federal law does not recognize a proprietorship as a separate legal entity.

Therefore, you're not selling Sam's Place as a whole.

You're selling its parts—its inventory, equipment, good-will, accounts receivable, and so on.

Should you sell everything, you'd calculate the value of each individual part. Then the proceeds from the sale of each item would be taxed differently. For example, your gain from the sale of inventory would be taxed to you as ordinary income, but the gain from the sale of land held for more than one year would be taxed as a long-term capital gain.

A corporation, a partnership, or an S corporation, on the other hand, is a legal entity. So, if Sam's Place were organized as any one of these three, the law would treat its sale as the sale of stock or a partnership interest. And as the owner of Sam's Place, you would ordinarily benefit from capital gains treatment on the entire sale.

_____ **TAXTIP** _____

If you operate your business as a sole proprietorship and are married, consider forming a general partnership and making your spouse a working partner. Your spouse may then participate in your company's retirement or profit-sharing plan and qualify for his or her own Social Security benefits.

PERKS

No doubt about it, operating as a proprietor does involve some painful trade-offs. Here's an example: Sole proprietors may not deduct as an ordinary business expense the cost of life or disability insurance for themselves. Also, they may write off as a business expense only 25 percent of their medical insurance policies. (Uncle Sam provides a special line on Form 1040 for writing off these insurance premiums.)

They may, however, write off the full cost of these policies for employees, which is one reason most companies are willing to provide this insurance coverage for workers.

Another reason: Providing insurance to employees allows proprietors to participate in a group insurance plan, which costs proprietors much less than an individual policy. (See chapter 15 for a discussion of fringe benefits.)

Retirement plans for sole proprietors are now subject to the same high ceiling as plans for corporations—a major change from the old days. Nowadays, benefits from a defined-benefit Keogh plan are limited to $90,000 or 100 percent of compensation, whichever is less. The cap on contributions to a defined-contribution Keogh plan is $30,000 or 25 percent of compensation, again, whichever is less.

As for profit-sharing plans that serve as retirement programs, they are subject to a whole set of special regulations. Among these rules: Contributions to profit-sharing plans may not exceed 15 percent of the average compensation of your entire workforce or 25 percent of any one employee's earnings. (See chapter 17 for more on retirement planning.)

_____ **TAXTIPS** _____

If you have the option, work for someone else part-time until you get your business up and running. Then your part-time employer can pick up your medical, life, and disability insurance tab.

Also, don't forget to deduct the medical insurance premiums you pay on your personal tax return—if your premiums, plus all other medical expenses, exceed 7.5 percent of your adjusted gross income.

PRIVACY

When proprietors apply for bank loans, they are asked for financial statements. Because, as a proprietor, you are not legally separate from your business, those statements almost always include a list of personal assets—everything from the furniture in your den to the ring on your finger.

To a great many businesspeople, this request is an unacceptable violation of privacy. It's also a pain in the neck to comply with.

Incorporating your business or forming a partnership does not necessarily help you escape this intrusion. Owners of businesses with revenues of less than $500,000 and start-ups are often asked for personal financial statements when they apply for business loans.

Whether or not a lender will ask about your personal assets is determined more by the size and stability of your business operation than by its form of organization.

SHELTER

If the net income from your business adds up to less than $75,000 a year, operating as a proprietorship may mean you're passing up tax-saving opportunities that a corporation could provide. A corporation pays less tax than a proprietorship on the first $75,000 of income. (See chapter 5 for more information on corporate tax rates.)

Just keep in mind that income is trapped inside a corporation—that is, you pay an additional tax on it at the personal level when it is withdrawn.

TAXES

Paradoxically, one of the primary drawbacks of operating a business as a sole proprietorship is also one of its chief advantages—business income is recorded on your personal tax return.

There is no corporate income tax form to file and no corporate tax to pay. You are taxed only once on your profits.

Another important feature: Sole proprietors are taxed on the amount of money their businesses actually earn, not on the amount they withdraw from their companies.

————————— CASE IN POINT —————————

As a house painter, your revenues total about $30,000 a year. Periodically, you transfer money from your business bank account to your personal account.

You use the cash for a variety of personal and business purposes: you pay household bills, buy groceries, fill up the car with gasoline, even purchase paint.

Under the law, when you write a check to yourself on your business account, the money is not treated as wages and recorded as taxable income to you. So, at the end of the year, you pay taxes not on the total of the checks that you have written to yourself but on the amount your business earns after you deduct your costs.

Sole proprietors pay capital-gains taxes at the same rates as an individual taxpayer. In 1987, the maximum capital-gains rate was 28 percent, but in 1988, with the 5-percent surtax, the rate on capital gains goes as high as 33 percent. The same holds true for 1989.

Also, as a proprietor, you pay lower Social Security tax (or self-employment tax, as it is called) on your earnings than you would as the owner of a corporation. The 1988 rate for a sole proprietor is 13.02 percent on earnings up to $45,000. For a corporation, it is 15.02 percent on an individual's income up to $45,000.

But this savings is illusory.

Here's why: Half the Social Security taxes levied on a corporation are paid by employees and half by the corporation itself. The portion of Social Security taxes paid by the corporation (7.51 percent) may be deducted by the corporation. By contrast, none of the Social Security taxes paid by proprietors may be deducted.

_____ CASE IN POINT _____

Say you're a plumbing contractor and operate your business as a sole proprietorship. Your taxable income from the business is $150,000.

Your 1988 self-employment tax, therefore, would total $5,859 (that is, $45,000—the maximum self-employment income subject to taxation—times 13.02 percent).

If you incorporated and took a salary of $45,000, your Social Security tax liability would be higher—$6,759 ($45,000 times 15.02 percent).

But you would pay half that amount ($3,379.50) through payroll withholding, and your corporation would pay the other 50 percent. Then it would deduct that amount on its tax return.

Since your corporation is paying income tax at the maximum marginal corporate rate of 39 percent, 39 cents of every dollar goes to the government. So, for every dollar you write off, you save 39 cents in taxes.

In this case, your corporate income tax liability would be reduced by $1,318 by deducting $3,379.50 in Social Security taxes (39 percent times $3,379.50 equals $1,318).

The result: Your actual Social Security cost is $5,441 (the $6,759 you pay minus your tax savings of $1,318). This amount contrasts with the $5,859 ($45,000 times 15.02 percent) you'd pay as a sole proprietor.

Of course, both these tax bills are considerably higher than they would be if you worked for somebody else. Since an employer pays half an employee's Social Security, the employee is responsible for only 7.51 percent.

In 1989, the self-employment tax rate becomes twice the Social Security rate for employees. But if you're self-employed, you'll be able to deduct half the tax from your earnings. So the net effect will be almost the same for a self-employed person as for a corporation.

_____ TAXTRAP _____

Sole proprietors, beware. With changes in the tax law, you're more likely than ever before of finding yourself subject to the alternative minimum tax (AMT).

What is the AMT?

It's the part of the tax code that says, in effect: Every individual and corporation is going to pay *some* tax on their income even if, by the usual rules, they owe little or nothing. The tax is an attempt—largely successful—to insure that taxpayers who take perfectly legal deductions to minimize their tax bills won't avoid paying taxes altogether.

Think of the AMT as a completely different tax system. First you figure your taxes under the normal tax code. Then you refigure them under a different set of rules.

What you get is something called the tentative minimum tax (TMT). If the TMT is greater than your normal tax, the difference between the two is your AMT. This, generally speaking, is the amount you'll pay on top of your normal tax, if any.

The only way to know positively if you're subject to this tax is to do the calculations. But if you took a substantial number of write-offs on your personal return, you should check with your tax adviser.

YEAR

Owners of proprietorships, unlike owners of regular corporations, don't have the option of electing a fiscal year that differs from the calendar year—a disadvantage in some cases.

CASE IN POINT

Suppose you set up shop in October 1988. In your first three months of operation, your revenues total $30,000 and your expenses $5,000.

In your second three months of operation, the exact opposite occurs. Your revenues dip to $5,000 and your expenses climb to $30,000.

After six months, your business breaks even.

As a proprietor, you'd be required to file a return in early 1988 and pay taxes on your taxable earnings—$25,000 ($30,000 minus $5,000)—during your first three months.

If you incorporated, however, you'd be off the hook. You could elect a fiscal year that began October 1 and ended September 30. (This scenario assumes that your corporation is not an S corporation or a so-called personal-service corporation and, thus, may still use a fiscal year. A personal-service corporation is, as its name suggests, a corporation whose sole purpose is to provide services, rather than products. Corporations that qualify include those made up of lawyers, doctors, or accountants. For more information on personal-service corporations, see chapter 5. For more information on S corporations, see chapter 6.)

You wouldn't have to file a tax return until after the close of your fiscal year. And you wouldn't have to pay income taxes on your first-quarter "profit." Your business would have the use of your money, not Uncle Sam.

BOTTOM LINE

Because they are so easy to set up and maintain, sole proprietorships are perfect for small one-person businesses and for people who moonlight.

Sole proprietorships are also simpler for businesses that are operating in the red, since proprietors include business losses on their personal tax returns. These losses offset income from other sources, and that helps sole proprietors slash their overall income tax liabilities.

This form of organization is right, too, for attorneys and physicians, since the law specifically exempts these professionals from the liability shield of a corporation in malpractice cases.

As a rule, though, individuals who need protection from liability beyond what they can obtain from insurance should not operate their businesses as sole proprietorships, no matter how small their enterprises.

FOR MORE INFORMATION

See these IRS publications:

- *Your Federal Income Tax* (Number 17)
- *Tax Guide for Small Business* (Number 334)
- *Farmers' Tax Guide* (Number 225)
- *Tax Guide for Commercial Fishermen* (Number 595)
- *Tax Information for Direct Sellers* (Number 911)

Try these IRS Tele-Tax tapes:

- *Business Income* (Number 136)
- *Sole Proprietorship Income* (Number 137)
- *Rental Income and Expenses* (Number 143)
- *Farming and Fishing Income* (Number 202)
- *Self-Employment Tax* (Number 300)
- *Small Business Tax Workshops—Tax Help for the New Businessperson* (Number 102)

Chapter 4

SIDE BY SIDE

Unlocking the Secrets of Partnerships

"I'm proud to be paying taxes in the United States," Arthur Godfrey once quipped. "The only thing is—I could be just as proud for half the money."

So, it seems, could a lot of other people.

But how do you pare down your tax liability? For many business owners, the partnership form of organization is the place to start.

In practice, taxation of a general partnership is identical to taxation of a proprietorship. Partners report their share of the partnership's profit or loss directly on their income tax returns. But partnerships are more flexible than proprietorships or corporations.

Smart business owners take advantage of that flexibility. They create partnerships tailored to meet specialized needs by bringing together both general and limited partners in a single business enterprise.

In this chapter, we'll explain how small business owners and professionals make limited partnerships pay. We'll also see how partnerships compare with other forms of organization.

CAPITAL

For the most part, partnerships are capitalized with money that is borrowed or contributed by the general or limited partners.

As we've already seen, general partners are fully responsible for the liabilities of their business, but limited partners are not.

The limited partners are legally responsible for the debts of the partnership only to the extent of their actual investment and any other commitments that they may have made, such as the promise to contribute more money. That one rule has opened the door for thousands of small business owners to use limited partnerships as tools for raising capital.

CASE IN POINT

Say your dream is to start a radio station in your hometown. You have the credentials for the job but not the cash.

You form a partnership and list yourself as the general partner. That means management control remains firmly in your hands.

You then sell 10 limited-partnership interests at $25,000 a piece. The investment entitles each partner to a 5 percent interest in the station.

In its first year of business, your station operates in the red. Half the losses are passed on to the limited partners.

They report these losses on their personal tax returns. The amounts offset their other passive income—meaning income from businesses in which they do not actively participate—and enable them to slash their tax liabilities.

In the second year of operation, your radio station posts a profit. That money is credited to the capital accounts of the limited partners.

The result: Everyone wins. The partners earn an acceptable return on their investment, and your station gets the seed money it needs.

FYI

Limited partnerships are used most commonly by real estate developers, corporations engaged in oil and gas exploration, and motion picture producers to raise investment capital. But they are in no way restricted to these industries. Nor should they be.

COMPLEXITY

Since you must create your own partnership agreement, partnerships, whether limited or general, are usually more complex than a sole proprietorship. That complexity alone discourages many proprietors from creating a partnership.

Another potential drawback to consider: Increased bookkeeping. Although a partnership pays no income tax on its own, it still must file a tax return (Form 1065).

It also must provide each partner with a Schedule K-1 that details his or her share of partnership income, deductions, and tax credits.

The partnership files a copy of each Schedule K-1 along with its tax return. Uncle Sam wants to know how the partnership allocates its earnings, deductions, and credits to the partners. That way, the agency can make sure that the partners are accurately reporting income on their personal returns—and catch any tax cheats.

─────────────────── **TAXTIP** ───────────────────

A partnership return can be even more complicated than a corporation return. Seek accounting help, especially if limited partners are involved.

CONTROL

Business owners relinquish some authority when they organize their enterprise as a partnership. For one, a partnership agreement may limit each partner's power.

It also may specify how decisions are made and who is allowed to make them. So you may find your hands tied from time to time.

For example, partnership agreements frequently require a unanimous vote of the partners before the business enters into a new venture or purchases equipment or machinery. You can get around this stumbling block by appointing a managing partner and granting him or her the authority to make day-to-day business decisions.

─────────────────── **FYI** ───────────────────

Although some partnerships function perfectly well without a written agreement, savvy businesspeople learn to anticipate problems.

That's why we advise all our partnership clients to adopt and periodically review a partnership agreement. At a minimum, this document should state:

• The purpose of the business
• The authority and responsibility of each partner
• The division of profits and losses

It's also a good idea to spell out the circumstances under which you will take new people into the partnership and the scenario if a partner dies or resigns.

We suggest you first hash out the key issues, then have an attorney draft an agreement for you. There is no sense paying a lawyer for work you can do.

COST

Partnerships are expensive. You're subject to legal fees and, in the case of limited partnerships, state filing fees. In addition, you're saddled with the cost of preparing a partnership tax return. What's more, the law won't allow partners to deduct many of the expenses they've incurred selling partnership interests.

Let's return to our example of the entrepreneur who sold limited partnerships to capitalize his small radio station.

Under the law, neither he nor any other partner may deduct the costs associated with selling those limited partnership interests. And those costs can mount up. They include commissions to brokers, legal and accounting fees, and the expense of distributing and printing a partnership prospectus.

There is a bright note: ultimately, when the partners sell their interests, or the partnership is liquidated, the costs may be deducted in computing the gain on the sale as part of the costs of the partnership interests.

FLEXIBILITY

Most people assume that income and deductions from a partnership are allocated to the partners based on their percentage of ownership.

If, say, you have a 10 percent stake in the enterprise, you're entitled to withdraw 10 percent of the profits or write off 10 percent of the losses.

But partnerships actually give you a great deal of flexibility in divvying up profits, losses, and tax benefits.

Specifically, IRS rules allow you to make extra payments or "special allocations" to certain partners based on their contributions to the enterprise.

These rules are complicated, but the effect is to enable you to pay a partner an amount that—on a percentage basis—is larger than his or her ownership share. In case of a loss, this partner gets to deduct more than his or her share.

For example, a partner who puts no money in the partnership but contributes her services instead may be given a big chunk of the partnership's earnings.

Another partner who puts up the capital for the venture but provides no services may, in turn, receive the lion's share of the partnership's losses.

Partners may also receive "guaranteed payments" in addition

to a portion of the profits. Guaranteed payments are, for practical purposes, salaries paid to partners.

But salaries paid to partners differ from salaries paid to employees in one key respect—the payments are not subject to withholding for Social-Security and income taxes.

For the most part, guaranteed payments are made to compensate partners for the extra work they do. For instance, a partner who assumes the additional role of managing partner might receive a guaranteed payment.

Partners also may be paid flat fees for services they render that are not related to their roles as partners. An example would be a partner-attorney who does legal work for a partnership involved in constructing apartment buildings. The attorney would be paid as if he were an outside contractor, and his fee would be treated as an ordinary business expense.

While partnerships provide plenty of flexibility in allocating income and losses, they do have a drawback: they limit your ability to withdraw money or distribute profits at will. Most partnership agreements, for example, allow partners to take money out of the business only with the permission of the other principals.

LIABILITY

General partners face unlimited liability for the debts their business incurs. Thus, they lack an important protection that owners of corporations have.

As we've seen, however, the law caps liability for a special kind of partner—a limited partner—who simply invests money in a company and takes no active role in management.

If a limited partner puts up, say, $5,000, her liability may not exceed that amount plus any additional sums she has promised. The same holds true no matter how large or small the investment.

--- **FYI** ---

If limited partners do take an active role in management, the court may rule that they aren't limited partners at all but general partners and hold them fully liable for all debts.

LIFE

Under federal tax law, a partnership ceases to exist when "no business is being carried on"—that is, when you've closed up shop.

Depending on the structure of the partnership agreement, a partnership also may come to its end when a partner dies or resigns.

Your partnership agreement should address what happens in these circumstances. Remember, the best time to work out these problems is before they crop up.

LOSSES

If a partnership produces a loss, that amount is deductible on the personal tax returns of partners who materially participate in the business. It is also deductible for partners who don't materially participate—as long as they have passive income from other investments to offset the losses.

In most cases, the partnership determines each partner's share of the loss by dividing the amount by his or her ownership interest.

A person who owns, say, 10 percent of a company that reports a loss of $100,000 would write off $10,000 on his or her personal income tax return—as long as he or she materially participates in the company's management.

Also, partners may carry forward or backward their business—or net operating—losses to offset profits in past or future years (what the IRS calls a "loss carryback" and "loss carryforward").

A partner's net operating loss is the difference between his or her gross income and deductions after he or she makes certain adjustments. For example, in computing a net operating loss, a partner usually may not add in personal deductions, such as mortgage interest or state taxes.

—————————— **CASE IN POINT** ——————————

Say you and your partner sustain a total loss of $4,000 from the operation of your small retail clothing store.

You have no other personal income, and your only allowable deductions are for mortgage interest—$1,100— and property taxes—$450.

Your share of the net operating loss—meaning the amount you may carry forward or backward to offset future income—is $2,000.

—————————— **TAXTRAP** ——————————

A note of caution, however: The at-risk rules that apply to proprietorships also apply to partnerships. That is, you may not deduct losses greater than the amount you have invested or for which you have assumed liability.

OWNERSHIP

It makes no difference to the IRS whether your partnership consists of two people or a thousand. No ceiling exists on the number of partners in a partnership.

You should know, though, that businesses organized as partnerships can be harder to sell or bequeath to heirs than corporations—though easier than proprietorships.

Why? For starters, to transfer ownership of a partnership, most agreements require that all the principals and members of management agree to the move. And, in some instances, bringing in a new partner means the creation of a new partnership. That alone can spell problems.

On the plus side, a partnership may help you shift income to family members whose tax brackets are lower than your own. You may make a family member—your spouse, child, or even a parent—a partner in your business. The income your relative receives from the enterprise is taxed in his or her bracket.

TAXTRAP

Beware. Special rules apply to family partnerships. For example, you may not simply assign to a family member the right to receive a portion of your company's income. You must make the person your actual partner. That is, you must transfer ownership of a portion of the business to the individual.

What's the difference between assigning the right to receive income and giving someone a piece of the pie? The answers are ownership and authority.

With an ownership interest, a family member may participate in business decisions. So the owner of the company surrenders a certain amount of control. (For more information on the right way to split income among family members, see chapter 16.)

PERKS

Partners are subject to the same limitations as proprietors on the type of fringe benefits they may provide for themselves.

Like proprietors, partners may not write off the cost of their life or disability insurance. However, again like proprietors, partners may deduct 25 percent of their medical insurance premiums on their personal tax returns. The other 75 percent is deductible to the extent that it—plus other medical expenses—tops 7.5 percent of the adjusted gross income. (You'll find a detailed discussion of fringe benefits in chapter 15.)

PRIVACY

Unlike a proprietorship, a partnership is a separate legal entity. Therefore, owners may not have to reveal the state of their personal finances to secure loans.

Remember, however, whether or not a lender requests a personal financial statement depends more on the size and stability of your business than on its form of organization.

SHELTER

Partnership income is reported by the partners directly on their personal returns. As a result, it is not possible to shelter income within the partnership.

TAXES

Like a proprietorship, a partnership passes all profits, losses, and tax deductions directly through to the partners' personal returns.

You need not worry that income will be taxed once as corporate profits and again as personal income when it is paid out as dividends. And, if your partnership produces a loss, you may write it off on your personal return—a real benefit if you have other income to offset.

Also, partners, like proprietors, pay income taxes on their actual earnings, not on money as it is withdrawn from the business.

A partnership, then, may write checks to its partners, and the money is not automatically viewed as compensation or a distribution of profits by the IRS.

Partners pay the same Social Security tax rates as proprietors—13.02 percent in 1988 versus 15.02 percent for corporations. But unlike owners of corporations, partners may not deduct the Social Security taxes they pay on their own earnings. (They may, however, write off Social Security taxes paid on employees' wages.)

The result: Partners, like proprietors, save nothing personally, even though they seem to benefit from a lower rate.

_____ **TAXTIP** _____

Starting in 1989, partners—like sole proprietors—may write off half their Social Security taxes.

YEAR

Traditionally, most partnerships used the calendar year, because that's how the partners filed their personal tax returns. But even partnerships that previously used fiscal years have had to switch to calendar year ends. The reason: The 1986 Tax Reform Act mandates that almost all partnerships use a calendar year. The IRS does allow some partnerships to use a fiscal year that differs from the calendar year; consult your tax adviser.

BOTTOM LINE

Partnerships are ideal for small businesses that are owned by more than one person and don't need the liability protection of a corporation.

Finally, partnerships—through limited partnership arrangements—offer small business owners a creative way to raise capital for their enterprises.

Limited partnerships are an attractive way to finance, say, your introduction of a new product or your research-and-development efforts.

FOR MORE INFORMATION

See these IRS publications:

- *Tax Information on Partnerships* (Number 541)
- *Your Federal Income Tax* (Number 17)
- *Tax Guide for Small Business* (Number 334)
- *Farmers' Tax Guide* (Number 225)
- *Tax Guide for Commercial Fishermen* (Number 595)
- *Tax Information for Direct Sellers* (Number 911)

Try these IRS Tele-Tax tapes:

- *Business Income* (Number 136)
- *Rental Income and Expenses* (Number 143)
- *Farming and Fishing Income* (Number 202)
- *Self-Employment Tax* (Number 300)
- *Small Business Tax Workshops—Tax Help for the New Businessperson* (Number 102)

Chapter 5

TO INC. OR NOT TO INC.

So You Want to Be a Corporation

On the wall behind the counter of a Washington, D.C., diner hangs a hand-lettered sign, a Christmas gift to the owner from his wife.

"What's the difference," the sign asks, "between a taxidermist and a tax collector?" The answer: "The taxidermist takes only your skin."

First posed by Mark Twain, this riddle still strikes a familiar chord today. Regardless of how fat our paychecks, most of us believe taxes gobble up far too much of our incomes. We all want to find ways to pare down our income tax liabilities. For many people, a corporation can serve as a tax-cutting tool.

Here's why: Under the law, a corporation may hold onto as much as $250,000 in profits before it must justify to the IRS why it is not paying dividends to shareholders.

These so-called accumulated earnings are subject to taxation on the company's return but not on the personal returns of its shareholders. In contrast, any profits earned by a proprietorship or partnership are taxed immediately on the owner's personal return.

Moreover, corporate tax rates on the first $75,000 of income are much lower than personal tax rates. For example, the first $50,000 of taxable corporate income is taxed at a rate of 15 percent. The first $29,750 of taxable personal income (if a person is married and files a joint return) is taxed at an overall rate of 15 percent.

But here's the real kicker: The next dollar of corporate income over $50,000 is taxed at a rate of 25 percent. And that 25-percent rate applies to the next $25,000 of corporate income. Married individuals filing jointly, however, pay a 33-percent marginal rate on income between $71,900 and $171,090.

The result: With a corporation, you pay less income tax on that big chunk of earnings you hold onto as, say, an emergency fund or as a means to finance growth through equipment purchases or acquisitions. But you pay a personal income tax on the money when you withdraw it from your corporation.

——————————— **CASE IN POINT** ———————————

Say you're a grocery wholesaler. In 1988, your corporation earns $75,000 after paying you a salary of $100,000. Your corporation pays taxes on its $75,000 profit. Here's how its bill adds up:

- A tax of 15 percent on its first $50,000 of earnings or $7,500
- Plus a tax of 25 percent on the remaining $25,000 of earnings or $6,250
- For a total tax bill of $13,750.

That means your company pays tax at an overall rate of only 18.33 percent—that is, your tax bill of $13,750 divided by your $75,000 profit.

Of course, you also pay taxes on your $100,000 salary. As a married taxpayer filing a joint return, you fork over $22,601 or some 22.6 percent of your pay to Uncle Sam. Your total tax liability: $36,351 ($13,750, your corporate tax bill, plus $22,601, your personal tax liability).

If you had operated your wholesale business as a sole proprietorship, you would have paid an overall personal income tax of $47,351 on earnings of $175,000. The result: You trim your current tax bill by $11,000 by doing business as a corporation.

There's one catch in this scenario, though.

If you accumulate more than the permitted $250,000 in earnings ($150,000 for certain personal-service businesses, such as law, accounting, consulting, and medical practices), be prepared to justify the accumulation to the IRS.

If you do not have good business reasons for the excess—you need the money to finance growth, for example—you may be slapped with an accumulated earnings tax. This tax equals 27.5 percent of the first $100,000 of taxable income that is "unreasonably accumulated" within the year and 38.5 percent on amounts in excess of that $100,000—and it is not deductible.

How does the IRS discover that you've accumulated more than you should? If you're audited, odds are the agent will immediately spot your excess earnings and try to slap you with the penalty.

"Hold on," you say. "Can't I get around this rule just by saying I need to accumulate earnings to finance growth? Who will be any wiser if I don't use my earnings for that purpose?"

Theoretically, the answer is nobody. But, keep in mind, tax returns are audited two to three years after they are filed. By that time, the proof is in your expenditures.

Our advice: Don't wait for your accountant or book-keeper to alert you to the fact that you have too much money in the corporate pot.

Keep tabs yourself on accumulated earnings, and make sure you don't go over the limit unless you have a valid business reason.

Something else you should do: Familiarize yourself with the so-called personal-service corporation rules.

TAXTRAP

Personal-service corporations don't benefit from the lower corporate rates on the first $75,000 of income. In fact, all their corporate income is taxed at the top corporate rate of 34 percent—a rate that usually applies to income of $75,000 and up.

A corporation falls into the category of a personal-service corporation if it meets all these requirements:

- The business is a C or regular corporation and not an S corporation.
- The principal activity of the corporation during the previous taxable year was the performance of personal services. These include services in the fields of health, law, engineering, architecture, accounting, actuarial science, the performing arts, and consulting. Uncle Sam says that personal services constitute the principal activity if more than 50 percent of the corporation's revenues comes from providing these services.
- Employee-owners hold more than 10 percent of the fair market value of the outstanding stock on the last day of the previous taxable year.
- The services are "substantially performed" by employee-owners—that is, more than 20 percent of the compen-

sation paid to employees providing these services goes to employee-owners.

─────────────── **TAXTRAP** ───────────────

The consulting category is tricky.

For instance, an incorporated financial planner whose compensation is based on hourly rates is classed as a consultant performing personal services. But a planner who is compensated by receiving commissions from products sold to clients is not.

The reason: The law does not classify corporations that receive commissions—real estate and insurance brokers, for example—as personal-service corporations.

CAPITAL

Corporations usually raise capital by borrowing money or selling stock. Ownership of the stock is transferred by handing over stock certificates—it is as simple as that. Corporations issue common or preferred stock or both.

What is common stock? My favorite business quipsters, Jim Fisk and Robert Barron, say it's American Telephone & Telegraph.

Jokes aside, any stock, whether common or preferred, represents the holder's share of ownership in a company. These owners have certain legal rights. For instance, common stockholders are usually entitled to:

- Elect the company's board of directors
- Receive dividends when dividends are declared by the board of directors
- Profit from the growth of the company through the appreciation of stock values
- Transfer ownership of any of their shares

Owners of preferred stock have legal rights, too. But they usually give up some privileges to gain preferential treatment in other areas.

For example, preferred stockholders often forgo voting rights in exchange for the privilege of receiving dividends before owners of common stock do.

Being first in line can be a big plus, especially if you own stock in a company that is strapped for cash and paying meager dividends.

Another advantage of owning preferred stock: If a business is liquidated, preferred stockholders usually have priority over common stockholders in the distribution of assets. The exact order in which creditors and owners are paid off is dictated by state law, but it generally goes like this:

- Employees (wages—but not bonuses—due them)
- Uncle Sam
- Creditors
- Bondholders
- Preferred stockholders
- Common stockholders

This advantage, however, can be illusory. In the case of bankruptcy, I know of very few instances where anyone below the level of creditor received any amount of compensation.

FYI

Because it is so easy to transfer ownership of stock, you should consider incorporating if you plan to raise new capital in the near future.

Also, as the principal owner of a private corporation, you can exercise some control over who owns your company's stock. For example, you are perfectly within bounds if you ask shareholders to sign an agreement giving you the right of first refusal should they decide to sell out.

COMPLEXITY

Remember the old saying, "Anyone who acts as his own attorney has a fool for a client"? Well, this maxim applies in spades when it comes to incorporating.

A corporation is formed under the laws of a specific state. As a result, it is subject to any number of state-imposed rules and regulations. Moreover, a corporation is a complicated form of organization that may be structured in any number of ways.

Our advice: If you plan to incorporate, seek the help of an attorney.

CONTROL

As with everything else related to taxes, there are as many drawbacks to operating as a corporation as there are advantages.

Among the disadvantages: Like the partnership form, the corporate form limits an owner's autonomy. A chief executive is ruled by the corporate laws of the state in which his or her business is based and, in some cases, by a company's board of directors.

Most states, for instance, require chief executives to seek the approval of their board before entering into a new venture.

Capital projects—such as the purchase of large machinery or expensive equipment—also normally require board action.

Of course, you eliminate these problems if you operate a one-person corporation.

COST

Operating your business as a corporation involves added expense. For one, you're more likely to require professional help in preparing your corporate tax return and in keeping board minutes and filing the required corporate reports.

In addition, some cities and states impose income taxes on corporations but not on sole proprietorships and partnerships. In Florida, for instance, corporations must pay a state corporate income tax. But proprietors and partners escape state taxation, because Florida has no personal income tax.

Then there's the cost of incorporating in the first place. This cost varies by the state in which you are organized and the size of your company.

At the very least, you should expect to pay legal fees and state filing fees, which can run anywhere from $100 to $750 or more. You can count on these expenses multiplying if you do business in more than one state.

To make matters even more costly, you may not deduct any expenses associated with selling shares of stock to capitalize your company. These costs include commissions paid to investment bankers, legal and accounting fees, and the expense of printing prospectuses—costs that can quickly add up to a hefty total.

TAXTIP

As a rule, you can't justify the costs of incorporation unless the move saves you $3,000 a year or more in taxes.

However, other considerations—such as limited liability—may be overriding. In other words, there are reasons to incorporate that have nothing to do with taxes.

FLEXIBILITY

Corporations are not, by their natures, flexible. To begin with, taking money out of a corporation is no simple task.

As you know, when a corporation pays a dividend, that money is subject to double taxation: the corporate income tax when the company earns the income, the personal income tax when the shareholder receives the dividend.

But you may ease the pain in many ways.

You may:

- Pay yourself, as owner of the corporation, a generous salary, thus minimizing corporate profits. You'll shell out more on your personal return. But it's better to pay taxes once—on the personal level—than twice (once on the personal level and once on the corporate level).
- Give yourself a liberal fringe benefits package.
- Put family members on the payroll—if they actually perform services for the business.

_____ **TAXTRAP** _____

Be sure the salary you set for yourself is "reasonable"—meaning it is in line with what other people in similar positions earn.

Otherwise, you may be subject to the government's "unreasonable compensation" rules. In such cases, the IRS may disallow the deduction for part of your salary.

The result: That portion is treated as a dividend and subject to taxation on both your corporate and personal returns.

LIABILITY

One of the biggest pluses of doing business as a corporation is that owners are shielded from liability. The debts of a corporation are not considered the debts of its owners.

Shareholders, like limited partners, are at risk only for the money they invest in the company, plus any obligations for which they are personally liable, such as a bank note they have guaranteed.

_____ **CASE IN POINT** _____

Say a customer slips and falls on the front steps of your small store. Subsequently, he sues for medical expenses, plus the cost of "pain and suffering." The court awards him $200,000 or about $100,000 more than the value of your entire store.

The court may order the seizure of your store and any assets attached to it, such as a company car. But your own assets are safe, since your business is incorporated. The court may not touch your house or any other personal holdings. And it may not go after the assets of your spouse.

One big exception to this rule: If you were personally negligent, you, as well as your corporation, may be held liable for damages.

Also, protection from liability does not extend to malpractice claims against individual professionals—physicians, attorneys, accountants, and so on.

But the corporation may shield some professionals who are part of the same firm but not personally involved in the case where malpractice is alleged.

_____ CASE IN POINT _____

You and another surgeon practice together in California, and you do business as a corporation. Your colleague and your corporation are sued for malpractice, and the court rules against him.

Under the law, your colleague is liable for his wrongdoing, but you are not. His assets and the assets of the corporation may be seized by the court. However, your personal assets are protected.

_____ FYI _____

The owners of a corporation aren't required to repay the debts of their companies. But they can assume these liabilities if they choose and, in certain circumstances, deduct the cost.

Consider the case of Conway Twitty.

When Twitty, the famous country-western singer, founded Twitty Burger Inc., in 1968, he envisioned a whole string of fast-food restaurants bearing his personal logo— a small yellow bird (the Twitty bird) strumming a guitar. But less than three years later, the company went bust.

Twitty, to his credit, decided to repay the people who invested in his hamburger chain—some seventy-five friends and business associates. The only problem was, the entertainer took an income tax deduction for the $96,492.46 he shelled out in repayments.

The IRS balked, and the case wound up in tax court.

Uncle Sam argued that Twitty was not obligated to repay the money, so he wasn't entitled to a deduction. But Twitty's attorney maintained the singer had good reason to reimburse investors. "Imagine," he told the court, "trying to keep a band together [when] somebody has stiffed the drummer's mother."

The tax court sided with the singer. And the judge concluded his decision with his own "Ode to Conway Twitty." To wit:

Twitty Burger went belly up
But Conway remained true
He repaid his investors one and all
It was the moral thing to do.
His fans would not have liked it
It could have hurt his fame
Had any investors sued him
Like Merle Haggard or Sonny James.
When it was time to file taxes
Conway thought what he would do
Was deduct those payments as a business expense
Under section one-sixty-two.
In order to allow these deductions
Goes the argument of the Commissioner
The payments must be ordinary and necessary
To (the) business of the petitioner.
Had Conway not repaid the investors
His career would have been under a cloud,
Under the unique facts of this case
Held: The deductions are allowed.

LIFE

The corporation is a bona fide legal entity owned by its stockholders. It has a life of its own and is immortal. When its owner dies, it continues to exist.

LOSSES

If your company is losing money, chances are you would be better off operating as a proprietorship, partnership, or S corporation. That way, you could claim the losses on your personal tax return.

Under the law, owners of a corporation may not deduct the company's losses on their personal tax returns, although they may take a personal write-off of their investment in the corporation if the corporation goes broke. This deduction is subject to strict at-risk rules, which means your write-off is limited to the amount you have invested or are responsible for.

_____ **FYI** _____

Like a proprietor and a partner, a corporation may carry

its losses back no more than three years and forward no more than fifteen years to offset profits in those years.

But it does have a choice. It may carry these losses forward *or* backward, depending on which method saves the most money for the company.

OWNERSHIP

It's easy to bequeath a corporation to your heirs. A corporation continues to live when you die, while a proprietorship dies when you do. Thus, a corporation guarantees at least the nominal survival of the business.

It can also help reduce income taxes.

If you sell stock in your corporation, the profits are usually taxed as long-term capital gains. That means they can be used to offset capital losses.

Another important point: Corporations may be sold or merged with other companies more easily than sole proprietorships and partnerships.

They also may offer employees stock—an excellent motivational tool. This offer generally takes the form of incentive stock options or an Employee Stock Ownership Plan. (See chapter 17.)

PERKS

Corporations may write off benefits of all sorts—medical and life insurance, company cars, athletic facilities, and so on.

The only major requirement: Most fringes must be doled out in a way that does not discriminate in favor of highly compensated employees, such as shareholders and top executives. (See chapter 15 for a full discussion of fringes.)

PRIVACY

A corporation can protect your privacy.

Unlike the owners of a proprietorship or partnership, you may not have to submit a summary of your personal assets in order to secure business loans.

But, again, whether or not a lender requests a personal financial statement depends more on the size and stability of your business than on your organizational form.

SHELTER

As we've seen, you can't accumulate an infinite amount of money in a corporation. If a corporation piles up more than $250,000 in earnings and there's no sound business reason for the accumulation, such as financing equipment purchases, the corporation is subject to an accumulated earnings tax.

Money your corporation pays out in dividends is, of course, subject to double taxation. First, it's taxed on the corporate tax return. Then, when you and other shareholders receive the money in the form of dividends, it is taxed on your personal returns.

TAXES

When you incorporate your business, your status under the tax laws change. You are no longer self-employed. Rather, you are an employee of your own corporation.

The corporation deducts the salary it pays you. You report that income, plus any corporate dividends you receive, on your personal tax return. And dividends are subject to double taxation.

Why, then, would you want to incorporate?

The answer is actually quite simple.

For the most part, corporate tax rates are lower than personal tax rates—at least on the first $75,000 of income. As we've seen, corporations are subject to a tax of 15 percent on the first $50,000 of earnings, and earnings between $50,000 and $75,000 are taxed at the rate of 25 percent.

So a corporation with income of $50,000 would fork over $7,500 to the government (that is, $50,000 times 15 percent). By comparison, a single taxpayer with $50,000 in taxable income would shell out $12,023 in income taxes—or about 24 percent of his or her earnings.

As a rule of thumb, businesses that earn less than $75,000 a year after owners' salaries and want to retain a portion of their profits to finance growth benefit from doing business as a corporation. Businesses that earn more than $75,000 or want to distribute most of their earnings to owners don't gain from doing business as a corporation.

_____ **CASE IN POINT** _____

Say you and your wife own a chain of five hairstyling salons. The company pays you salaries of $30,000 each.

You file a joint tax return and claim some $10,000 in personal deductions and exemptions. These bring your joint taxable income down to $50,000. On that amount, you pay $10,133 in income taxes. But, at the end of the year, after subtracting your salaries and other business expenses, your company reports a profit of $75,000.

What are the tax consequences? If your company is

incorporated, and you do not pay out any of its earnings as dividends, your personal tax bill remains unchanged.

Your corporate tax liability, meanwhile, totals $13,750. So your total tax bill—adding together your personal and business liabilities—comes to $23,883.

That figure is less than you and your spouse would pay if your business were a partnership. As a partnership, you would have to report the entire $75,000 in profits as income on your personal return. Your tax, then, is computed on earnings of $125,000—that is, the personal taxable income of $50,000 plus business profits of $75,000.

So your tax bill soars.

Instead of handing over $23,883 to the government ($10,133 in personal taxes plus $13,750 in corporate taxes), you pay $9,905 more—or a whopping $33,788.

TAXTIPS

The only way to know if you would save money by incorporating is to sit down with a pencil and a piece of paper, and "run the numbers." You'll find a table of corporate tax rates on the opposite page.

With a corporation, you do pay higher Social Security taxes on your own earnings—15.02 percent compared to 13.02 percent for sole proprietors and partners. But your corporation may deduct the employer's portion of Social Security tax payments.

TAXTRAP

Say you used a number of devices—accelerated depreciation of assets, for example—to lower your corporate tax bill dramatically. Don't breath a sigh of relief just yet. Your company may still be subject to the alternative minimum tax (AMT).

As we saw in chapter 3, the AMT ensures that individuals and corporations pay some tax, even if their legal deductions reduce their tax bill to zero.

Which companies pay the AMT? There's no hard and fast rule. But take a look at your tax calculations. Has your company avoided or deferred taxes on substantial amounts of income? If so, the odds are good that you'll be subject to the AMT.

Whether you think your company is subject to the AMT

or not—and even if it's never had to pay the AMT before—don't ignore the possibility.

Check with your tax professional and get some advice. If the news is bad, at least you can turn the hard part—the figuring—over to him or her.

Corporate Income Tax Rates

Taxable Income	Tax Rate
Up to $50,000	15%
$50,000 to $75,000	25
$75,000 to $100,000	34
$100,000 to $335,000	39
More than $335,000	34

Note: Corporations pay a 5-percent surtax on income between $100,000 to $335,000. The effect of this surtax: to eliminate the benefits of lower rates once income reaches a certain level. By ponying up the surtax, corporations effectively pay 34 percent on all their taxable income once they earn more than $335,000.

TAXTIP

Another benefit of incorporation is that corporations may exclude from taxation 80 percent of the dividends they receive from investments in other corporations in which they own 20 percent or more of the stock. Corporations may exclude 70 percent of the dividends they receive from companies in which they own less than 20 percent interest. Companies typically cash in on this provision by investing their idle cash in stocks of big public companies.

TAXTRAPS

Some states also tax corporations heavily. So be sure to check your state's laws when you contemplate setting up a corporation.

Another word to the wise: Federal laws won't allow you to split your company into several corporations just to take advantage of the accumulated earnings rule, nor will it allow you to split your company into several parts to profit from the lower taxes imposed on earnings of less than $100,000.

YEAR

A corporation (other than a personal service corporation) may adopt a fiscal year that does not mirror the calendar year. So it may start its fiscal year at any time.

BOTTOM LINE

Small companies profit from the corporate form of organization, because it allows them to reduce the tax on earnings that are reinvested in the company and not distributed to shareholders. Under the guidelines, a company may hold onto as much as $250,000 ($150,000 for certain personal-service businesses) in earnings without passing the money on to its stockholders.

As a rule, you should generally consider forming a corporation if:

- Your corporation's earnings add up to less than $75,000 a year.
- You want to reduce the taxes you pay on income you retain for business growth.
- You can benefit from the legal liability limitations of a corporation.

TAXTRAP

Converting an existing business to a corporation is complex. You may wind up owing tax on "income" you receive from the conversion, even though you do nothing but transfer your own assets and liabilities to the new corporation.

If you contribute assets to the corporation in exchange for stock, and if you own the corporation after the transfer, chances are the conversion should produce no taxable income.

But if, for example, you transfer a building to the corporation on which there is an outstanding debt—and that liability exceeds your basis—the IRS will conclude that the corporation has given you something valuable. It has taken over your net debt. And you'll have to report income on your personal return equal to the excess of your debt over your basis.

CASE IN POINT

Say you transfer to your corporation equipment that you purchased for $5,000 and financed at a local bank. The debt on the machinery is $4,000.

Your basis in the equipment is only $3,000. Your basis is the purchase price—$5,000—minus the depreciation you've claimed to date—$2,000.

The result: You must report as income the difference between your basis and the liability the corporation assumed—in this case, $1,000.

FOR MORE INFORMATION

See these IRS publications:

* *Tax Information on Corporations* (Number 542)
* *Your Federal Income Tax* (Number 17)
* *Tax Guide for Small Business* (Number 334)
* *Farmers' Tax Guide* (Number 225)
* *Tax Guide for Commercial Fishermen* (Number 595)
* *Tax Information for Direct Sellers* (Number 911)

Try these IRS Tele-Tax tapes:

* *Business Income* (Number 136)
* *Rental Income and Expenses* (Number 143)
* *Farming and Fishing Income* (Number 202)
* *Small Business Tax Workshops—Tax Help for the New Businessperson* (Number 102)

Chapter 6

WHAT'S IN A NAME?

S Corporation S Marvelous

Owners of S corporations pay taxes like proprietors and partners. Profits and losses go directly on their personal returns, and they are generally subject to no separate, federal business income tax.

But their owners enjoy the same protection as owners of ordinary corporations. Shareholders bear no personal responsibility for the liabilities of their businesses.

Still, S corporations aren't what they used to be. Rather, they are, for the most part, better than they used to be.

In the past few years, Congress has substantially changed the laws governing this type of organization. Uncle Sam has even renamed them. What used to be known commonly as "Subchapter S" or "small business" corporations are now officially called S corporations.

What else has changed about them?

Losses and capital gains are treated more favorably than they were in the past, and there's an increase in the amount of passive income (such as interest, rents, and royalties) an S corporation may receive. There's also a hike—from twenty-five to thirty-five—in the number of shareholders an S corporation may have.

The majority of these changes came about when Congress adopted the Subchapter S Revision Act in 1982. This law simplified tax treatment for S corporations.

It also eliminated—or substantially reduced—many of their disadvantages. So how do S corporations now stack up against other forms of organizations?

Let's take a look.

CAPITAL
Like owners of regular corporations, owners of S corporations

frequently raise capital by selling company stock. However, owners of S corporations don't have to worry about stock types, because their businesses issue only one class of stock—common.

TAXTRAP

S corporation stock is subject to three restrictions:

* Unlike the stock in a regular corporation, it may be owned only by individuals, estates, and certain types of trusts. So you can't sell stock to another corporation and remain an S corporation.
* Nonresident aliens may not own stock in an S corporation.
* Ownership of an S corporation is strictly limited to 35 shareholders. (But the law counts a husband and wife who each own stock as one shareholder.)
* An S corporation may not set up an active subsidiary.

COMPLEXITY

S corporations are not simple entities.

To begin with, you may not elect S-corporation status unless the owners of your company unanimously consent to the move—a headache if you have as many as thirty-five shareholders.

Also, the law says, you lose your S-corporation status the moment your company does something it is not allowed to do, such as setting up an active subsidiary or exceeding the allowable number of shareholders.

In any case, correct your mistake at once. Ask the IRS for a ruling that an inadvertent termination took place.

Document the corrective actions you took. Then, if the IRS calls you on the carpet, you have some defense. (Have no proof? Remember the old saying, "When in charge, ponder. When in trouble, delegate. When in doubt, mumble.")

TAXTRAP

You may run into the problem of "built-in" capital gains when you convert a regular corporation to an S corporation. You'll pay taxes on these gains, once you realize them, as if your company were still a regular corporation.

Here's how it works. Say your corporation owns a small office building, and its basis in the building comes to $100,000. Now you convert your regular corporation to an S corporation. At the time you convert, the market value of your building is $150,000.

Under the rules, if you sell your building at a gain any time in the next ten years, $50,000 of that gain—that is, the difference between your $100,000 basis and the market price at the time you converted—is taxed as if you were still doing business as a regular corporation. It makes no difference to Uncle Sam that you are an S corporation at the time of the sale.

The rest of the gain is taxed in the same way as other earnings from your S corporation—it is passed along to you and reported on your personal return.

––––––––––––––––––– **TAXTIP** –––––––––––––––––––

One way to get around this problem: Rather than convert an existing corporation, create a new one and opt for S status.

It's also smart to consult your accountant before you switch to S corporation status. That way, you'll avoid potentially costly mistakes.

––––––––––––––––––– **FYI** –––––––––––––––––––

To convert a regular corporation to an S corporation, you must file Form 2553 by the fifteenth day of the third month of the tax year in which you want to convert.

You may revert back to the status of a regular corporation at any time. You just file a statement that you wish to revoke the choice of S status on a particular date. State the number of shares outstanding, and submit statements of consent from owners of more than 50 percent of the corporation's stock.

Keep in mind, however: Once S status has been terminated, you may not elect to operate as an S corporation for the next five years—without permission from the IRS.

CONTROL

Shareholders of an S corporation exercise no more control over the management of the company than do shareholders of a regular corporation. Operation of the business rests where it should—with its management.

COST

The cost of setting up an S corporation is the same as the cost of creating an ordinary corporation. That's because an S corporation is nothing more than a regular corporation that has elected S status by filing Form 2553 with the IRS.

FLEXIBILITY

Like regular corporations, S corporations are created by law and subject to restrictions imposed by the state in which they are incorporated.

For the most part, money cannot be withdrawn from an S corporation at will. It must be paid out either in the form of salaries or distributed as profits.

LIABILITY

S corporations provide business owners with the same protection as ordinary corporations. Owners are not held personally liable for the debts of the business.

However, as with corporations, this protection from liability does not extend to malpractice claims against individual professionals—physicians, attorneys, accountants, and so on.

But the S corporation—again like regular corporations—may shield some professionals who are firm members but not personally involved in the malpractice case.

LIFE

Under the old law, many business owners believed they were properly operating as S corporations, only to learn during the course of an IRS audit that their S status had been terminated due to a technical violation of the S-corporation rules. As a result, they were taxed as an ordinary corporation.

The old law allowed no relief to taxpayers in such cases. If your corporation technically failed to qualify as an S corporation, regardless of the intent of the shareholders, it lost its S-corporation status for the entire year in which the termination took place, as well as for five subsequent years.

Under the current law, S-corporation status may still be terminated when a business ceases to qualify, but the penalties are less severe.

For example, companies no longer lose their S-corporation status for the whole year. Rather, the termination takes effect on the day the company ceased to qualify under the rules.

Also, now, if the company corrects the problem that caused the disqualification within a year, it may continue to operate as an S corporation.

Even if S-corporation status is terminated, the company's life as a legal entity is not affected. Now, as in the past, it simply becomes a regular corporation.

LOSSES

Say your S corporation reports a $5,000 loss. As its owner, you simply subtract that amount from any other income you report on your personal tax return.

There is one important catch: You may not deduct an amount that is greater than your "basis in stock and debt."

As we saw in chapter 3, basis is the sum of:

- The original cost of your stock
- Plus any loans that you have made to the corporation (but not loans you have guaranteed)
- Plus any profits the corporation has accumulated
- Less any money the corporation has previously distributed
- Less any previous losses you've claimed to date.

Under the Subchapter S Revision Act, this "basis" limitation holds true for any one taxable year. But the law provides a tax break: it allows you to carry forward any losses in excess of your basis in stock and debt indefinitely to offset future S corporation income.

Take heed, though: The IRS is strict about what it considers a loan and therefore your basis.

——————————— **CASE IN POINT** ———————————

Shareholders in the Flint Motor Inn, an S corporation, deducted on their personal returns three years' worth of the company's operating losses.

The shareholders claimed that their basis included their portion of a $400,000 loan that the company had obtained from the Westinghouse Credit Corp. Since the shareholders had to guarantee this loan, they argued, the transaction actually amounted to a loan from Westinghouse to them.

This reasoning, the appeals court judge concluded, was, at best, "contorted." The shareholders, he maintained, "are liable for the tax consequences of the transaction they actually executed; they may not reap the benefits of some other transaction they might have effected instead."

This ruling, the judge pointed out, was in line with judgments in similar cases. In short, "the courts have consistently required some economic outlay by the guarantor in order to convert a mere loan guaranty into an investment."

OWNERSHIP

Ownership of an S corporation is transferred in essentially the same way as ownership of a regular corporation—through shares of stock.

But as we've seen, a host of restrictions apply to S corporations that do not apply to regular corporations. To review them quickly:

- An S corporation may not have more than thirty-five shareholders.
- An S corporation may not have nonresident aliens as shareholders.
- An S corporation may be owned by individuals, estates, and certain trusts but not by other corporations.
- An S corporation may not set up an active subsidiary.

PERKS

The 1982 law changed the fringe benefit rules—for the worse. S corporations are now treated as partnerships and proprietorships, as far as perks are concerned.

That means health, disability, and group life insurance purchased for shareholders with a 2-percent or greater stake in the corporation aren't deductible by the company. (See chapter 15 for a full discussion of fringe benefits.)

PRIVACY

An S corporation generally protects a shareholder's privacy. Most lenders do not require shareholders in a large or established S corporation to reveal their personal assets when the company applies for a loan, but they may request information on the personal financial status of owners if a business is small, is a start-up, or is owned by one person.

SHELTER

Since an S corporation's profits and losses are passed on to its shareholders, this form of organization provides no possibilities for protecting business income from taxation. You can't cash in on low corporate tax rates that apply to the first $75,000 of income.

TAXES

With an S corporation, income is reported on the personal tax returns of shareholders, just as it would if the business were a sole proprietorship or a partnership.

In this respect, an S corporation is the same old Subchapter S: the absence of a corporate income tax on earnings continues to be its primary selling point.

Also, S corporations are still subject to Social Security taxes on wages paid to employees—including shareholder employees—at the same rates as ordinary corporations. That is, they must pay 15.02 percent of the first $45,000 in income compared to 13.02 percent on the income of sole proprietorships and partnerships.

As we've seen, though, this is a plus, not a minus.

S corporations, like regular corporations, actually pay only half of the 15.02 percent bill. The other 7.56 percent is deducted from the employees' salaries.

TAXTRAP

The following states do not recognize S corporations. Thus, they'll charge you corporate taxes even if you choose S status at the federal level:

- Connecticut
- District of Columbia
- Louisiana
- Michigan
- New Hampshire
- New Jersey
- North Carolina
- Tennessee

Owners of S corporations in these states pay taxes like proprietors at the federal level and like ordinary corporations at the state level. The S corporation does deduct its state tax bill on its federal returns. In most cases, however, owners of S corporations would be better off if they could simply pay state taxes like sole proprietors and partners—and skip the deduction on their corporations' federal returns.

TAXTRAP

Here's more bad news: some states that do recognize S corporations impose a corporate tax on them, though the tax is lower than the regular corporate rate.

In California, for example, regular corporations pay a tax of 9.3 percent on their earnings, while S corporations pay 2.5 percent.

YEAR

Normally, S corporations may not elect a fiscal year that differs from the calendar year.

BOTTOM LINE

Companies that benefit most from operating as S corporations are start-ups and mature no-growth businesses. Here's why:

- Start-ups usually operate in the red during their first two or three years. S-corporation rules allow owners to claim business losses on their personal returns.
- Mature companies benefit from S-corporation status. They have no need to accumulate earnings to finance growth—a primary reason for forming a corporation. Moreover, they avoid the accumulated earnings tax.

Finally, by operating as S corporations instead of ordinary corporations, mature companies bypass having to pay taxes at both the corporate and personal level.

FOR MORE INFORMATION

See these IRS publications:

- *Tax Information on S Corporations* (Number 589)
- *Your Federal Income Tax* (Number 17)
- *Tax Guide for Small Business* (Number 334)
- *Farmers' Tax Guide* (Number 225)
- *Tax Guide for Commercial Fishermen* (Number 595)
- *Tax Information for Direct Sellers* (Number 911)

Try these IRS Tele-Tax tapes:

- *Business Income* (Number 136)
- *Rental Income and Expenses* (Number 143)
- *Farming and Fishing Income* (Number 202)
- *Small Business Tax Workshops—Tax Help for the New Businessperson* (Number 102)

Chapter 7

THE NUMBERS GAME

Cashing In on Cash and Accrual
Accounting

"Next to being shot at and missed," someone once quipped, "nothing is quite as satisfying as an income tax refund."

I couldn't agree more—with one caveat.

The goal of tax planning is not to get a sizable check back from Uncle Sam. (After all, why should you let the government keep a big chunk of your money—on which it pays no interest—for the better part of a year?) Instead, the object is to pay no more in income taxes than you should and to pay no sooner than you're required.

As we've seen, the first step in achieving these ends is to pick the best form of organization for your business. The second step is to select the right accounting method.

The choice usually isn't too difficult.

For starters, you have only two options. You must select either cash or accrual accounting. And, as we'll see, many types of businesses don't have a choice at all.

IN GOD WE TRUST—ALL OTHERS PAY CASH

Cash accounting is the simpler of the two methods.

With cash-basis accounting, income is recorded when it is actually received; expenses are reported when they are actually paid.

But only certain types of businesses may use the cash method. The law says that businesses selling services—such as insurance agencies, freight lines, travel agencies, and consultants—are permitted to use this method. Other people who fall into this category: lawyers, accountants, doctors, writers, and owners of hotels and motels.

Farming and timber businesses may use the cash method. So may businesses, other than tax shelters, that have average annual gross receipts of $5 million or less. But the law prohibits the following types of businesses from using the cash method:

- Companies that maintain inventories
- Regular corporations with gross receipts of more than $5 million
- Partnerships with one or more regular corporations as a partner or partners
- Tax shelters
- Trusts, such as charitable trusts, that are taxed on income that is unrelated to the main purpose of the trust

For example, say a nonprofit country club, operated by a trust, pays taxes on revenues it derives from renting out its restaurant for special events.

The club must use the accrual method to keep tabs on this unrelated business income. But the club may use the cash basis to account for revenues from its related activities—greens' fees, meals in the restaurant, and so on.

The primary advantage of the cash method: Your income is not subject to taxation by Uncle Sam until the money is in hand.

The primary disadvantage: Cash-basis accounting tells you when income is collected and paid out but not when money is earned or expenses incurred. As a result, your records provide you with an accurate picture of cash flow but no information on how your business earns and disburses money over the long run.

HOW TO PLAY THE GAME

First, the good news: Even if you use the cash method, you may write off some expenses before you actually fork over any money to a vendor.

Say you buy office supplies with a credit card. You make the purchase in December, but you don't write a check for the amount you spent until January when you receive your credit card bill.

Under the rules, you may write off the expense in December anyway. Technically, the credit card company is loaning you the money for the purchase.

Since the IRS doesn't care if the expense is taken care of with borrowed funds or money out of your own pocket, it views your purchase as paid.

So if you want to accelerate deductions but are strapped for cash, use credit cards to purchase items at year's end.

Now, the bad news: Even though you use the cash method of accounting, you may have to report money you have not actually received as income.

The federal government's "constructive-receipt" rules state that income is yours the minute you have "control" over it.

If you receive a check, you must treat the income as if it were yours—even if you don't deposit the money in your bank account for weeks.

Also, if you appoint someone as your agent and he or she receives money for you, you're considered to have earned the cash the minute your agent has it in hand.

Why? The IRS assumes you control your agent and the money is yours for the taking.

FYI

As a rule, you, as a cash-basis taxpayer, may consider an expense paid on the date you write a check or purchase a money order.

If the check bounces, you may not claim your expense until you deposit sufficient funds in your account or you arrange for the bank to cover your overdraft.

If you make payments by telephone or computer, you may deduct the amount on the date the financial institution actually pays the bill. This date is reported on your bank statement.

Another rule: If you receive income in the form of property—in a barter deal, say—you must report as earnings the fair-market value of that property once it is in your hands.

DANCING TO ANOTHER TUNE

The accrual method is just the opposite of cash accounting.

With accrual accounting, revenues are recorded as they are earned, regardless of when the money is actually collected. Similarly, expenses are recorded as they are incurred, without regard to when the cash is paid out to meet an obligation.

The accrual method has some disadvantages. Primary among them is that you pay income taxes on revenue before it is actually in hand—a real drain on cash flow.

But accrual accounting does paint a more accurate picture of how well a business is doing overall than does cash-basis accounting. The reason: Accrual-basis financial statements show the income you've produced and the expenses you've incurred; cash-basis financial statements show only cash flow.

Under IRS regulations, any business may use accrual accounting, but all businesses carrying inventories—from tiny retail stores to giant manufacturing companies—*must* use the accrual method. The government is dead serious about this rule.

_____ CASE IN POINT _____

A funeral home, which employed the cash method of accounting, deducted the cost of caskets in the year it paid for them—whether they used them or not.

The amount the funeral home charged for its coffins included not only the cost of the box itself but the expense of providing certain services.

For example, the home added in the cost of embalming, a charge for the use of its chapel, plus a fee for transporting the deceased to the grave site.

When the IRS audited the funeral home's return, it balked at the undertaker's use of the cash method. The caskets, the IRS ruled, must be regarded as inventory.

Why?

The funeral home always kept an ample supply on hand. Furthermore, the sale of the caskets was an integral part of the funeral home's business and "of an income-producing nature," which is how the IRS defines inventory.

Moreover, only on rare occasions, when a body would be shipped to the funeral home from another part of the country, would the home furnish funeral services without the use of its own caskets. So the home was not, as it claimed, simply a service business. It sold a product, too—coffins.

For all these reasons, the tax court judge concluded, the funeral home was obliged to use the accrual method of accounting.

TIMING IS EVERYTHING

For the most part, payments that accrual-basis taxpayers receive in advance are treated like payments cash-basis taxpayers receive in advance. That is, they are counted as income in the year they are received. Among the few exceptions to this rule: fees paid for future services and fees paid before the manufacture of special-order or custom-made items.

But as far as advance payments for future services go, the

IRS allows you, an accrual-basis taxpayer, to defer reporting them only on one condition: you must provide the services for which the advance payment is made before the end of the next tax year—not several years down the road.

Also, in order to put off reporting these advance payments as income, you must be able to identify when the services will actually be rendered.

Another requirement: The amount of income you defer must equal the value of the services that you have yet to deliver.

_____ CASE IN POINT _____

Say that in November 1988 you sign a one-year contract to provide forty-eight dancing lessons to a group of young-sters.

You collect your money for the full contract thirty days later—December 30. You give eight dancing lessons in 1988 and forty in 1989.

Under the rules, you may, if you wish, report the value of eight dancing lessons as income in 1988 and defer the remainder until 1989.

_____ FYI _____

If you own rental property, two rules apply to the receipt of advance payments:

* You may not defer reporting as income any advance rent or interest payments you receive.
* You don't have to include in income security deposits that are refundable to your tenants.

GOOD, BAD, AND INDIFFERENT

When it comes to writing off bad debts, the law is strict: you may deduct as bad debts loans and amounts you previously reported as income.

As a result, the write-off is generally available only to accrual-basis taxpayers. It may not be taken by anyone who uses the cash method.

_____ CASE IN POINT _____

Say you're an accountant who uses the cash method, and you submit a bill for $560 to one of your clients. The bill is never paid.

Under the rules, you are not entitled to a bad debt deduction. The reason: You never reported the $560 as income.

One exception to the rule: Cash-basis taxpayers may deduct as bad debts cash advances and expenses they incur in providing services to people or companies that don't pay up.

_____ **TAXTRAP** _____

In the past, you could set aside a so-called reserve for bad debts based on your past collection experience. Then you could deduct your addition to this reserve each year.

But no more. Our legislators eliminated the reserve method of accounting for bad debts in 1986 for tax years after 1986. Now you may write off a bad debt only when it becomes partially or totally worthless.

IF EVER TWO WERE ONE

Many companies that may use either the cash method or the accrual method divide their operations into two parts. They then use the cash method of accounting for one portion of their business and the accrual method for the other.

Their reason for combining methods is simple: they are required to use accrual accounting for any part of their business that maintains inventories.

Since they don't want to pay taxes on income before it is actually received, they choose to use cash accounting for the remainder of their operations.

This tactic is perfectly legal.

Hotels, for example, frequently take advantage of this strategy. Typically, they use the accrual method for their food services (where they maintain inventories) but use the cash method for keeping track of room rentals.

The reason? It sometimes takes hotels weeks to collect their money from customers who rent meeting rooms and other convention facilities. By using the cash method, they don't have to report that money as income until they actually receive it.

VARIETY IS THE SPICE OF LIFE

Congress has provided several variations on the two basic accounting methods to benefit businesses in a few select industries.

Publishing is an example.

_____ **CASE IN POINT** _____

As a publisher of a skiing magazine, you collect your subscription fees in advance.

Under the rules, you may report your subscription income over the period you are obligated to deliver the magazine—not when the money is received.

That means you record income from a subscriber each time you mail your ski publication to that subscriber and no sooner. The result: You defer paying taxes from one year to the next on a sizable portion of your subscription income.

ANOTHER DIFFERENCE BETWEEN DEATH AND TAXES: DEATH IS FREQUENTLY PAINLESS

Businesses that use the cash method may issue financial statements under the accrual method yet still file their income tax returns using the cash basis.

The benefit of mixing methods is clear.

Your company pays taxes under the cash method—meaning your tax liability is computed on income as it is received, not when it is recorded. But you prepare financial statements using the accrual method, so your records present an accurate picture of your day-to-day operations.

However, businesses that use the accrual method of accounting and want to change to the cash method must seek permission from the IRS.

Nowadays, Uncle Sam allows you to make the change on one condition: you must prepare all financial statements, including those provided to creditors, on a cash basis.

TAXTRAP

If you think you can switch accounting methods without gaining permission from the IRS, you're wrong.

If you do, and IRS auditors spot your change—not an uncommon occurrence—you'll probably pay dearly for your transgression.

Under the rules, Uncle Sam can slap you with a negligence penalty (5 to 50 percent of the taxes you owe) for changing accounting methods without approval.

FYI

For permission to switch your accounting method, file Form 3115 no later than the 180th day of the year for which you are requesting the change.

IN THE BEGINNING

It makes no difference which accounting method you use: you may not write off business expenses until your company is actually in operation.

The dollars you shell out before your business is up and running are, in the eyes of the IRS, start-up expenditures.

And start-up costs, such as employee training and market research, must be amortized or written off over a period of time, in this case, not less than sixty months. This period begins the day you actually open your doors for business.

The one exception: Taxes, interest expenses (except those that you must depreciate as part of the cost of an asset), and research-and-development costs may be written off in the year in which they are incurred.

―――――――――― **TAXTIP** ――――――――――

You may write off the costs of expanding an ongoing business in the year in which you shell out the money.

―――――――――― **CASE IN POINT** ――――――――――

An existing operating subsidiary of a corporation was allowed to deduct all the expenses associated with opening its new restaurants. The costs included salaries and travel expenses for restaurant managers and wages paid to new employees during their training.

However, when a new subsidiary was formed to comply with a law requiring local ownership of liquor licenses, expenses incurred before opening couldn't be deducted. They had to be amortized.

―――――――――― **TAXTRAP** ――――――――――

Unfair as it seems, start-up costs are deductible only if the business actually gets off the ground.

The IRS, for example, wouldn't allow a taxpayer to write off the money he spent developing hunting camps in Alaska, since the camps never opened for business.

It also wouldn't let a taxpayer depreciate the cost of equipment purchased for a video company. The reason: The man couldn't prove he ever started his business.

TAX STRATEGIES

Here's an idea worth considering: Installment sales enable you to defer income from one year to the next and may be used by both accrual- and cash-basis taxpayers.

With installment sales, buyers spread out their payments to you over a specified period of time rather than paying you in one lump sum.

It makes no difference if you're an accrual-basis taxpayer. You still report the money as income as you actually receive it.

_____ **CASE IN POINT** _____

Say you own an antique car that you purchased for $24,000. In November 1988, you sell it for $30,000. That makes your profit on the deal $6,000.

If your customer pays you $30,000 on the spot, you must report the entire $6,000 profit on your 1988 income tax return.

But if your customer pays you $3,000 a month for ten months, you report your profit as it comes in—$600 a month for ten months.

If your customer makes two payments in 1988 and eight payments in 1989, you'd report income of $1,200 in 1988 and $4,800 in 1989.

In fact, you could, if you wish, defer your entire profit until 1989 by contracting at the outset to make no payments on the car until then.

_____ **TAXTRAP** _____

The 1986 Tax Reform Act and the 1987 Revenue Act zapped the use of installment sales by dealers.

For example, if you sell furniture, you're not allowed to use the installment method to report your furniture sales. But say you sell your old cash register. You may use the installment method for this transaction, because selling cash registers is not your primary line of business.

The rules say you may also use the installment method if you sell residential lots, timeshares, and farm land. Real estate sales are also eligible as long as the property costs less than $150,000. If it costs more than $150,000, you may still use the installment method, but you have to pay interest on the tax you've deferred.

Here's how it works.

You must calculate how much tax you'd pay if you reported the sale not on the installment method. Then you must pay interest to Uncle Sam on that amount.

Finally, you may not use installment sales for securities traded on an established market.

One final strategy: If your business uses the cash method of accounting, we suggest you reexamine your choice from time to time. You may find that a switch to accrual accounting could prove beneficial.

CASE IN POINT

Years ago, a client of ours adopted the cash method to track income and expenses for his apartments and other rental properties.

The primary reason he opted for cash accounting: The method allowed him to write off mortgage interest payments he made in advance.

Congress nixed this practice in the 1970s. Still, the client stuck with cash accounting until we advised him to adopt the accrual method.

Accrual accounting let him write off expenses for services as they were incurred, not when he actually paid for them. As a result, he was able to accelerate the amount he deducted for such big-ticket items as repairs and maintenance.

Also, he was able to write off gas, electric, and water bills that were actually paid in January but covered services that were provided during a period ending in December.

And, since most of his tenants paid their rents on time, the amount of rental income he reported each year didn't change significantly with his accounting method.

FOR MORE INFORMATION
See these IRS publications:

- *Accounting Periods and Methods* (Number 538)
- *Your Federal Income Tax* (Number 17)
- *Tax Guide for Small Business* (Number 334)
- *Farmers' Tax Guide* (Number 225)
- *Tax Guide for Commercial Fishermen* (Number 595)
- *Tax Information for Direct Sellers* (Number 911)

Try this IRS Tele-Tax tape:

- *Small Business Tax Workshops—Tax Help for the New Businessperson* (Number 102)

Chapter 8

THE PAPER CHASE

Understanding LIFO and FIFO

The tax laws provide two methods of accounting for inventory: First In First Out or FIFO inventory accounting and Last In First Out or LIFO inventory accounting.

- A supermarket puts last week's potato chips in front of today's, so customers will buy the older chips first and they won't go stale. Accountants call this system FIFO inventory management.
- A coal yard dumps incoming coal on a pile. Whenever a customer buys a ton, workers simply shovel out the most recently delivered coal. Accountants refer to this system as LIFO inventory management.

If your business carries inventories, mastering the distinctions between the FIFO and LIFO methods is important to you. The difference between the two approaches may seem unrelated to taxes. But, in reality, the tax implications are enormous.

Why? How you account for your inventory determines how you calculate your costs. Your costs, in turn, affect the size of your profit.

The smaller the profit you make, the less tax you pay.

FIRST THINGS FIRST
Before deciding whether to choose LIFO or FIFO, you should know the IRS's definition of inventory. Uncle Sam regards as inventory:

- Any item that you plan to resell in the normal course of your business
- Any item that ultimately will become part of a product that you resell

So inventory includes:

- Finished goods
- Partly finished goods, or work in process, such as a partially sewn pair of pants
- Raw materials (such as iron ore, steel, and so on) and supplies that either will become part of your merchandise or be used in the manufacture of products

Legally, your inventory does not include items you don't own. For example, used clothing you accept on consignment has no inventory value to your store—from the tax collector's point of view, anyway.

But here's the flip side: Merchandise remains part of your inventory as long as you continue to own it. Say, for example, that you sell antiques on consignment. The antiques remain part of your inventory, whether they're in your warehouse or in a customer's shop.

_____ **FYI** _____

Inventory doesn't include the cost of items you wouldn't resell in the normal course of business. For instance, you'd consider typewriter ribbons, envelopes, and other office supplies ordinary business expenses and write them off as such.

Also, real estate is never considered inventory, even if your primary business is selling homes. So homebuilders may not use the LIFO method.
_____

CHOICES, CHOICES

Uncle Sam provides a great deal of latitude when it comes to choosing how to calculate the value of your inventories.

A supermarket owner who, in fact, sells the oldest items in her stock first, may pretend for tax purposes that her inventory moves Last In First Out (LIFO). The coal yard owner who sells his newest coal first may pretend that he manages his inventory on a FIFO basis.

Here's the bottom line on how you should report: You want to choose the method that allows you to claim the least profit—and pay the least amount in taxes.

WILL IT BE FIFO OR WILL IT BE LIFO?

Any business that carries inventories may select either the FIFO or the LIFO method of accounting for inventories.

Let's go back to the supermarket owner who decides to use

FIFO—both on her shelves and on her books. The supermarket owner—or any FIFO taxpayer—can easily calculate the price she paid, and thus the value for tax purposes, of her stock on hand.

Under the FIFO rules, she values her potato chips at the amount she originally paid for them. She has only to count the bags of potato chips in stock and multiply by her purchase price to learn the value of her inventory.

If she has been buying potato chips for 50 cents a bag and has 100 bags in stock, her inventory is worth $50. If she sells these 100 bags of potato chips for 75 cents each, her profit is 25 cents per bag—or a total of $25.

But FIFO can get more complicated if you've been in business more than a year. In that case, your business—to arrive at its profit—must compute its beginning inventory, its ending inventory, the goods available for sale, and the cost of goods sold.

Here's an example of how it all works.

Say the supermarket owner has been in business more than a year. She starts the year with 150 bags of chips on hand, and the chips are valued at $72.50. During the year, she purchases 100 bags of chips for $50 or 50 cents a bag, and 400 bags for $220 or 55 cents a bag.

She calculates her goods available for sale by adding her beginning inventory—$72.50—to her purchases during the year—$220 plus $50. The result: $342.50.

Now, she counts up her ending inventory. She has 200 bags of chips on hand. She calculates the value of her inventory by tracing her purchases.

Her last order was for 200 bags, and she paid 55 cents for each bag. So she values the 200 bags in inventory at 55 cents a bag or $110.

Finally, she figures her cost of goods sold. She subtracts her inventory—$110—from the goods available for sale—$342.50. The result—$232.50 is her cost of goods sold.

Why is the cost of goods sold important? As the cost of goods sold goes up, income goes down. If the cost of goods sold goes down, income goes up.

WHAT A DIFFERENCE LIFO MAKES

Now let's look at a company handling inventory accounting on a LIFO basis. Again, we'll use the supermarket owner as an illustration.

Say the owner is in her first year of business. Under the LIFO rules, she values the chips in her ending inventory first at the price she paid for chips during the year, not at the amount she paid. To learn the value of her inventory, she multiplies the number of bags of potato chips in stock times the current price.

What if she's been in business more than a year? The calculation is more complicated.

She starts with a beginning inventory—in her case, $65 or 150 bags of potato chips times at a beginning price of 43 cents a bag.

During the year, she purchases an additional 500 bags of chips. She pays 50 cents a bag or $50 for the first 100 bags, then 55 cents a bag for the remaining 400 bags.

That means she has 650 bags of chips available for sale during the year—that is, her inventory of 150 bags plus 500 new bags.

So her goods available for sale adds up to $335. Next, she adds up her ending inventory, and it comes to 200 bags.

Now, here's where LIFO differs from FIFO. Under the LIFO rules, she treats 150 bags as being the same 150 bags she started the year with. She values the remaining 50 bags by multiplying them by the earliest price paid that year—50 cents a bag.

So her ending inventory adds up to $90—that is, $65 (her beginning inventory) plus $25 (50 cents times 50 bags) or $90.

Her cost of goods sold comes to $245—or her goods available for sale of $335 less her ending inventory of $90.

BOTTOM LINE

The main trick to choosing between LIFO or FIFO is remembering a couple of rules of thumb:

When prices are rising, LIFO gives you a lower profit figure. So you pay less tax.

Under these same conditions, FIFO produces a higher profit figure. So you pay more tax.

When prices are falling, the opposite holds true. You pay less tax under FIFO than you do under LIFO.

—————————————— **TAXTIPS** ——————————————

LIFO doesn't make sense if you're in an industry, such as high technology, where the price of products drops as they become more common.

Another important point: The law lets you use different methods for different inventories. For example, a car dealer may use LIFO for his new car and auto parts inventories, but he may use FIFO for his inventory of used cars.

_____ **TAXTRAP** _____

Usually, Uncle Sam makes you wait ten years to readopt LIFO once you switch to FIFO, so you should carefully weigh your decision to change methods.

_____ **FYI** _____

To switch from FIFO to LIFO, you must file Form 970, "Application to Use LIFO Inventory Method," with your return. To switch from LIFO to FIFO, file Form 3115, "Application to Change an Accounting Method," in the first 180 days of the tax year in which you want to make the change.

FOR MORE INFORMATION
See these IRS publications:

- *Accounting Periods and Methods* (Number 538)
- *Your Federal Income Tax* (Number 17)
- *Tax Guide for Small Business* (Number 334)
- *Farmers' Tax Guide* (Number 225)
- *Tax Guide for Commercial Fishermen* (Number 595)
- *Tax Information for Direct Sellers* (Number 911)

Try this IRS Tele-Tax tape:

- *Small Business Tax Workshops—Tax Help for the New Businessperson* (Number 102)

Chapter 9

SAFETY IN NUMBERS

Locking In Depreciation Deductions

When you purchase machinery or equipment for your business—a company car or a computer, say—the IRS generally won't allow you to write off the cost of that item all at once. Instead, Uncle Sam requires that you deduct it over a specified number of years. This gradual write-off is known as depreciation.

By definition, depreciation is a tax deduction you take for the effects of decay, corrosion, wear and tear, and obsolescence on your business equipment and machinery.

Items qualify for depreciation if, in the eyes of the IRS, they have a useful life of more than a year. Telephones and typewriters qualify for depreciation. Office supplies do not.

As a rule, any item of small value—less than $100 or so—may be written off completely in the year it is purchased. However, if you purchase several items for $100 each—a dozen chairs, say, or six small tables—you'll probably have to depreciate them.

Any item that you hold for resale or material that you use in the manufacture of a product you sell doesn't have to be depreciated. So inventories don't qualify for depreciation.

It Takes Two
Current tax laws provide two methods for depreciating newly acquired equipment and machinery—the straight-line method and the accelerated method. (Real estate depreciation is a different kettle of fish. See chapter 10 for a discussion of these special rules.)

These two methods are part of the Modified Accelerated Cost Recovery System (MACRS), which was created under the 1986 Tax Reform Act.

Straight-line is the easiest of the methods.

You simply divide the cost of the item you're depreciating

by the number of years over which the law allows you to recover the purchase price. (Uncle Sam furnishes clear guidelines for the recovery time of different categories of items. You'll find these tables at the end of this chapter.)

You deduct that amount from your taxable income each year—except in the first and last years that you write off the equipment.

In those years, you write off half the amount.

───────────── **CASE IN POINT** ─────────────

Say you shell out $10,000 for a business computer and printer. The law tells you to write off the cost of these items over five years.

So you divide the purchase price—$10,000—by five and get $2,000. In the first year, you write off half that amount—$1,000.

In the second, third, fourth, and fifth years, you deduct $2,000. In the sixth year, you write off the remaining $1000.

Whoa! I hear you say. That's six years, not five.

Well, not exactly. According to the rules, you're entitled to six months depreciation in year one and a full year in years two, three, four, and five. Then you pick up the final six months in year six. (This rule is known as the midyear convention.)

That adds up to five full years of depreciation.

───

The second depreciation method—accelerated—is slightly more complicated. If you use it, you may take larger deductions in the early years of ownership, a big plus for taxpayers.

The tax code defines two types of accelerated depreciation—the 200-percent-declining-balance method and the 150-percent-declining-balance method.

Which method do you use? It depends on the type of property you're depreciating. You use the 200-percent method for everything except 15- and 20-year property. For 15-year and 20-year property only, you use the 150-percent method. To figure out how much to depreciate each year, you simply look up the correct percentage in the tables we've reproduced at the end of this chapter.

───────────── **CASE IN POINT** ─────────────

Again say that you shell out $10,000 for a business computer and printer. This time, however, you write off their cost using the 200-percent double-declining balance method. How do you calculate your depreciation deductions?

A computer is five-year property. Since you bought your equipment in January—and you made no other capital expenditures during the year—the half-year convention applies. So you consult Table 1 at the end of this chapter. It says that you write off 20 percent of the purchase price—or $2,000—in the first year.

In the second year, you claim 32 percent of the purchase price, or $3,200. In the third year, you deduct 19.2 percent of the purchase price or $1,920.

In the fourth and fifth years, you write off 11.52 percent annually or $1,152. Finally, in the sixth year, you write off the remaining 5.76 percent or $576.

The advantage of this method over straight-line depreciation is clear. You write off an extra $1,000 in year one and an additional $1,200 in year two. In years three, four, five, and six, you write off less than you would under the straight-line method.

But no matter. You have to consider the time value of your money. It's better to get the larger write-offs—and pay less tax—sooner rather than later. That way you have extra money in your pocket to save or invest.

TAXTIPS

One way to trim your current tax liability is to accelerate equipment purchases. Buy machinery and equipment in late 1988 rather than early 1989.

Also, you may, if you wish, deduct equipment and machinery over longer periods. This tactic benefits taxpayers who know they'll need depreciation deductions to offset substantial income further down the road.

But there are rules governing the use of longer depreciation schedules, too. For one, you must use the straight-line method. So if you plan on going this route, see your accountant.

FYI

Use Form 4562 to report your depreciation deductions.

WHAT A DIFFERENCE A DAY MAKES

In most cases, it makes no difference if you owned the equipment for the entire year or only on the last day of the year. You are entitled to the same amount of depreciation.

As you recall, however, a midyear convention applies when you depreciate property. Under it, you claim a half year's depreciation in the first and last years, no matter when you actually bought the property.

The law also mandates a midquarter convention.

You must figure your depreciation using this convention if more than 40 percent of your capital expenditures take place in the last quarter of the year.

How does the convention work? You identify when—by quarter—you purchased each item. Then you depreciate the property according to a schedule that assumes you bought it in the middle of the quarter.

Specifically, you use Table 2 for property purchased in the first quarter, Table 3 for property bought in the second quarter, Table 4 for property purchased in the third quarter, and Table 5 for property bought in the fourth quarter. (The IRS tables are given at the end of this chapter.)

--- **TAXTIP** ---

You can use the midquarter convention to your advantage. Say you make a large purchase in the first quarter. You buy nothing in the second and third quarters. You plan to purchase a needed piece of equipment in the fourth quarter.

Should you buy it this year or next?

If you spend enough in the fourth quarter to make you subject to the midquarter convention, you get more depreciation for the year. How? You get 10.5 months of depreciation—instead of 6 months—on the property you acquired in January.

PLAY BALL

When we think of depreciable items, we usually have in mind such tangible property as tractors, computers, office furniture, and so on. But you may also depreciate such intangible assets as the value of sales territories as well as ballplayers' contracts.

Under the rules, you may depreciate an intangible asset only if it has a limited useful life that can be estimated with some accuracy.

Goodwill, for example, is classified by the law as an intangible asset. It is not depreciable, however, because its useful life is as long as a company exists. How you write off those intan-

gible assets that qualify for depreciation can make a big difference in your tax bill.

_____ **CASE IN POINT** _____

On April 1, 1970, Allan "Bud" Selig and his partners put
up $10.8 million to buy the floundering Seattle Pilots
and move them to Milwaukee, where they became the
Milwaukee Brewers.

The contract between the Pilots and the Brewers
allocated $100,000 of the purchase price to equipment and
supplies, $500,000 to the value of the franchise (including
membership in the American League), and $10.2 million—
or 95 percent of the total—to player contracts.

The IRS had no trouble accepting the equipment valuation, but when it came to the franchise and player allot-
ments, Uncle Sam cried foul.

Here's why: Selig depreciated the $10.2 million in his
ballplayers' contracts over five years—the accepted useful
life of the right to a baseball player's services.

The $500,000 allocated to the franchise could not be
depreciated, since the franchise had "no definable limited
useful life." So Selig benefited by allocating as much of
the purchase price as possible to the value of the contracts.

In 1979, the IRS disallowed the entire $10.2 million
allocation and attributed zero value to the player contracts.

As a result, the Brewers' owner anted up more than
$141,000 in extra taxes, plus interest. Then he sued. On
appeal, the court held that Selig's allocation was, in fact,
proper.

Selig offered in evidence appraisals of the Brewers' 149-
man roster plus proof of the high cost of player development. He also pointed to the amount of insurance he had
to carry on his men and the big bucks ballplayers were
commanding.

An economics expert testified that Milwaukee's small
population and its many sports franchises made Selig's
own franchise not very valuable.

The government, in turn, tried to convince the appeals
court that the fair-market value of the franchise was more
than 5 percent of the club's purchase price.

"Why," the government's lawyers asked, "would anyone

pay more than $10 million for a team when the franchise is essentially worthless?"

But the appeals judge remained unswayed.

For starters, he said, Selig did allocate $500,000 to the franchise. "You take $500,000 here and $500,000 there," he noted, "and pretty soon you're talking about real money."

Moreover, he noted, the original franchise wasn't as valuable as the government claimed, since the baseball climate in Milwaukee was relatively poor.

Besides, the judge said, "Players are principally responsible for winning games, drawing fans, and maintaining the financial health of the franchise."

The judge wrapped up the case by quoting the immortal lines of another baseball fan, Ernest L. Thayer:

> But there is no joy in Mudville—
> Mighty Casey has Struck Out.

With his favorable ruling, the judge concluded, "There should be joy somewhere in Milwaukee."

WHOSE LIFE IS IT, ANYWAY?

Before the passage of the Economic Recovery Tax Act (ERTA) in 1981, you depreciated machinery and equipment over a period that was supposed to represent its actual useful life. But, in 1981, Congress gave up trying to guess the useful lives of each individual item and adopted the Accelerated Cost Recovery System (ACRS).

The present system—MACRS—sets forth, by category, the amount of time over which you may write off new equipment and machinery, regardless of which depreciation method you use.

These recovery periods range from three to twenty years. Three-year property covers small tools. Five-year property includes light trucks, cars, and computers.

In the seven-year category are office furniture and fixtures and most other equipment and machinery. In the ten-, fifteen-, and twenty-year classes are a small number of specialized assets, such as industrial steam and electric generating equipment and cable television lines.

SLEIGHT OF HAND

If you sell machinery and equipment at a profit, you must comply with tough regulations designed to allow the government to recapture excess depreciation.

Here's how these rules work: Every item you depreciate has a value for tax purposes—its basis. This basis is the purchase price minus the depreciation you've taken.

When you sell business equipment for less than its basis, you write off the difference as a loss. When, however, you sell business equipment for more than its basis but less than its original cost, you must report the difference—a gain—as ordinary income.

TAX STRATEGIES

In the 1970s, Congress provided small businesses, especially proprietorships, with a tax break: a capital investment "expense allowance."

With the allowance, small businesses could deduct as a business expense 100 percent of the cost of equipment in the year they bought it.

They didn't have to worry about complex accounting rules that required them to spread out deductions over several years. Rather they could take the write-off in one bite and improve cash flow. The only catch: The limit on this allowance was a meager $2,000.

In 1980, small business trade groups began promoting the idea of increasing the expense allowance, and the politicians joined in.

The push on behalf of small companies resulted in a graduated allowance that began in 1982 at $5,000. The allowance now stands at $10,000. You may claim the full allowance as long as your equipment purchases don't add up to more than $200,000 a year.

TAXTRAP

Recapture rules apply to items deducted under the special $10,000 write-off provision for small businesses.

If you buy a desk for $500, write it off immediately, then later sell it for $200, you must pay ordinary income tax on the $200 you receive.

Another important point: This deduction is available to you only if your business posts a profit. You may not use the write-off to boost your company's loss for the year.

Table 1. General Depreciation System
Applicable Depreciation Method: 200 or 150 Percent
Declining Balance Switching to Straight Line
Applicable Recovery Periods: 3, 5, 7, 10, 15, 20 years
Applicable Convention: Half-year

If the Recovery Year is:	3-year	5-year	7-year	10-year	15-year	20-year
			the Depreciation Rate is:			
1	33.33	20.00	14.29	10.00	5.00	3.750
2	44.45	32.00	24.49	18.00	9.50	7.219
3	14.81	19.20	17.49	14.40	8.55	6.677
4	7.41	11.52	12.49	11.52	7.70	6.177
5		11.52	8.93	9.22	6.93	5.713
6		5.76	8.92	7.37	6.23	5.285
7			8.93	6.55	5.90	4.888
8			4.46	6.55	5.90	4.522
9				6.56	5.91	4.462
10				6.55	5.90	4.461
11				3.28	5.91	4.462
12					5.90	4.461
13					5.91	4.462
14					5.90	4.461
15					5.91	4.462
16					2.95	4.461
17						4.462
18						4.461
19						4.462
20						4.461
21						2.231

Table 2. General Depreciation System
Applicable Depreciation Method: 200 or 150 Percent
Declining Balance Switching to Straight Line
Applicable Recovery Periods: 3, 5, 7, 10, 15, 20 years
Applicable Convention: Midquarter (property placed in service in first quarter)

If the Recovery Year is:	3-year	5-year	7-year	10-year	15-year	20-year
			the Depreciation Rate is:			
1	58.33	35.00	25.00	17.50	8.75	6.563
2	27.78	26.00	21.43	16.50	9.13	7.000
3	12.35	15.60	15.31	13.20	8.21	6.482
4	1.54	11.01	10.93	10.56	7.39	5.996
5		11.01	8.75	8.45	6.65	5.546
6		1.38	8.74	6.76	5.99	5.130
7			8.75	6.55	5.90	4.746
8			1.09	6.55	5.91	4.459
9				6.56	5.90	4.459
10				6.55	5.91	4.459
11				0.82	5.90	4.459
12					5.91	4.460
13					5.90	4.459
14					5.91	4.460
15					5.90	4.459
16					0.74	4.460
17						4.459
18						4.460
19						4.459
20						4.460
21						0.557

Table 3.   General Depreciation System
Applicable Depreciation Method: 200 or 150 Percent
Declining Balance Switching to Straight Line
Applicable Recovery Periods: 3, 5, 7, 10, 15, 20 years
Applicable Convention: Midquarter (property placed in service in second quarter)

If the Recovery Year is:	and the Recovery Period is:					
	3-year	5-year	7-year	10-year	15-year	20-year
			the Depreciation Rate is:			
1	41.67	25.00	17.85	12.50	6.25	4.688
2	38.89	30.00	23.47	17.50	9.38	7.148
3	14.14	18.00	16.76	14.00	8.44	6.612
4	5.30	11.37	11.97	11.20	7.59	6.116
5		11.37	8.87	8.96	6.83	5.658
6		4.26	8.87	7.17	6.15	5.233
7			8.87	6.55	5.91	4.841
8			3.33	6.55	5.90	4.478
9				6.56	5.91	4.463
10				6.55	5.90	4.463
11				2.46	5.91	4.463
12					5.90	4.463
13					5.91	4.463
14					5.90	4.463
15					5.91	4.462
16					2.21	4.463
17						4.462
18						4.463
19						4.462
20						4.463
21						1.673

Table 4.   General Depreciation System
Applicable Depreciation Method: 200 or 150 Percent
Declining Balance Switching to Straight Line
Applicable Recovery Periods: 3, 5, 7, 10, 15, 20 years
Applicable Convention: Midquarter (property placed in service in third quarter)

If the Recovery Year is:	and the Recovery Period is:					
	3-year	5-year	7-year	10-year	15-year	20-year
			the Depreciation Rate is:			
1	25.00	15.00	10.71	7.50	3.75	2.813
2	50.00	34.00	25.51	18.50	9.63	7.289
3	16.67	20.40	18.22	14.80	8.66	6.742
4	8.33	12.24	13.02	11.84	7.80	6.237
5		11.30	9.30	9.47	7.02	5.769
6		7.06	8.85	7.58	6.31	5.336
7			8.86	6.55	5.90	4.936
8			5.53	6.55	5.90	4.566
9				6.56	5.91	4.460
10				6.55	5.90	4.460
11				4.10	5.91	4.460
12					5.90	4.460
13					5.91	4.461
14					5.90	4.460
15					5.91	4.461
16					3.69	4.460
17						4.461
18						4.460
19						4.461
20						4.460
21						2.788

Table 5. General Depreciation System
Applicable Depreciation Method: 200 or 150 Percent
Declining Balance Switching to Straight Line
Applicable Recovery Periods: 3, 5, 7, 10, 15, 20 years ·
Applicable Convention: Midquarter (property placed in service in fourth quarter)

If the Recovery Year is:	3-year	5-year	and the Recovery Period is: 7-year	10-year the Depreciation Rate is:	15-year	20-year
1........	8.33	5.00	3.57	2.50	1.25	0.938
2........	61.11	38.00	27.55	19.50	9.88	7.430
3........	20.37	22.80	19.68	15.60	8.89	6.872
4........	10.19	13.68	14.06	12.48	8.00	6.357
5........		10.94	10.04	9.98	7.20	5.880
6........		9.58	8.73	7.99	6.48	5.439
7........			8.73	6.55	5.90	5.031
8........			7.64	6.55	5.90	4.654
9........				6.56	5.90	4.458
10........				6.55	5.91	4.458
11........				5.74	5.90	4.458
12........					5.91	4.458
13........					5.90	4.458
14........					5.91	4.458
15........					5.90	4.458
16........					5.17	4.458
17........						4.458
18........						4.459
19........						4.458
20........						4.459
21........						3.901

FOR MORE INFORMATION
See these IRS publications:

- *Travel, Entertainment, and Gift Expenses* (Number 463)
- *Depreciation* (Number 534)
- *Sales and Other Dispositions of Assets* (Number 544)
- *Basis of Assets* (Number 551)
- *Business Use of Home* (Number 587)
- *Your Federal Income Tax* (Number 17)
- *Tax Guide for Small Business* (Number 334)
- *Farmers' Tax Guide* (Number 225)
- *Tax Guide for Commercial Fishermen* (Number 595)
- *Tax Information for Direct Sellers* (Number 911)

Try these IRS Tele-Tax tapes:

- *Business Use of Car* (Number 215)
- *Office-in-the-Home Expenses* (Number 237)
- *Investment Credit* (Number 311)
- *Basis of Assets* (Number 401)

- *Depreciation—General* (Number 402)
- *Depreciation—Accelerated Cost Recovery System* (Number 403)
- *Small Business Tax Workshops—Tax Help for the New Businessperson* (Number 102)

Chapter 10

THE PROMISED LAND

How to Use Business Real Estate As a Tax Shelter

My grandfather, a man of uncommon common sense, invested only in real estate. When I was still a young fellow, he advised me to do the same.

"I never knew a piece of land," he used to quote John Adams as saying, "to run away or break." I couldn't argue with him then, and I can't argue with him now.

GIVE ME LAND, LOTS OF LAND

People who invest in real estate, whether it's commercial or industrial properties, can profit enormously, particularly with the help of the tax laws.

Here's how: Say it's January of 1989, and you purchase a small storefront for $50,000. You apply for a loan at your local bank, specifying that you will pay $10,000 down.

Your $40,000, twenty-five-year mortgage is approved at an annual interest rate of 10 percent. That makes your monthly mortgage payment $364.

Next, you add up all the other expenses: $800 in property taxes, $400 for insurance, $500 for maintenance and repairs, $200 for water and sewage.

At the end of the year, you will have spent $6,268 on the property—that is, mortgage payments of $4,368 plus other expenses of $1,900.

The best you can do, you assume, is cancel out your mortgage payments and other expenses. So you set the rent on the building at $523 a month ($6,268 divided by 12).

You figure you've broken even. But when you look at your tax situation, you'll see you actually come out way ahead.

Here's how: You deduct the interest you paid as part of the mortgage payment each month—$3,983 the first year. You also write off the local real estate taxes ($800).

Since you are renting out your property, you may also deduct expenses for insurance, maintenance, repairs, water and sewage ($1,100).

But here's where your real savings come in.

You depreciate the building—as the tax laws allow—under the theory that your property will decline in value from year to year as a rental unit.

Land is not depreciable. So you subtract the value of the land—in this case, $5,000—from the amount you depreciate. And you end up depreciating $45,000 of the purchase price.

The amount you deduct in the first year for depreciation is $1,369, or 3.042 percent of the cost of the building since you held it since January. (As we'll see, Uncle Sam mandates a set percentage you may depreciate each year. See below for an explanation of how much you may write off annually.)

Together, these write-offs provide you with a tax deduction of $7,252 for the first year you own the rental property.

This amount, however, is offset by your rental income—$6,268 in year one. You subtract your total income from your deductions—$7,252—to get a $984 loss on the property.

Assuming you're in the 33-percent tax bracket, this $984 loss reduces your income taxes by $325 (33 percent of $984). And you still have the storefront building, which, if you have invested well, should appreciate in value over time.

TAXTRAP

When Congress adopted the 1986 Tax Law, it capped deductible losses from rental real estate at $25,000 a year. This full amount may be claimed only by taxpayers whose adjusted gross income is $100,000 or less. And only if they actively participate in the property's management.

THE OBJECT OF THE GAME IS TO MAKE MONEY

As our example shows, one advantage realized by owners of commercial and industrial property under current law comes in the form of depreciation deductions.

These cost-recovery rules apply to any investment in real estate—a factory, warehouse, or retail space or rental houses, apartments, and condominiums.

Under the depreciation rules, your cost recovery usually takes place over a 31.5-year period (27.5 years for residential rental property).

That means you may deduct from your taxable income each year for 31.5 years a portion of the cost of the property you purchased. At the end of 31.5 years, of course, you will have written off the total cost of your investment property.

The law allows you to depreciate property over as long as 40 years. Increasing the cost-recovery time period might prove helpful if you want to spread out tax deductions over many years. Our advice: As a rule, most people will be better off following the 31.5-year depreciation schedule.

WRITE IT OFF, WRITE IT ALL OFF

As we saw in the last chapter, you must use the straight-line method to depreciate real estate. With the straight-line method, you divide the cost of the property by the number of years over which the law allows you to recover your purchase price.

Then you write off the same amount from year to year—with the exception of the year you purchase the property and the year you sell it. In those years, you're entitled to claim depreciation deductions only for the months you actually own the property.

Moreover, under the so-called midmonth convention, you may claim only a half month's depreciation in the first and last months you own the property. For example, if you purchase a building on February 1, 1989, you may claim only 10.5 months' worth of depreciation that year.

To calculate deductions, you take as your starting point the month you first acquired the property. Then, for commercial property, use the following schedule:

- Deduct 0.1322 percent of the cost of the building the first month you own the property
- Deduct 0.2645 percent a month for the remainder of the year
- Deduct 3.1746 percent a year for each full year you own the property
- Deduct 0.1322 percent the month you sell your property
- Deduct 0.2645 percent a month for the remainder of the year in which you sell

For residential real estate, use this schedule:

- Deduct 0.1515 percent the first month you own the property
- Deduct 0.303 percent a month for the remainder of the year

- Deduct 3.6363 percent a year for each full year you own the property
- Deduct 0.1515 percent the month you sell your property
- Deduct 0.303 percent a month for the remainder of the year in which you sell

TAX STRATEGIES

Don't overlook the rehabilitation tax credit.

When Congress adopted the 1981 Economic Recovery Tax Act (ERTA), it put in a tax credit for people who rehabilitate or restore aging commercial structures.

Tax credits are better than tax deductions. That's because a tax credit is subtracted from your tax bill. A tax deduction merely reduces your taxable income.

The credit, combined with depreciation deductions, produces big tax savings for the owners of these rental properties. The credit equals:

- 10 percent of the cost of redoing structures placed in service before 1936
- 20 percent of the cost of redoing certified historic buildings

So an outlay of $100,000 for renovating a commercial building will produce tax credits of:

- $10,000 if the building was erected before 1936
- $20,000 if the structure is historic

A "certified historic structure" is defined by the government as any building and its structural components that is listed on the National Register or located in a registered historic district.

_____ **TAXTRAPS** _____

Uncle Sam won't allow you to claim a 20-percent credit simply for rehabilitating a building that's a certified historic structure. To qualify for the credit, your plans must also meet the approval of local and federal authorities.

A couple of other special requirements for taking a rehabilitation credit: To earn the credit, a building's owners must leave 75 percent of the square footage of the exterior walls standing after renovation.

Another potentially sticky point: The IRS sets a minimum amount a person or company must spend to qualify for the tax credit.

This amount is the greater of $5,000 or an amount equal

to the adjusted cost basis of the property. In most cases, of course, the adjusted cost basis is the amount the person or business pays for a building.

For example, if a small company pays $200,000 for a building, it must spend $200,000 on renovations to qualify for the credit. The exception to this rule: If an individual or company has owned property for some years and depreciated a portion of it, the adjusted cost basis is computed differently.

Say you purchased a building thirty years ago for $50,000. Under pre-1981 depreciation rules, you depreciated it until its book value is now $12,500. That figure becomes your adjusted basis. So, to qualify for the credit you must spend at least $12,500 rehabilitating the structure.

To make sure no snafus arise, be sure you can prove to the IRS that you have restored the structure, not simply performed a number of repairs. The most convincing evidence is a set of architectural drawings or engineering plans, outlining the renovation or restoration project.

The amount you or your company spends on your restoration project may also be accepted as proof by an IRS examiner.

For example, if you buy a building for $100,000, then put $200,000 into renovating it, not many IRS examiners will argue with you for taking the credit.

FOR MORE INFORMATION
See these IRS publications:

- *Rental Property* (Number 527)
- *Depreciation* (Number 534)
- *Sales and Other Dispositions of Assets* (Number 544)
- *Basis of Assets* (Number 551)
- *Business Use of Your Home* (Number 587)
- *Your Federal Income Tax* (Number 17)
- *Tax Guide for Small Business* (Number 334)
- *Farmers' Tax Guide* (Number 225)
- *Tax Guide for Commercial Fishermen* (Number 595)
- *Tax Information for Direct Sellers* (Number 911)

Try these IRS Tele-Tax tapes:

- *Rental Income and Expenses* (Number 143)
- *Renting Vacation Property, Renting to Relatives* (Number 200)

- *Office-in-the-Home Expenses* (Number 237)
- *Investment Credit* (Number 311)
- *Basis of Assets* (Number 401)
- *Depreciation* (Number 402)
- *Small Business Tax Workshops—Tax Help for the New Businessperson* (Number 102)

Chapter 11

HOME SWEET HOME

A Home Office Is Where
the Deductions Are

A few years back, a man strode into one of our East Coast offices and asked to see an accountant. He was referred to me.

"I need help with my taxes," he told me rather plaintively.

And indeed he did. For more than two years, the man had maintained an office in his house, but he hadn't written off a cent in home office deductions.

"Why not?" I asked him.

"I was afraid to," he told me. "I'd always heard that claiming a home office means an automatic tax audit."

"Nonsense," I responded flatly. Contrary to the accepted wisdom, a home office deduction will not automatically trigger an IRS examination.

"If you're honestly entitled to the deduction," I told the man, "take it. The trick," I added, "is knowing whether you're genuinely eligible."

WHAT QUALIFIES AS A HOME OFFICE?

No doubt about it, the regulations governing home office deductions are harsh. It makes no difference whether you rent or own your home, the same strict rules apply. Under the law, you may write off a home office only if it meets one of three tests:

- It must be your principal place of business.
- It must be used to meet regularly with clients, patients, or customers.
- It must be located in a separate building that is not attached to your house.

In the first two instances, your home office also must be

necessary to the pursuit of your trade or business. For example, a U.S. Tax Court judge recently disallowed a physician's home office deduction. The reason: The doctor maintained the home office simply for his personal convenience; his main office was elsewhere.

Another requirement: Your home office must be used strictly for business. In another recent case, a law student was not allowed to deduct a portion of his rent when he used an area of his apartment to study and write his thesis. The young man was unemployed, said the court, and not required to go to law school. So his expenses were considered purely personal.

Under the rules, the space you write off as a home office doesn't have to be a separate room. You may use half your basement as an office and half as a workshop and still take a deduction.

However, we advise our clients to furnish their home offices as offices. Granted, many people could happily use an old card table as a desk, and their work wouldn't suffer in the slightest. But appropriate furnishings—a real desk, a filing cabinet, a telephone—help demonstrate the legitimacy of a home office deduction to Uncle Sam.

Unsavory as it seems, IRS agents do occasionally come to taxpayers' homes during audits to examine the evidence.

--- **TAXTIPS** ---

For the most part, the IRS and the courts nix write-offs for home offices that are used by taxpayers to manage investments, unless managing those investments is their primary occupation.

Also, be sure your home office is used exclusively for business. The IRS disallows deductions for offices that are also used for personal purposes—a bedroom, say, that is an office by day and sleeping quarters by night.

IT'S NOT THE MONEY, IT'S THE PRINCIPLE
OF THE THING

When the government says that your home office must be your principal or primary place of business, it isn't kidding.

Take the case of the woman who sold homemade baked goods at a stand near her home. True, she prepared her products in her own kitchen, and she used one room of her house exclusively to manage the books of her burgeoning business. But she was not allowed a home office deduction. The small wooden roadside stand, the court ruled, was her principal place of business—not her kitchen and not the room where she did her books.

She's not the only person to be tripped up by the principal-place-of-business rule. Two other unhappy taxpayers who lost their home office deductions:

- A high school track-and-field coach who used a room in his house to do paperwork and review films of his students in action.
- A real estate broker who designated a room in her home as a sales office. (The office of the broker for whom she worked was considered her primary place of business.)

Not only was the office not her main place of business, the court decided, it wasn't even necessary to her business.

But hold on a minute, you say. What about those tens of thousands of people who are engaged in more than one line of work? How do they go about determining their primary place of business?

An individual may legitimately have more than one business. In that case, the person may write off the cost of maintaining more than one office.

_____ **CASE IN POINT** _____

Not too long ago, a dermatologist purchased six rental units and set aside one bedroom of his condominium as an office to manage these properties.

Mindful of the IRS requirement that a home office be used exclusively for business, he furnished the room with a desk, bookcase, filing cabinets, calculator, and answering machine. He kept no television, sofa, or bed in the room. Nor did he allow overnight guests to stay there.

In the closet, he stored such items as lamps, rugs, advertising materials, and cleaning supplies—all used for his rental business.

Despite his precautions, his home office deductions were disallowed during an audit. The doctor's principal place of business was the hospital, the IRS said.

The court, however, didn't buy this argument.

It ruled that the doctor was engaged in two separate businesses and was therefore entitled to deduct the expense of using a portion of his house as an office.

_____

Under unusual circumstances, you may also write off the

expense of maintaining a home office even if you are employed full-time by someone else.

_____ **CASE IN POINT** _____

"What's the best way to get to Carnegie Hall?" a confused tourist asks a New York City native. "Practice! Practice!" comes the reply.

And the courts, it seems, would agree.

Four musicians, employed by the Metropolitan Opera, deducted from their gross incomes the rent, electricity, and maintenance costs of the rooms they set aside in their New York City apartments for practicing. Each of the musicians spent from thirty to thirty-two hours a week studying and playing in these rooms.

But the IRS zapped the deductions.

The musicians were Met employees, the IRS argued. So their principal place of business was Lincoln Center—the same as their employer's.

The tax court thought otherwise.

For a performing musician, the judge said, practice is not simply the best way to get to Carnegie Hall. It is the only way.

Moreover, he added, practice is the only means of ensuring that, having arrived, a musician remains at center stage. Since the Met provided no practice facilities for its musicians, their home studios "were not purely a matter of personal convenience, comfort, or economy. Rather, they were business necessities."

This case represents one of the instances where an employee's principal place of business is not that of his or her employer.

Another example: The owner of a Wisconsin laundromat was allowed to deduct her home office expense because, in part, she spent most of her work time there—paying bills, doing payroll, and so on.

_____ **TAXTIP** _____

As in the above examples, you may write off the cost of your home office if you spend more time there than at your other business locations.

No Getting Around It

Even if they are the owners of the business, employees must meet one other condition before they write off home office expenses: they must maintain a home office for the convenience of their employer.

Say your company sells paper products to restaurants. Office space at your headquarters is limited, so you use your home as your office.

Since this office in your home is clearly for the convenience of the company, you may—as long as you meet the other tests—write off your home office expenses.

TAXTRAP

What if your home office isn't your principal place of business or you don't meet regularly with clients or customers there?

"In that case," you might say, "I'll simply lease space in my house to my corporation and write off my rental expenses. That way, I'll collect a deduction and bypass the home office rules entirely."

Sorry, but no dice. True, the tax court ruled in 1985 that this tactic was perfectly legal. But the Tax Reform Act of 1986 overruled the court's decision.

Now, an employee who leases part of his or her home to an employer may not take home office deductions. Period. The same rule applies to independent contractors who lease space to the clients for whom they perform services.

THE CUSTOMER IS ALWAYS RIGHT

Make no mistake, the government is serious when it says that you qualify for a home office deduction only if you meet regularly with clients, patients, or customers. For example, the court recently threw out the claim of a businessperson who deducted as a home office the room where he took telephone calls from clients.

TAXTIP

If you're claiming a deduction because you meet with clients or customers in your home, be sure you can prove it.

Our advice: Keep a log with your visitors' names, their times of arrival and departure, and the business nature of their visits.

NO PLACE LIKE HOME

Say your property includes a building that's physically separated from the rest of your house—a detached garage, guest house, or maid's quarters, for instance.

An office in this separate area is deductible even if it isn't your principal place of business or if you don't use it to meet with clients, patients, or customers.

TAXTIP

If you maintain an office in a building that is not attached to your house, you may want to ask utility companies to bill you separately for that structure. You'll get a more accurate picture of how much it costs to keep up your office, and the separate bills will help substantiate deductions if you're audited.

HOW DO YOU CALCULATE YOUR HOME OFFICE DEDUCTION?

Naturally enough, the first step in calculating a home office deduction is to decide what portion of your home is used for business.

If you've set aside one room in a seven-room house and that room is comparable in size to the other rooms, the answer is simple—one-seventh.

But suppose the room you choose for your office is smaller or larger than the others in your house. In that case, measure each room in your house to get a total square-footage estimate. Then figure what percentage of this total floor space is used for your office.

After you've determined the portion of your house allocated to business, figure the amount of depreciation that you're entitled to claim.

The law says you must use the straight-line method for writing off your property—that is, you must write off the same amount each year. (The 1986 Tax Reform Act zapped the use of accelerated depreciation, which allowed you to take larger deductions in the first years of ownership.)

Let's assume you acquired your home in January 1987. In this case, you must write it off over 31.5 years. (See chapter 10 for the details on depreciating real estate.)

First, multiply the percentage of your house that is used for business times the total purchase price minus the value of the land. (As we've seen, land is not depreciable.)

Next, calculate what share of your mortgage interest (you can't deduct principal payments) and real estate taxes you may deduct. (The remaining interest and real estate taxes may be written off on your personal return if you itemize your deductions.)

Then figure the amount of other expenses you may write off. If one-seventh of your home is allocated to the business, you may deduct one-seventh of your household expenses—heat, electricity, phone, and so forth—on your tax return.

You may write off other expenses, too. For example, do you plan to paint the bathroom? Include the proportional cost in home office expenses, since you obviously use the bathroom when you're working.

Don't, however, include any landscaping expenses. The IRS specifically forbids inclusion of these costs in a home office deduction. Too many people, it seems, tried to write off the cost of landscaping their backyards, because they took business calls by their swimming pools.

_____ **TAXTIP** _____

The IRS doesn't allow double-dipping.

You may not write off your full mortgage interest and taxes on your personal return, then also deduct these amounts as business expenses.

So don't try it.

Also, be sure to keep records throughout the year of all utilities and other household expenses, such as cleaning and maintenance. The IRS examines these receipts carefully in an audit.

_____ **FYI** _____

If you rent your home, you simply deduct that percentage of your rent payment that may be allocated to your home office.

HERE TODAY, GONE TOMORROW

The fact is, you may not deduct more on your tax return for an office in your home than the net income you generate there. Net income, in this instance, means your total income minus your expenses—with the exception of your home office costs.

So if you sell $3,000 worth of vitamins from your home and rack up $1,000 in expenses, you may deduct only $2,000 in home office costs.

If you generate $40,000 worth of legal fees from an office downtown and net $4,000 from your home office, you may write off only $4,000 in home office expenses.

SPECIAL RULES FOR DAY CARE CENTERS

If you care for other people's children, the rules for home office deductions are more generous than they are for other businesspeople.

Child-care providers may write off the cost of a portion of their house even if the room is not used exclusively for business.

You may, for instance, use your living room for day care in the morning and for television viewing at night and still deduct the expenses.

Just be sure that your day care business is licensed if your state requires it.

You calculate your deduction by using this formula: First, estimate the portion of your home used for day care activities, using the methods we've discussed. Then jot down how much time per week you're providing day care. Multiply to get the share of your expenses you may deduct.

For example:

- 40 percent of your home is used for day care 40 hours a week.
- 40 hours a week equals 24 percent of the week's 168 hours.
- Therefore, you may allocate 0.40 times 0.24 or 9.6 percent of your home's total cost (including utilities and maintenance) to day care.

Day care providers may also take a home office deduction for any part of their house used exclusively as an office. In these cases, the regular rules apply.

FOR MORE INFORMATION

See these IRS publications:

- *Miscellaneous Deductions* (Number 529)
- *Depreciation* (Number 534)
- *Business Use of Your Home* (Number 587)
- *Your Federal Income Tax* (Number 17)
- *Tax Guide for Small Business* (Number 334)
- *Farmers' Tax Guide* (Number 225)
- *Tax Guide for Commercial Fishermen* (Number 595)
- *Tax Information for Direct Sellers* (Number 911)

Try these IRS Tele-Tax tapes:

- *Office-in-the-Home Expenses* (Number 237)
- *Investment Credit* (Number 311)

- *Basis of Assets* (Number 401)
- *Depreciation—General* (Number 402)
- *Depreciation—Accelerated Cost Recovery System* (Number 403)
- *Small Business Tax Workshops—Tax Help for the New Businessperson* (Number 102)

Chapter 12

DRIVING FOR DOLLARS

The New Rules for Writing Off
Business Cars

In 1984, Congress stirred up a hornets' nest when it adopted a strict new law governing tax deductions for business cars. The law mandated that individuals who drive company cars must maintain a detailed daily diary listing mileage, date, place, and purpose of business travel.

Moreover, the legislators insisted, this log had to be kept contemporaneously. Otherwise, the cost of operating the automobile could not be deducted.

The protest from outraged taxpayers was immediate, loud, and unrelenting. And, in due time, Congress responded. It recognized that not even accountants have the necessary discipline for such meticulous recordkeeping. So, in early 1985, it erased the "contemporaneous" provision.

But it kept a whole host of other requirements. In this chapter, we examine these harsh rules and suggest ways to maneuver around them.

EASY STREET

When you deduct car expenses, you have two choices: you or your company may write off the actual costs of operating the automobile or claim a flat amount for each business mile you drive.

At present, the standard mileage rate is 22.5 cents a mile for the first 15,000 miles of business travel and 11 cents a mile for mileage in excess of 15,000.

There's one catch, though: You may not use the standard 22.5-cents-a-mile deduction on cars that you have fully depreciated. For these cars, you may claim only 11 cents a mile.

TAXTIPS

As a rule, actual expenses will exceed the standard mileage deduction. So we ask our clients to keep track of actual costs, then use whichever method produces the higher deduction.

A portion of all of the following is deductible (the percentage you write off equals the percentage of your car's mileage attributable to business):

- Automobile club memberships
- Driver's license
- Registration and other licensing fees
- Gasoline
- Lubrication and repairs
- Washing
- Insurance
- Tires with a life of less than one year (tires that last longer and are purchased separately from the car should be depreciated)

Also, you may write off parking fees and tolls incurred when you travel on business, even if you opt for the standard mileage deduction. However, the cost of parking a car at or near your office is not deductible by you personally. It may be written off by your company, as long as you do business as a corporation or partnership.

If your company does write off your parking, the value of this fringe benefit is not taxable to you, so it is not reported as income on your W-2 or 1099 Form. (Fines for violating traffic and parking laws are not deductible.)

FYI

Uncle Sam means it when he says you may write off only business-related travel in your company car. Recently, a cartoonist portrayed the government's attitude thusly: A terrified taxpayer is confronted by a stern IRS auditor. The auditor leans menacingly over our trembling citizen and screams, "You took the SCENIC route!"

CAUGHT IN THE CLUTCH

Formerly, you or your company could write off actual automobile expenses one year, then switch to the standard mileage deduction the next. Under the new rules, you may still switch back and forth, but some restrictions apply.

If you take the standard mileage deduction in year one, then write off actual costs in year two, you must depreciate the car using the straight-line method.

If you opt to deduct actual costs from the start, you may depreciate the value of your car using the more favorable accelerated method. (See chapter 9 for more information on depreciation.)

DRIVING FOR DOLLARS

Under the old rules, if a car was used solely for business, the entire purchase price—no matter how large—was depreciable. You or your company wrote off the cost over three years.

Now, you or your company must write off the cost over five years. Moreover, the law limits depreciation deductions for cars used full-time for business to $2,560 in the first year, $4,100 in the second year, $2,450 in the third year, and $1,475 each subsequent year. (See chapter 9 for more information on depreciation deductions.)

The result: Since most companies keep automobiles only three years, the move, in effect, eliminates the tax advantages of providing business owners and employees with cars that cost $12,800 or more.

The purpose of this particular provision was, of course, to eliminate tax breaks for owning so-called luxury cars.

There's only one problem with this reasoning: You don't have to own a Mercedes-Benz to have a luxury automobile. These days, practically any roomy midsize car costs more than $12,800.

CRASH TEST

In the old days, the government left it up to individual taxpayers to report on their personal returns the dollar value of driving company cars during off hours. But 1984's Tax Reform Act shifted the burden to you, the employer. Now, you must list the value of so-called personal usage on each employee's W-2 Form.

And that's not all.

You also must withhold from workers' payroll checks a full 20 percent of the dollar value of taking company automobiles on personal trips. (See chapter 15 for more on the withholding rules.)

There is, however, one way around this requirement: you must notify workers in writing on January 31 of each year that you have elected not to withhold income taxes from the value of driving business cars during off hours. That means employees fork over the tax themselves.

How do you compute the value of personal usage?

In a complicated set of regulations, the IRS ties the value of personal usage to the annual cost of leasing an automobile.

Uncle Sam even provides a chart listing lease values for automobiles that cost as much as $60,000. (You'll find a copy of this chart beginning below.)

—————————— **CASE IN POINT** ——————————

Say the fair-market value of your company automobile is $15,000. The IRS sets the annual lease value of that vehicle at $4,350.

Say, too, that you use the car a quarter of the time for personal reasons. That means you will incur taxable income equal to 25 percent of the lease value—$1,087.50.

This amount must be included on your W-2 Form if you are an employee of your corporation. If you're a proprietor or partner, you add the amount to your income.

But what happens if the only personal usage of the company automobile is for commuting? Another batch of rules applies.

The person who drives the car to and from work incurs an extra $3 a day in taxable income. A one-way commute is valued at $1.50.

The exception to the regulation: If the driver of the car is an officer or shareholder, no flat dollar amount of extra taxable income is reported.

Instead, the mileage to and from work is added up at the end of the year. It is used to help compute how much of a car's time is used for business and how much for pleasure—and what percentage of the car's value must be reported as taxable income to the officer or shareholder.

Annual Lease Value

Fair Market Value	Lease Value
$ 0 to 999	$ 600
1,000 to 1,999	850
2,000 to 2,999	1,100
3,000 to 3,999	1,350
4,000 to 4,999	1,600
5,000 to 5,999	1,850
6,000 to 6,999	2,100
7,000 to 7,999	2,350
8,000 to 8,999	2,600
9,000 to 9,999	2,850
10,000 to 10,999	3,100

Fair Market Value	Lease Value
$11,000 to 11,999	$3,350
12,000 to 12,999	3,600
13,000 to 13,999	3,850
14,000 to 14,999	4,100
15,000 to 15,999	4,350
16,000 to 16,999	4,600
17,000 to 17,999	4,850
18,000 to 18,999	5,100
19,000 to 19,999	5,350
20,000 to 20,999	5,600
21,000 to 21,999	5,850
22,000 to 22,999	6,100
23,000 to 23,999	6,350
24,000 to 24,999	6,600
25,000 to 25,999	6,850
26,000 to 27,999	7,250
28,000 to 29,999	7,750
30,000 to 31,999	8,250
32,000 to 33,999	8,750
34,000 to 35,999	9,250
36,000 to 37,999	9,750
38,000 to 39,999	10,250
40,000 to 41,999	10,750
42,000 to 43,999	11,250
44,000 to 45,999	11,750
46,000 to 47,999	12,250
48,000 to 49,999	12,750
50,000 to 51,999	13,250
52,000 to 53,999	13,750
54,000 to 55,999	14,250
56,000 to 57,999	14,750
58,000 to 60,000	15,250

For those who own vehicles that cost more than $60,000—and you know who you are—lease values can be figured by using this simple formula: multiply the fair-market value (purchase price) of the car times 25 percent, then add $500.

WRECKLESS DRIVING

The law also imposes new rules when business usage falls below 50 percent.

Among these: Although the depreciation schedule remains

five years, you must depreciate the automobile's cost using the straight-line method rather than the accelerated method. (You'll find a complete explanation of depreciation methods in chapter 9.)

TAXTIP

Commuting is not considered business use, even if you install a telephone and transact business while you're driving. But not every trip that starts from your home is necessarily "commuting."

CASE IN POINT

A physician was recently allowed to write off the cost of traveling between his home and his rental properties.

The automobile expenses, the court ruled, were not commuting costs, since the office in his house was the principal place of his rental business.

The trips to and from his rental properties were "ordinary and necessary" to carrying on his business as a landlord.

ON EMPTY

Warning: The rules say you may not write off automobile expenses on your personal return if your company would have reimbursed you.

Sometimes, however, the tax court is forgiving.

CASE IN POINT

An attorney frequently used his own car to drive to and from court and to travel to nearby towns to take depositions. In one year alone, he racked up 7,500 business miles and spent $375 for parking fees and tolls. Consequently, he wrote off $1,650 on his 1977 tax return (7,500 miles at the 1977 rate of 17 cents a mile plus $375).

The IRS disallowed the deduction. The attorney, the IRS argued, could have been reimbursed by his law firm for at least part of the expense.

However, the tax court found otherwise.

The judge pointed out that the attorney's firm had a written policy not to reimburse automobile expenses unless they were chargeable to specific clients. So the lawyer was allowed his $1,650 write-off.

─────────────────────── **FYI** ───────────────────────

The IRS—as its representatives will be the first to tell you—applies the same strict yardstick to its employees as it does to you and me.

Consider the case of Horace Podems.

An IRS field examiner, Podems frequently had to drive from Orange, New Jersey, where his office was located, to the homes or businesses of the taxpayers he was auditing. He used his own automobile for these trips, and his duties never took him away from Orange overnight.

For three years, Podems filed vouchers with his employer, the IRS, for reimbursement of his travel expenses on a cents-per-mile basis. All the vouchers were promptly honored.

There was only one problem: Podems was a tad lazy and bothered to submit requests for payment only a few months out of each year. He deducted the rest of his unreimbursed expenses from his gross income. At his audit, these deductions were disallowed.

The IRS ruled that the expenses were not ordinary and necessary. Why? Podems could have been reimbursed for his costs had he taken the trouble to file his expense reports.

On appeal, the judge agreed—but only to a point.

Since Podems's reimbursements were on a mileage basis, he would not have been fully compensated for the use of his car even if he had regularly filed vouchers.

A large part of the total amount he wrote off consisted of parking and depreciation, and, the judge concluded, he should be allowed to deduct these additional costs.

TAX STRATEGIES

As we've seen, people who drive company cars don't have to keep track of each and every trip they take. Instead, they may log only personal trips or follow the 70–30 rule. That rule allows full-time sales and service personnel to claim 70-percent business usage and 30-percent personal usage on their company cars without maintaining a daily log.

Our advice: Proceed with caution.

You still must prove that you used the car 70 percent of the time for business, so you must keep some kind of diary.

As we've seen, this diary doesn't have to be kept contemporaneously—meaning you don't have to write down trips on the day that you take them.

You may, if you choose, log your trips once a week. However, the longer you wait to make note of your travels, the more likely you are to lose track of your mileage.

────────────────── **TAXTIPS** ──────────────────

Mileage logs aren't required if:

- Your business has a written policy prohibiting employees from using company cars during off hours.
- Business automobiles remain on your company's premises when they are not in use.
- No employee lives on your business premises. (This rule forces people who maintain offices at home to keep logs.)
- Personal usage of the company car is limited to commuting, and the driver incurs an extra $3 a day in gross income for the trip to and from work.
- The vehicle, such as a forklift, dump truck, or tractor, is not susceptible to personal use.

FOR MORE INFORMATION
See these IRS publications:

- *Travel, Entertainment, and Gift Expenses* (Number 463)
- *Depreciation* (Number 534)
- *Basis of Assets* (Number 551)
- *Sales and Other Dispositions of Assets* (Number 544)
- *Your Federal Income Tax* (Number 17)
- *Tax Guide for Small Business* (Number 334)
- *Farmers' Tax Guide* (Number 225)
- *Tax Guide for Commercial Fishermen* (Number 595)
- *Tax Information for Direct Sellers* (Number 911)

Try these IRS Tele-Tax tapes:

- *Business Use of Car* (Number 215)
- *Business Travel Expenses* (Number 216)
- *Basis of Assets* (Number 401)
- *Depreciation—General* (Number 402)
- *Depreciation—Accelerated Cost Recovery System* (Number 403)
- *Small Business Tax Workshops—Tax Help for the New Businessperson* (Number 102)

Chapter 13

MANY HAPPY RETURNS

Capturing Attractive Travel and Entertainment Deductions

In days long past, you could write off travel and entertainment (T&E) expenses with abandon. You were not required to account for the legitimacy of every cent you deducted.

Known as the "Cohan rule," this favorable tax treatment stemmed from a case involving the legendary Broadway entertainer and songwriter, George M. Cohan.

Cohan wrote off thousands of dollars in travel and entertainment expenses, little of which he documented. The IRS challenged the deductions.

The case wound up in the U.S. Tax Court, where the first judge ruled against Cohan. But the entertainer won on appeal.

The appeals judge simply ordered the lower court to "make as close an approximation" as it could of Cohan's expenses. In other words, Cohan—with the help of the court—was allowed to make a rough estimate of his expenditures and write off that amount.

Nowadays, of course, the law is much stricter and more straightforward. For starters, you may deduct only 80 percent of your meal and entertainment expenses—that includes all business meals, even those eaten on the road.

Also, if you can't substantiate a T&E deduction, the rules say, you can't take it. If you go ahead and take a write-off that you can't document, the IRS may slap you with a penalty for "negligence" or "intentional disregard of rules and regulations."

This penalty is 5 percent of any extra tax you owe, plus a whopping 50 percent of any interest on the amount you owe since the date your return was due. So you end up paying the extra tax, plus 5 percent more, plus the accumulated interest (the IRS compounds daily), plus a penalty of 50 percent on any accumulated interest.

---------------------- **CASE IN POINT** ----------------------

Say you owe an additional $400 in tax. You pay the government $420 ($400 plus 5 percent). If a year has passed since you filed your return, you also owe at least $40 in interest (assuming an interest rate of 10 percent). So you fork over an additional penalty of $20 (50 percent of the interest). The result: You're out $480.

But wait. There's more. The IRS also imposes a penalty for substantially understating your tax. It equals 25 percent of the understatement.

The IRS may hit you with still another penalty if it determines that you were fraudulent, as well. This penalty adds up to as much as 50 percent of the extra tax you owe.

More bad news: The rules don't precisely define "negligence" or "intentional disregard." So the IRS has plenty of rope with which to hang you.

WHEN IN DOUBT LEAVE IT OUT

To substantiate your T&E deductions, the rules require you to maintain two kinds of records.

The first consists of documentary evidence—receipts, paid bills, or canceled checks—that proves you actually spent the amount you claimed. (Receipts are required only if the amount exceeds $25.)

The second is a log or diary in which you list:

- The cost of the travel or entertainment
- The date
- The place
- The business purpose of the travel or entertainment
- The general topic of business conversation, if there was one
- Your relationship to the people entertained

The order in which you list these items is not important, but the log or diary should be kept contemporaneously. It should look something like this:

Wed., Feb. 5. Entertained representatives of ABC Manufacturing—David Butler, president; John Edwards, vice president. Dinner at Charlie's on Newbury St. in Boston—$76.25 including tip. Theater tickets—$95. Drinks at Michael's on Commercial

Wharf—$32.50. Cab fares to/from restaurants: $18.00. Discussed sale of our valves to ABC for use in its plant.

Thurs., Feb. 6. Meeting with representatives of ABC (same people as listed above). Mileage to/from ABC plant—82 miles at 22.5 cents/mile. Total: $18.45. More discussions of use of our valves by ABC.

TAXTIPS

Instead of maintaining a log, you may write down the required information on the back of restaurant and charge card receipts. Also, the IRS will accept an oral log. So if you want to dictate your expense record, feel free.

A word of warning: Don't underestimate the importance of recording this information in some way. Without documentation, the IRS will probably disallow your perfectly legitimate deductions.

CASE IN POINT

Over the course of ten years, Joseph Mann had built a small contracting business into a thriving and profitable operation. By the time he had his day in tax court in 1981, he considered himself one of the largest contractors in Shelby County, Tennessee.

Mann generated most of his revenues by contracting for the concrete work in the construction of new apartment buildings. Not surprisingly, he spent a great deal of time—and money—wining and dining clients and contacts. Most of these associates hailed from out of state, so he also put in his share of hours on the road. Like many business-people, Mann charged his entertainment expenses to his MasterCharge credit card.

On the same card, he put expenses for gasoline and auto repairs, office supplies, construction materials, and personal items.

At year's end, the company bookkeeper would break down the charges into their proper categories.

In 1974 and 1975, the years for which he was audited, Mann claimed $5,599.36 and $2,729.75, respectively, for travel and entertainment—not unusually high sums considering his line of work. To demonstrate that his expenses were on the up and up, he put into evidence copies of his MasterCharge statements.

The court didn't consider his expenses excessive.

Nonetheless, they disallowed the entire deduction.

Mann, they said, was required by law to show the amount, time, place, and business purpose for his entertainment and travel.

In order to prove the validity of his entertainment charges he had the further burden of establishing the business relationship with his guests. Mann did not keep a contemporaneous expense record, such as a diary or an accounting book. And the MasterCharge statements alone, the judge ruled, were inadequate.

To make matters worse, Mann could neither recall the identity of his guests nor the business purpose of their meetings.

The contractor's excuse for his meager evidence—that he simply disliked keeping records—failed to sway the judges, and he lost his write-off.

CASE IN POINT

A lawyer, who entertained frequently at home and at private clubs, characterized his expenses as "courtesy and promotion" and attempted to deduct them.

The tax court said no dice. His expenses, the judge ruled, were not clearly related to a trade or business nor were they properly substantiated.

The court was singularly unimpressed by the attorney's argument that the large number of people he entertained made it economically unfeasible for him to keep detailed records.

His situation, the court said, was "similar to that of other professionals and businesspeople who find it advisable to entertain."

TAXTRAP

The law won't allow you to construct a diary or log years after the fact, unless your records were destroyed in a fire, flood, or earthquake. So don't try it. (Chemical analysis will reveal the age of your diary.)

FYI

Don't be surprised—or insulted—when your tax preparer asks you to sign a written statement that you can substantiate your deductions. Some type of confirmation is required by law.

EAT, DRINK, AND BE WARY

"Our country wouldn't be where it is today," someone once said, "if Commodore Vanderbilt had to account for every cent he spent on entertainment."

Nowadays, of course, there's a whole host of regulations that must be followed—and followed to the letter—when you write off T&E expenses.

Among them: You may not deduct travel-and-entertainment expenses that are, in the eyes of the IRS, "lavish or extravagant."

Unfortunately, Uncle Sam doesn't explain what he considers lavish or extravagant. He doesn't need to. "I know it when I see it," an IRS agent once told me.

Take heart. For the most part, the IRS won't disallow expenses simply because they top a certain dollar amount or take place at a high-priced hotel or restaurant.

We advise our clients to travel and entertain in the style to which they have grown accustomed—so long as they document their expenditures.

Another requirement: You may deduct T&E entertainment expenses only if they are "ordinary and necessary" to your business or trade.

Again, the IRS doesn't explain what it means by "ordinary" or "necessary." But, in case after case, the courts have defined these two terms liberally.

_____ **CASE IN POINT** _____

In 1939, two Greek immigrants, Harry Kanelos and Aristidis Radopolis won $137,986.25 in the Irish Sweepstakes.

Notified of their good fortune by letter, they promptly consulted a lawyer. He, in turn, immediately contacted two banks.

What facilities, the attorney wanted to know, could the banks offer for collecting the winnings?

Officials at both banks said they would not be responsible if the ticket were lost en route to Dublin, where sweepstakes regulations required it to be presented. So the lawyer advised his clients that they should travel to Dublin to collect the windfall, which they did.

On their 1939 tax returns, Kanelos and Radopolis each deducted half of the trip's total expense—$2,218, including steamer charges, hotel rooms, food, drinks, and tips—from their share of the winnings.

These deductions were upheld on appeal.

The judge pointed out that the two friends, having placed their confidence in the lawyer, quite naturally accepted his conclusion that the trip was necessary to collect the money. Moreover, the judge pointed out, "there is no suggestion that the trip was made for any purpose aside from the collection of the sweepstakes winnings.

"No time was consumed in unrelated travels or sight-seeing, and the usual and customary modes of transportation were used."

Accordingly, the judge ruled, the expenses fully met the law's requirement: they were "ordinary and necessary for the collection of income."

And the two friends were allowed their deductions.

THAT'S ENTERTAINMENT

You may deduct entertainment expenses only if they are

- Directly related to the active conduct of your business or
- Associated with the conduct of your business

Any entertaining you do during which you discuss or conduct business is considered "directly related" by the IRS. Typical examples include rental of a hospitality suite at a convention and a Saturday golf outing where business is a topic of conversation.

To substantiate an expense as directly related entertainment, you must, under the rules, be able to show that

- The main purpose of the business entertainment was the business, not the entertainment.
- You had "more than a general expectation" of getting income or some other specific business benefit (such as information that would help you in planning expansion down the road).
- You discussed business with the person you were entertaining.

Associated entertainment is a bit more complicated. To claim a deduction under this rule, you must be able to prove that your entertaining had a "clear business purpose."

What must you offer as evidence?

If your entertainment immediately precedes or follows a

substantial business discussion—for example, if you take a client to a show when he's in town to sign a major deal—an IRS agent will assume that a clear business purpose existed. If you take a client sailing on a Sunday, however, you may have problems.

"Business is not considered to be the main purpose when business and entertainment are combined on hunting and fishing trips," the IRS says in its *Small Business Tax Guide,* "or on yachts or other pleasure boats, unless you can show otherwise."

It also is difficult, under the "clear business purpose" rule, to write off the cost of a lavish party to which you happened to invite some business associates.

_____ **CASE IN POINT** _____

Manfred and Anne Brecker got short shrift from the tax court when they tried to deduct a portion of the cost of their son's Bar Mitzvah party as a business expense.

Manfred, head of a four-member partnership that operated several discount department stores, invited 19 employees and a handful of business associates to his son's Bar Mitzvah. These business contacts accounted for 38 out of 193 invited guests, and Manfred argued that he should be able to deduct 38/193 or $653 of the total cost of the party.

The judge didn't buy it.

Looked at on its own terms, he said, a Bar Mitzvah party is personal in nature and has no business connotation whatsoever. There were no facts to indicate that this particular party was motivated by anything other than personal reasons.

Nor was the judge impressed by Manfred's argument that the partners' practice of inviting employees to such family gatherings as "weddings, anniversary parties, and funerals" bolstered morale. The employees who attended with their wives, pointed out the judge, were basically supervisory personnel.

"It would seem," he concluded, "the morale of those not attending would be adversely affected rather than fortified by these facts."

In sum, the judge said, "The primary purpose of the Bar Mitzvah was not related to business, the surroundings did not provide an atmosphere conducive to business discussions, and the expenditures were not part of a business program."

You may, however, sometimes deduct 80 percent of the cost of entertainment that is designed simply to create goodwill—that is, entertainment where a direct business benefit (such as making a sale, negotiating a contract, or gathering business intelligence) does not exist. But you may deduct the expenses only if the entertainment:

- Takes place in an obvious business setting, such as a convention (here, the IRS assumes that business is being conducted, and the entertainment qualifies as a directly related expense)
- Directly precedes or follows a substantial business discussion—in this case, the entertainment qualifies under the "associated" rules

Simply taking the mayor of your town to a baseball game to cultivate good feelings wouldn't qualify as business entertainment, for example. However, if you discussed before the game your plans to build a big office building in the city, you could write off the costs.

_____ **TAXTRAP** _____

Taking clients to sporting events and theatrical performances has long been a popular form of business entertainment.

But you may deduct only the face value of the tickets. You may not write off a scalper's markup or fees charged by ticket agencies.

Business Meals

"A dinner lubricates business," Samuel Johnson told his biographer James Boswell back in the eighteenth century. The same holds true today.

Fortunately, the government agrees. Uncle Sam is surprisingly liberal when it comes to deductions for business meals. You may write off 80 percent of the expenses for food and beverages consumed—as long as you discuss business during the meal.

Similarly, under most circumstances, you can take an employee to lunch or dinner and write off 80 percent of the cost. As Andy Warhol once put it: "Employees make the best dates. You don't have to pick them up, and they're always tax-deductible."

_____ **TAXTIP** _____

The law does make some exceptions to the 80-percent rule. You may still deduct 100 percent of the cost of a holiday party you throw for your employees. And you may fully deduct samples and promotional items—for example, food passed out at supermarkets. Also, restaurants are allowed to write off 100 percent of the cost of the meals they prepare and sell—labor, food, and so on.

No Free Lunch

Under current tax law, you may not deduct the cost of a meal you eat alone unless it is part of an overnight business trip. Even under those circumstances, you may deduct only 80 percent of its cost.

Say you're the owner of an advertising agency in Illinois and have three clients in a city that is 180 miles away. One day a month, you hop in your car and pay them a visit. Between stops, you pick up a hamburger and a soft drink, which you consume in your car.

Unfair as it may seem, the price of that meal is no more deductible than the salad or sandwich you may eat at your desk.

The reason: It is not an overnight business trip.

I Scratch Your Back, You Scratch Mine

Friends often take turns picking up the tab for meals, but you may not write off lunches or dinners if they have no business purpose.

Say you and another businesswoman eat lunch once a week. You talk about personal matters only, and you take turns paying.

The meals are not deductible under the so-called "reciprocal" entertainment rules, which state that these regularly scheduled meals must have a legitimate business purpose.

However, if you actually talk business—and she takes you out every so often and you take her out once in a while—then you could write off 80 percent of the cost of the meal.

Guess Who's Coming to Dinner

The IRS doesn't advertise the fact, but it does allow you to deduct 80 percent of the cost of business meals you prepare and serve in your own home.

_____ **CASE IN POINT** _____

Once a month, a taxpayer invited associates to his home for dinner. At the end of the year, he deducted the costs of the dinners as a business expense.

The IRS questioned the validity of the deductions, and the case wound up in tax court.

The man argued that he invited only people who could be helpful to him in his company, and that the parties kept him up-to-date on a host of business topics. Besides, he maintained, his quiet spacious home was much more conducive to discrete business conversation than noisy crowded restaurants.

Finally, he pulled out his ace in the hole. He also gave social dinner parties once a month to which he invited some of the same people, and these costs he did not deduct.

He won the case.

_____ **TAXTIP** _____

IRS auditors go over deductions for meals prepared at home with a fine-tooth comb, so it is essential that you maintain good records. Jot down in a diary or notebook or keep on file the following information:

- The cost of the meal (add up the price of the groceries you bought and keep your receipts)
- The date
- The names of your guests
- The business relationship with your guests (it will be harder to justify deductions for dinner parties where you invite both business associates and people who are strictly friends)
- The topic of business conversation
- The business purpose of the meal

MEMBERS ONLY

You may deduct your own country club or social club dues only if you use the club at least 50 percent for entertainment that furthers your business.

Even then you may write off only your actual business use. Say, for example, that you use your country club 70 percent of the time for business. That means you may deduct 70 percent of your country club dues as a business expense.

Watch out. The government demands clear records that show when you use your club for personal purposes and when you use it for business.

WHERE'S THE PARTY?

For the most part, Uncle Sam won't allow you to deduct the cost of entertainment property, such as yachts, hunting lodges, tennis courts, and swimming pools, even if you entertain business associates in these surroundings.

However, you may write off the cost of meeting facilities you purchase in resort communities if you actually use the property for business purposes.

AND AWAY WE GO

When you travel on business, your write-offs are clear. You may deduct what you spend for meals (up to 80 percent), lodging, and travel—expenses you would not have incurred at home. But taxpayers can't willy-nilly deduct all expenses.

In a recent case, for example, a businessperson deducted long-distance telephone calls while away from home on business. The calls, however, were made to parents and friends, and the taxpayer presented no evidence indicating that the expenses were incurred for business reasons. So the cost of these phone calls were not deductible.

_____ TAXTRAP _____

When you stay at a hotel, you must separate your meal expenses from your overall bill. The IRS won't let you get around the 80-percent rule by deducting the entire bill as lodging expense.

A HOME AWAY FROM HOME

You may deduct your hotel and motel expenses. Or, if you regularly travel to one destination, you may instead write off the cost of renting an apartment or a house.

The only requirement: Your rental must make business sense. In other words, you should spend less on the apartment than you would on a hotel or motel plus meals.

IF IT'S NOT BUSINESS IT MUST BE PLEASURE

Your travel deduction becomes less clear-cut when you combine business with relaxation, sightseeing, or visiting old friends.

If you take a vacation or other primarily personal trip, you may not deduct any part of your transportation expenses. You may, however, write off any business expenses that you incur while on the trip.

If you want a significant tax deduction for a combined business and pleasure trip, you must prove that the trip was primarily (that is, more than 50 percent) for business. And take care. The IRS carefully scrutinizes these borderline "business" trips.

_____ **CASE IN POINT** _____

A Dearborn, Michigan, attorney tried to deduct $11,969 in T&E expenses for "business development." He spent the money, he said, to obtain new clients for his law firm.

Much of the deduction stemmed from a golfing trip to Palm Springs, California, that the attorney took with two college friends.

One of these buddies was now vice president of a Chicago manufacturing company, the other was regional manager for a Lowell, Massachusetts, computer company.

The purpose of the trip, said the lawyer, was to gently persuade these old friends to retain him as counsel. (The attorney claimed to take a subtle approach: "I wasn't beating their brains out on a daily basis in that regard," he said.)

Despite a daily round of golf, however, he was unsuccessful in snagging their business. He also failed to retain his write-off.

The attorney, the tax court judge ruled, did not convincingly establish that the trip was directly related to his trade or business. Rather, the evidence suggests that it "was nothing other than a spring golf outing with two college friends who just happened to be corporate managers."

The lawyer knew that one friend employed a full staff of attorneys to handle his legal work and the other, based in Chicago, probably did not require counsel in Dearborn.

Moreover, since the taxpayer had previously done no legal work for either of his friends' companies, it was unlikely that any business discussion could have lasted an entire week. And, the judge said, he couldn't understand "why it was necessary to conduct any such discussion several thousand miles away from the various individuals' offices."

The judge wasn't finished.

The pattern of expenses, he pointed out, suggested that the trip was entirely personal. The attorney put a deposit on a condominium; his friends paid the balance. The group played golf daily; the attorney shelled out for only two rounds.

Finally, the attorney paid for four dinners but didn't pick up the tab for any breakfasts or lunches, and he bought only one miserly after-golf snack.

The conclusion was inescapable. The attorney was "merely sharing expenses on a personal trip to southern California in anticipation of summer."

If you do convincingly document that the main reason for your trip was business, you may deduct the entire transportation cost, even if the trip includes some personal time.

One catch: This rule applies only to trips within the United States. For foreign outings, you must allocate the transportation costs between the business and personal portions of your trip. If a trip consisted of 70 percent business and 30 percent vacation, you could deduct only 70 percent of the travel cost.

Here's another special rule: A trip to a convention outside the United States, Canada, Mexico, or some nearby Caribbean countries may be disallowed if the IRS concludes that holding the convention in, say, Paris or Vienna was unreasonable from a business standpoint.

Obviously, international organizations may hold meetings in Paris, and you may deduct the cost of your participation. But if the Missouri Federation of Electrical Contractors decides to meet in Greece this winter, don't count on pocketing a big write-off.

CRUISE CONTROL

The IRS won't allow you to deduct trips on cruise ships to exotic places, no matter what a salesperson tells you. And it doesn't matter if the travel is supposed to be educational.

You may, under limited circumstances, deduct the cost of attending a convention or seminar aboard a cruise ship if you can show the convention was directly related to your trade or business. The conditions: The ship must be under United States registry, and you must not sail outside the United States or its possessions.

You may not deduct traveling and entertainment associated

Nor may you deduct the cost of a trip abroad, claiming that the trip itself is educational. For example, a French professor who travels to France to brush up his language skills may not write off the cost of his trip.

Another rule: Say you travel to London on business. Instead of flying, you go by luxury liner. Your deduction for travel is limited to twice the highest per diem rate—currently $126—allowed to employees of the federal government.

CASE IN POINT

It takes you six days to travel to England by ship. You may deduct two times $126, or $252, times six days. So you may deduct a total of $1,512.

Just keep in mind that the $1,512 also covers meals and entertainment while on the ship, not just transportation.

You must break out the cost of meals and entertainment, and you may deduct only 80 percent of these expenses.

YOU CAN'T TAKE THEM WITH YOU—USUALLY

Neither you nor your company may deduct your spouse's travel expenses unless you can show a clear business reason for his or her presence. Two examples follow.

CASE IN POINT

Volkswagen paid a husband and wife's expenses for a trip to Germany. The husband's reason for the trip: To decide whether to invest in a VW dealership.

Because he had a perfectly sound business reason for traveling abroad, his reimbursed trip expenses would not be included as taxable income to him, the court ruled.

His wife's trip, however, was another story. She, it seems, was just along for the ride. So the money VW forked over for her trip had to be declared as taxable income on the couple's joint return.

CASE IN POINT

Then there's the refund that Roy and Edna Disney pocketed.

Roy, the president and chairman of Walt Disney Productions, was frequently required to make business trips both within the United States and abroad.

His wife would almost always accompany him. On these

trips, he would meet with the company's far-flung sales forces; go to business meetings and conferences; and, with his wife, attend screenings, receptions, dinners, press conferences, and many other business-oriented social engagements.

The company regularly reimbursed Roy for both his traveling expenses and for Edna's.

The Disneys kept meticulous records and paid back Walt Disney Productions for any personal expenditures. On audit, however, the IRS told Disney he would have to include the reimbursements to his wife in the couple's gross income. The appeals court disagreed.

Disney's company, pointed out the appeals judge, had a longstanding policy that its executives take their wives along with them on extended business trips. (Remember, these events took place in the early 1960s, when men were men and women were wives.)

The wives' presence, thought company higher-ups, was critical in enhancing the Disney image. And the judge agreed. Mrs. Disney's appearances with her husband, he conceded, "invites additional publicity for women's pages and enhances the image of the company as a disseminator of family entertainment."

Nor did it matter that Mrs. Disney performed no duties of a "business-office nature, such as acting as her husband's secretary or attending daytime business meetings."

Indeed, she spent much of her free time attending to "such matters as the care of her husband's laundry, taking telephone calls at their hotel rooms, and the performance of other activities of a 'wifely' character," as Mrs. Disney herself put it.

But she also frequently attended luncheon meetings, helped entertain at social gatherings, took charge of arrangements for functions, and made goodwill visits to people in the industry.

In short, the judge found, the dominant reason for Mrs. Disney's presence on these trips was to further her husband's business purpose, and a substantial amount of her time was spent pursuing that end. The expenses for her trip, therefore, did not have to be included in the couple's income, and the Disneys were entitled to a hefty $3,154 refund.

FOR MORE INFORMATION
See these IRS publications:

- *Travel, Entertainment, and Gift Expenses* (Number 463)
- *Business Expenses* (Number 535)
- *Your Federal Income Tax* (Number 17)
- *Tax Guide for Small Business* (Number 334)
- *Farmers' Tax Guide* (Number 225)
- *Tax Guide for Commercial Fishermen* (Number 595)
- *Tax Information for Direct Sellers* (Number 911)

Try these IRS Tele-Tax tapes:

- *Business Travel Expenses* (Number 216)
- *Business Entertainment Expenses* (Number 217)
- *Small Business Tax Workshops—Tax Help for the New Businessperson* (Number 102)

Chapter 14

THE MANNER OF GIVING IS WORTH MORE THAN THE GIFT

The Right Way to Write Off Business Gifts

No doubt about it, when it comes to business gifts, the federal government is a Scrooge. Uncle Sam allows you to deduct no more than $25 for gifts to any one person during any one year.

It makes no difference whether the recipient is a customer of many years standing or a client from a country such as Japan, where gift-giving is practically a prerequisite of doing business.

Nor does it matter if the gift is perishable and has no lasting value. Fresh fruit, for example, is subject to the same $25 ceiling as, say, a monogrammed sweater.

Gifts to employees fall under the same miserly restrictions as presents to customers. You may deduct no more than $25 per employee per year.

Here's an example of how this rule can cost you dearly: Suppose you manufacture sportswear. Every year, as a Christmas present, you give each of your fifty employees a free jacket, which costs $40 to make. Under the rules, your business may write off only $25 of each $40 gift.

The remaining $15 per jacket—or a total of $750—may not be subtracted from your company's taxable income. In effect, that amount comes from your company's after-tax revenues.

Or say you're a distributor of leather goods—wallets, key cases, and so on. Every time you introduce a new product line, you hand out free samples to customers. This year, you give your thirty-eight retailers three gifts valued at $25 each, or a total of $75 worth of products per person.

Under the law, you may write off only $950 (that is, 38 times $25) in gifts on your tax return. Again, the remaining $1,900 is not deductible.

_____ **TAXTIPS** _____

In adding up the cost of a business gift, you may exclude incidental expenses, such as monogramming and engraving, that, in the opinion of the IRS, do not add value to a gift.

What's more, you may write off certain incidental expenses under other categories, such as office supplies or ordinary business expenses.

Believe me, no IRS auditor will question the $3.75 you spent mailing a business gift—the deduction is perfectly legal.

_____ **TAXTRAP** _____

If you think you can get around the $25 rule simply by reporting the value of expensive gifts as income to employees, think again.

A New York City company gave two newlywed employees $250 each. It wrote off the two payments as compensation and reported the amounts as income to the employees.

When the IRS audited the company's return, it balked at the deductions. It ruled that the two $250 payments were gifts, not pay or bonuses, and subject to the $25 limitation.

The U.S. Tax Court agreed.

NO RULE IS SO GENERAL, WHICH ADMITS NOT SOME EXCEPTION

Or so wrote clergyman Robert Burton back in the 1600s.

One exception to the $25-per-person rule is advertising materials—pens, pencils, calendars, posters, note pads, matchbooks, and so forth.

To qualify for the exclusion, however, items must cost less than $4 each and be imprinted either with your name or your company's name. You may pass out as many of these "gifts" as you want.

Another exception to the $25 limitation is point-of-purchase sales aids that are handed out to retailers for use at their places of business. Common examples include metal display racks and signs that are given by magazine distributors and publishers to bookstore owners.

Also excluded from the $25 rule are prizes passed out to employees in recognition of measurable accomplishments, such as productivity, safety, or length of service.

Under the tax law, awards may be either in cash or in the form of tangible property—the traditional gold watch, say, or silver bowl.

Whether money or property is given, however, you must report the value of awards that exceed $25 as income to employees by listing it on their W-2 Forms. The value of the gift may not exceed $400 unless it fits the government's definition of a so-called "qualified-plan award."

ARE YOU QUALIFIED?

What, you may ask, is a qualified-plan award?

To the IRS, it's an award that is given under an ongoing program of an employer. The plan must be spelled out in writing, and employees must be notified of its existence. A handout explaining the program, for example, could be posted on a bulletin board or included in an employee handbook.

Two other requirements: A qualified-plan award program may not discriminate in favor of top executives or shareholders, and the average cost of all awards made during the year under the plan may not exceed $400. Single awards, however, may be as large as $1,600.

FYI

Examples of companies with qualified-plan programs include:

- A company that awards employees an extra two weeks of vacation after twenty years of service
- A company that grants hourly workers three shares of company stock for each year of perfect attendance
- A company that awards employees an extra day's pay each year on their anniversary

---

THE PRIZE IS RIGHT

Also excluded from the $25 gift ceiling are grants, scholarships, prizes, and awards you hand out to outsiders in recognition of some special accomplishment.

For example, you may award an annual $5,000 college scholarship to a deserving local high school student and not run up against the business gift rules.

If you make the gift directly to the college or university and let it disburse the money to the recipient, you may write off the entire amount as a charitable contribution. If you make out the check to the recipient, you deduct the amount of the scholarship or award as an ordinary business expense under miscellaneous.

─────────────── **FYI** ───────────────

"What do you mean, 'clarify miscellaneous?'" an angry taxpayer asks an IRS auditor in a New Yorker cartoon. "What do you think that word is for?"

TAX STRATEGIES
One little-known but effective way to get around the $25 limit on business gifts to employees and customers is to establish a legitimate product-testing program for goods you make.

Items distributed to help you test a product are fully deductible. However, you must keep good records so you can prove your program is strictly on the up and up.

Under the IRS rules, testing and evaluation must be an ordinary part of your business. For instance, it makes sense for manufacturers to test products, but probably not most retailers.

Also, there must be a good reason why the product cannot be tested in-house. An example might be a jacket you want exposed to wear and tear under ordinary living conditions.

And, the law says, testers must furnish a written detailed evaluation report to the company that provided the product.

A final requirement: People must be chosen for the testing program on a nondiscriminatory basis. That means you may not favor your top executives.

But you may favor top customers. The discrimination rules, it seems, apply to people who work for you—not with you.

Another proven way around the $25 gift limitation: Whenever possible, treat items as business expenses instead of business gifts. (See chapter 13.)

─────────────── **CASE IN POINT** ───────────────

Suppose you shell out $50 for a bottle of champagne to reward your vice president of marketing for signing on a new client.

Under the business-gift rules, you could deduct only $25 of the $50. But if you spend $50 on champagne, which you share with everyone in the marketing department, you may write off the entire amount as a business expense.

The champagne, in this case, qualifies as a *de minimis* fringe benefit. (See chapter 15.)

You should also look for ways to deduct your business gifts as entertainment expenses. (Again, see chapter 13.)

_____ **CASE IN POINT** _____

You give a customer two tickets to a basketball game. You may now write off their price ($50) either as a business gift or as an entertainment expense.

Since there's no ceiling on entertainment expense deductions—though you may write off only 80 percent—you obviously come out ahead by deducting the tickets as entertainment.

PLAYING IT SAFE

IRS auditors scrutinize business-gift deductions carefully, so you should maintain records that show

- What you purchased
- The price of the gift (the IRS requires you to have receipts for items that cost more than $25 even though your write-off is limited to $25)
- The date you bought the gift
- The purpose of the gift (to mark the opening of a customer's new store, to recognize an employee's birthday, and so on)
- The name of the recipient
- Your relationship to the recipient (he or she could be a customer, an employee, even a business adviser)

FOR MORE INFORMATION

See these IRS publications:

- *Travel, Entertainment, and Gift Expenses* (Number 463)
- *Scholarships and Fellowships* (Number 520)
- *Your Federal Income Tax* (Number 17)
- *Tax Guide for Small Business* (Number 334)
- *Farmers' Tax Guide* (Number 225)
- *Tax Guide for Commercial Fishermen* (Number 595)
- *Tax Information for Direct Sellers* (Number 911)

Try these IRS Tele-Tax tapes:

- *Business Entertainment Expenses* (Number 217)

- *Scholarships, Fellowships, and Grants* (Number 207)
- *Contributions* (Number 234)
- *Small Business Tax Workshop—Tax Help for the New Businessperson* (Number 102)

Chapter 15

ADDING IT UP

How to Make Fringe Benefits Pay

In 1978, Congress ordered the Internal Revenue Service to stop issuing regulations on the income tax treatment of fringe benefits.

Lawmakers, it seems, wanted to decide the matter for themselves. But it took them a while—six years, to be exact— to make up their minds.

In the meantime, the taxability of these benefits—other than insurance, which was covered by existing legislation—remained open to question.

Most companies did more or less what they wanted—passing out fringes liberally without regard to the tax consequences. Business owners gave themselves everything from free rides on company airplanes to high-priced company automobiles and wrote off the costs. The IRS challenged few of these freebies.

When the Tax Reform Act finally came along in 1984, it changed this anything-goes atmosphere. True, the law listed specific benefits that employers could provide tax-free, but it also created several categories of fringe benefits that employers had to report as income to themselves and to other employees.

The law also mandated that any fringe benefit not covered by the act be treated as income to employees and be subject to income-tax withholding and Social Security taxes.

Recently, the IRS has come out with a whole new set of rules to clarify and, in some cases, elaborate on the provisions of the 1984 law.

In this chapter, we summarize the new fringe benefit regulations. We show you which benefits are tax-free or deductible to you and which are tax-free to your employees. And to help you sidestep the regulatory land mines, we outline some perfectly legal and effective strategies for getting around these strict new rules.

After all, providing yourself with a handsome array of fringe benefits is still one of the pluses—and pleasures—of being your own boss.

First, though, a few words about discrimination.

For the most part, you may not deduct the cost of a fringe benefit unless you make that perk available to all your employees.

Excepted from this rule are seasonal and part-time workers (those who work less than 1,000 hours annually) and employees who have been with you less than a year. Excluded, too, are individuals covered by collective bargaining agreements that don't specifically call for the provision of certain benefits.

Our advice: If you're determined to introduce an employee-benefit plan that will mainly help you or other key executives, play it safe and let a professional set it up. Otherwise, you may run afoul of the new regulations.

Now, let's take a look at the tax consequences of most common fringes.

DEATH BENEFITS

Survivor Benefits

A company may deduct payments of up to $5,000 to the survivor of an employee and not report that amount as income to the recipient. Death benefits in excess of $5,000 are also deductible by the company, but the amount over $5,000 is treated by the IRS as compensation to the recipient.

As a rule, the $5,000 death benefit may be funded with insurance (if so, all the premiums are deductible by the business) or drawn from the company's own coffers.

Restrictions apply to payments made to survivors of share-holders with a 2 percent or greater stake in the company—if the benefits aren't paid pursuant to a written plan, in such cases, death payments are included in the beneficiary's income.

Life Insurance

When it comes to life insurance, the law is clear. Corporations may provide life insurance coverage for owners and employees and write off the costs. Sole proprietorships and partnerships, on the other hand, may deduct only the cost of life insurance policies that cover employees.

Another rule: The cost of employer-paid life insurance must be reported as income to employees, unless the insurance is provided under a group-term policy. Even then, employees aren't home free. They pay taxes on amounts paid for coverage that tops $50,000.

But they do get a break. The cost of additional insurance that is reported as income to the employee is an amount based on an IRS table of "average premiums." These premiums amount to much less than the company would actually pay.

To constitute a group-term plan, a policy must be carried in the name of the employer, but its cost may be paid entirely by the company or jointly with employees.

Generally, a group-term policy must cover at least ten full-time employees. Participation in the plan may be limited by length of service.

Plans that cover fewer than ten employees must meet special rules. Among the requirements: All full-time employees must be covered by the plan, so long as they provide evidence of insurability.

You may prove insurability only through a medical questionnaire. You may not require employees to take a physical examination or any other special tests.

Also, as a rule, group-term life insurance plans may not discriminate in favor of business owners or key employees as to eligibility.

But these nondiscrimination rules aren't too onerous. The IRS realizes that you may have good reasons for excluding some employees from some benefits.

So, as a rule, you're welcome to pay benefits in proportion to salary received, thus automatically giving greater benefits to higher paid people. Any life insurance plan is assumed nondiscriminatory if it benefits at least 70 percent of your employees.

Another test: At least 85 percent of the covered employees must not be stockholders, officers, or other highly paid individuals.

_____ **TAXTRAPS** _____

Or, rather, two tax warnings.

If insurance you take out on the lives of your executives lists you or your company as the beneficiary, you are not allowed to deduct your premium payments.

Also, if a bank requires you to take out a life insurance policy as a condition to obtaining a loan, you may not deduct the premiums, even if it is a business loan.

However, a bank that takes out insurance on your life—

and a lender sometimes does—may deduct the premiums it pays as long as your loan is outstanding.

DEPENDENT-CARE PLANS

An employee may take a tax credit for child-care expenses. But what happens if a company provides child-care assistance for workers?

The expense is deductible by the business and not included in the employee's income to the extent that it doesn't exceed $5,000 ($2,500 for a married couple filing separate returns). It makes no difference who provides the care. A company may operate a child-care facility on its premises, or it may contract with a child-care center located nearby for such services.

To qualify as a nontaxable benefit, however, your business must provide dependent care under a written plan, and it must notify employees in writing that the program is available. It also must distribute to employees on or before January 31 of each year a statement outlining expenses incurred in providing care for employee's offspring.

In addition, a child-care program may not discriminate in favor of owners or officers of the company. In fact, no more than 25 percent of the amounts paid by an employer for child care each year may be for the benefit of an individual who owns 5 percent or more of a business.

This rule, in effect, precludes self-employed people who do not have employees from putting a dependent-care program in place.

Union employees may be barred from participation in a dependent-care program only if their collective bargaining agreement does not call for the provision of this fringe.

Another requirement: The value of qualified dependent-care programs may not exceed the total earned income—wages, salaries, plus other compensation and any self-employment income—of employees who benefit from the service.

—————————————— **TAXTIPS** ——————————————

There are two good reasons for setting up a child-care program. First, if money for child care is paid directly to employees, the payments are generally treated by the IRS as compensation. That means the money is deducted by the company and reported as income to the employee. Employees pay income tax on the benefit where otherwise they would not.

Moreover, research shows that these programs boost

employee morale and productivity, so their benefits usually far outweigh their costs. We recommend that businesses institute such programs.

Another idea: Companies may also help employees cover the cost of caring for ailing parents and other dependents. Like the rules governing child care, sums paid out under such programs may be deducted by the company but not reported as income to the employee.

HEALTH PLANS

Athletic Facilities

A company-operated athletic facility can be just about anything—a swimming pool, fishing lake, tennis court, even a golf course.

To be nontaxable, the facility need not be open to all employees or operated in a way that does not discriminate in favor of any particular group. That means you may set aside certain hours for the exclusive use of the facility by you and other owners or executives of your business. Or you may limit use of the facility entirely to top executives.

As a rule, a company athletic facility doesn't have to be located at your place of business. It can be a gym you own or lease a mile or two away.

But the facility must be used virtually all the time by you and your employees. So buying a batch of memberships for workers at a local health club won't enable you to claim a deduction for a company athletic facility.

What's more, company-paid memberships in health clubs are viewed as compensation by the IRS. That means the amounts are reported as income to employees and subject to taxation.

Also ineligible for write-offs on your company's tax return as athletic facilities: gyms, tennis courts, and similar facilities that are part of a resort or residential complex that you own and operate.

TAXTIP

The IRS defines a company-operated athletic facility as one that is either run by your employees or operated under a contract with a third party. All you need do to establish a health club is to contract with an outside company to set up the facility for you on your premises.

The amount you pay this third party to operate the facility is fully deductible. Also, you avoid forking over a big chunk of cash all at once for weights, stationary bicycles, rowing machines, saunas, and so forth—assuming the outside company is willing to foot the bill for the necessary equipment.

———————————————— **FYI** ————————————————

The law allows you to write off the cost of exercise equipment you purchase for branch offices and keep at those sites.

Also, the law says that company-operated athletic facilities may be—but don't have to be—open to the spouses and children of current employees and to retired and disabled workers. So be generous!

Disability Insurance

Owners of corporations may deduct on their income tax returns the cost of disability insurance coverage for their employees and themselves. However, sole proprietors and partners may not deduct the expense of these policies for themselves, although they may write off the cost of coverage for employees.

The reason for this rule?

Proprietors and partners report income from their businesses on their personal returns. They are taxed as individual taxpayers.

Individuals may not write off the cost of disability insurance. So, the reasoning goes, neither can proprietors and partners.

Under the regulations, disability coverage may be provided under a self-funded plan or a policy purchased from an insurance carrier.

The only catch: Workers must be told the plan is in place. To satisfy this requirement, simply post a notice of disability coverage on your bulletin board.

———————————————— **TAXTIP** ————————————————

We advise clients with corporations to buy disability insurance policies for themselves with their own money, not with funds drawn from their corporations.

Here's the reason: Payments you receive from a disability policy to replace wages are generally taxable to you if the insurance premiums were paid by your corporation. (Employees who become permanently disabled before they reach the age of sixty-five and receive less than $100 a week in benefits are excluded from this rule.)

You don't have to report disability payments as income, if you pay the insurance policy out of your own pocket.

Some of our clients, gambling that they won't become disabled, write off the cost of disability insurance on their corporate returns.

It's their choice. But we advise against it.

Employee Mental Health Services

Mental health coverage is a fast-growing fringe benefit. Indeed, some businesses credit the coverage with helping them slash their overall health-care costs.

Under the rules, businesses that provide free counseling for troubled employees may deduct the expense of assistance programs and not report these costs as income to recipients.

These mental health services may be provided in-house or by outside specialists. Payments for services may be made by the company or through an insurance carrier.

Exercise Classes

Most business owners are more than happy to provide space for on-site exercise programs. Many of them are even willing to foot the bill for an instructor.

And why not? The amount your company pays out for an exercise teacher is tax deductible, so long as the class is open to all employees.

_____ **FYI** _____

You may also write off floor mats and other class equipment.

Medical Insurance

For many small business owners, skyrocketing medical insurance premiums are a major budget item. Premiums for a typical family policy run upwards of $3,000 a year.

Owners of sole proprietorships and partnerships may deduct the cost of medical coverage for employees as a business expense on their returns. They also may deduct one-quarter of their own premiums.

They may write off the remainder of the premium cost as a medical expense, but only if that amount plus all other medical and dental expenses exceed 7.5 percent of their adjusted gross income.

Corporations, on the other hand, may write off the cost of

medical insurance for shareholder-employees and other workers as well.

However, the IRS may classify premiums for medical plans that are limited to stockholders as dividend income if the coverage is not tied to the provision of employee services. This rule is intended to prevent you from paying the medical-insurance premiums of shareholders who do no work for your corporation.

A corporation may choose to cover its employees' medical expenses in one of two ways—through an insurance policy or through a self-funded plan.

With either method, sums paid to reimburse employees for medical expenses are deductible by the corporation but need not be reported as income to employees. Employers may cover doctor, hospital and nursing bills, as well as the cost of diagnosing and treating illnesses and diseases.

You may also cover expenditures for hearing aids and eyeglasses, dental care, artificial teeth and limbs, guide dogs, rental of medical equipment and devices, and essential transportation costs, such as ambulance fees.

For the most part, medical benefits must be provided to employees in a nondiscriminatory fashion or costs may be taxable to recipients.

Companies may deduct the cost of annual physical examinations for employees and not report that benefit as income to workers.

Businesses also may write off amounts they pay out to equip and operate health care centers for employees and their dependents.

―――――――――――――― TAXTIPS ――――――――――――――

Trim your medical-insurance bills by limiting participation to employees who have worked for you a certain length of time.

The law allows you to exclude workers who have been employed by you less than three years. You may also exclude part-time and seasonal workers.

Another idea: If you employ only yourself (and you're young and healthy), purchase major-medical coverage or a policy with a high deductible—say, $2,000 to $5,000. You can cut your premiums in half.

―――――――――――――― FYI ――――――――――――――

An individual's medical expenses are deductible only to

the extent that they exceed 7.5 percent of adjusted gross income.

Therefore, if adjusted gross income is $50,000, a taxpayer has to shell out more than $3,700 in medical expenses (including health insurance and prescription drugs) before a penny can be written off. So it makes tax sense—for employees, at least—for a company to provide medical-insurance coverage.

Medical-Reimbursement Plans

In the good old days, a company could reimburse its owners and key executives for health care costs not covered by regular medical plans, then deduct those amounts as ordinary and necessary business expenses. But Congress nixed that practice a few years back. It mandated that businesses couldn't deduct these payments unless they were provided to all employees. The only workers who could be excluded were those who

- Had not completed three years of service
- Were under twenty-five years of age
- Were part-time employees
- Worked only on a seasonal basis
- Were covered under a collective-bargaining agreement that did not call for the provision of medical-reimbursement coverage

Some insurance carriers, however, have discovered a loophole in the law—a provision that allows companies to provide this particular benefit to owners and top executives if the reimbursements are made through insurance policies. Consequently, a couple dozen insurers have introduced what they call medical-reimbursement plans.

Essentially, the policies enable companies to provide business owners and executives with an additional fringe benefit that is both 100 percent tax deductible by the company and not reported as income to the individual.

As a rule, reimbursement plans cover only medical costs that qualify as deductible under the law. But that's not much of a restriction.

The Internal Revenue Service's list of deductible health care expenses includes everything from false teeth to—believe it or not—fees paid to an Indian medicine man.

A typical medical-reimbursement policy works like this: A business owner incurs an out-of-pocket health care expense, such as eyeglasses or dental work, that is not covered by his regular medical insurance. He forwards the bill to his medical-reimbursement insurance policy carrier. The carrier sends the business owner a check for the expense. Next, it forwards an invoice to the corporation for the amount of the bill, plus a 10 to 13 percent handling fee.

Also included in the plans is what is known as stop-loss insurance coverage—a rider that caps an employer's liability when claims exceed a certain present limit. The usual range is $2,500 to $10,000 per person for a group of six key executives.

The cost of reimbursement insurance varies slightly with each carrier. But most companies' standard plans charge a base fee of $175 per year for the first executive and $100 for each additional executive, plus the actual medical expenses.

When you figure in the tax savings, the plans usually more than pay for themselves.

Stop-Smoking Programs

Businesses may write off the cost of stop-smoking programs and not report the amount as income to employees. However, all employees must have access to the program, not just key executives or shareholders.

CASE IN POINT

Say you are the owner of a small retail clothing store that employs ten people, and you offer to foot the bill for a stop-smoking program.

If you are the only person who smokes, you wouldn't be able to write off the cost of the program as a business expense.

The IRS would argue that you set up the program with the knowledge that you would be the only person to benefit from it. Thus, it would be discriminatory.

Stress-Management Programs

The rules that apply to stop-smoking programs also apply to stress-management programs: costs may be deducted by the company and not treated as compensation to employees.

The only catch: The program must not discriminate.

Weight-Loss Programs

Businesses may deduct the cost of weight-loss programs and not report the amount as income to employees.

Again, the program may not discriminate in favor of top brass or company owners. It must be open to all employees.

RETIREMENT PLANS

Retirement planning is deductible by the company. It is not treated as compensation to employees if it is provided in a nondiscriminatory fashion.

We cover retirement plans in chapter 17.

OTHER PERKS

Company Airplanes

Federal law sets forth harsh valuation rules to calculate the value of personal flights by business owners and executives on company-owned aircraft.

Usually, the value of flying on a company plane is equivalent to the amount it would cost a person to charter a flight on a comparable aircraft for a comparable flight.

In most cases, this amount far exceeds the cost of a ticket from a commercial carrier. For example, a ticket on a commercial flight from New York to Los Angeles costs from $200 to $400. The cost of a charter flight between those two cities would run in excess of $2,000.

Our advice: Use company planes for business only.

Defensive Driving Courses

Businesses may write off the cost of defensive driving courses for employees whose jobs require them to spend a great deal of time on the road. The cost of the class is not reported as income to employees, so long as the benefit is provided by the company in a way that does not favor owners or key executives.

De Minimis Fringe Benefits

De minimis (Latin for "from the least") fringes are benefits whose value is so small—free coffee, free doughnuts, and so forth—that, in most cases, accounting for them on a per-employee basis is impractical. The law allows businesses to deduct the cost of these fringes and not report their value as income to employees.

Other examples of *de minimis* fringes:

- Occasional company picnics or parties
- Clinics held periodically on company property to check the blood pressure of employees
- Free taxi rides home for employees who attend office parties and are unsure of their ability to drive home
- Holiday turkeys or hams

The law also allows employers to provide public-transit

system passes to employees at a discount if the discount does not exceed $15 per employee per month.

Occasional tickets to movies and sporting events qualify as *de minimis* fringes, too, as do free photocopies and company cocktail parties.

However, photocopies are a *de minimis* benefit only if the photocopying machine is used at least 85 percent of the time for business.

CASE IN POINT

Say you own an insurance agency and purchase a small photocopier. You use the machine primarily to copy correspondence.

Your business usage adds up to about forty copies a month. But your two employees have access to the machine as well. They use it to photocopy everything from recipes to notices of club meetings.

Their usage totals about sixty copies a month.

The result: Business use of the copying machine totals only 40 percent. So you have to report as income to employees the value of each photocopy they make.

How, you may ask, will IRS agents know if someone uses their photocopier at least 85 percent of the time for business? The IRS won't unless someone tells them, which is why this rule seems so silly. Our advice: Consider whether you even need a machine if business usage falls below 85 percent.

What doesn't qualify as a *de minimis* fringe?

Benefits that do not fall into the *de minimis* category include such *maximus* benefits as season tickets to sporting or theatrical events, the use of a business car for commuting to and from work, membership in a country club, and the weekend use of a company-owned boat or vacation facility—a beach house, say, or a hunting lodge.

The primary factor in determining whether a benefit qualifies as a *de minimis* fringe is its monetary value. But the law provides no specific floor or ceiling. The result: We'll have to wait for the courts—or the IRS—to define the limits. In the meantime, our advice is to play it safe. Treat only benefits that are of little value as *de minimis* fringes.

Another factor to weigh in deciding whether or not a perk fits into the category of a *de minimis* benefit is the frequency with which it is provided to an employee or group of employees.

_____ **CASE IN POINT** _____

Suppose you serve free breakfast daily to your fourteen employees. You may deduct the cost, so long as you report the value of the meal as taxable income to your employees. You—or your employees—have, it seems, been shafted by the frequency rule: you provide breakfast every single day, so it is not a *de minimis* fringe.

You could, however, write off the cost of a breakfast you serve occasionally to employees or executives who attend an early morning meeting and not report its value as income to them.

_____ **CASE IN POINT** _____

Every two weeks, you purchase movie tickets for your controller. The tickets would not qualify as a *de minimis* fringe because you hand them out regularly.

Consequently, you would have to keep track of how much you spend on the tickets, then report it as income to the executive.

If you treat the movie tickets as a business gift, however, you may deduct the first $25 you spend and not report that amount as income to the executive.

_____ **TAXTIP** _____

Unlike most benefits, the law allows you to provide *de minimis* fringes on a discriminatory basis. Our advice is to cash in on this rule. Provide yourself and other key executives with as many *de minimis* fringes as possible.

For instance, you may furnish free coffee, soft drinks, and snacks to officers of your company and write off the cost. Or you may pay for an occasional meal for an executive who works overtime but not extend that benefit to other employees.

Demonstrator Automobiles

The 1984 Tax Reform Act singled out a number of specific groups for special scrutiny, among them, employees of automobile dealerships.

The act mandated that the tax-free personal use of demonstrator cars (those used for test drives by customers) is strictly limited to full-time salespeople.

Furthermore, salespeople may not drive demonstrator cars

outside the dealership's sales area—say, a seventy-five-mile radius of the automobile sales offices.

Full-time salespeople, say the regulations, are individuals who work a minimum of 1,000 hours a year and derive 85 percent of their income from selling cars.

The rules eliminate the use of demonstrators as a tax-free benefit for mechanics, bookkeepers, even the owners of the dealership.

Dining Facilities

Unlike company-provided athletic facilities, a dining facility must be open to all employees or you cannot write off its cost.

Also, a cafeteria must be located on or near the company's place of business and operated by either employees or under a contract with a third party.

Revenues from the food operation must be either equal to or exceed the cost of providing the service. What makes this last rule doubly difficult is that each cafeteria or dining room your company maintains is treated by the IRS as a separate entity. So you have to keep books for each site, and each site must pay its own way.

TAXTIP

Why not contract with a caterer to serve a buffet-style lunch to your employees every day? The price the caterer would charge would no doubt be less than the amount they would pay at a restaurant.

Education Programs

It used to be that companies could write off up to $5,000 a year in tuition assistance payments to employees and not treat that amount as compensation.

But no more.

The 1984 Act mandates that general tuition plans are tax-free only for employees of colleges and universities. Businesses that offer tuition-assistance programs for employees must report the sums they pay out as income to those employees.

The result: Employees who earn their college degrees at the expense of their employers will be taxed on the benefit.

However, businesses may still write off the cost of job-related training programs or courses and not report their value as income to employees.

Employees, meanwhile, are still entitled to deduct on their personal returns the cost of education that is related to their jobs. But they may write off these expenses only as miscellaneous itemized deductions (subject to a 2 percent floor) on their returns, which means that only high-paid employees are likely to capture these deductions.

FYI

An inexpensive way to keep employees up-to-date on business matters is to pay for their subscriptions to trade magazines or professional journals.

. Another way to stretch your education dollars: A client of ours, the chief executive officer of a small manufacturing company, spends several hundred dollars a year on trade publications and books.

He leaves the publications in his lunchroom for employees to read. The plan, he says, is an inexpensive but effective way to keep workers current on industry trends. What's more, his company gets to write off the cost of all those magazines and books as ordinary business expenses.

Employee Discounts

If you sell company products and services to your employees for a cut rate, you should know that Uncle Sam is strict about what you may—and may not—do.

A service business, for example, may not offer employees a discount of more than 20 percent. The discount ceiling for any other type of company is its gross profit percentage.

To compute your gross profit percentage, use operating results from the previous year. The following example illustrates how to perform this calculation:

Suppose your sales last year were $800,000 and your cost of goods sold was $600,000. You would subtract your costs—$600,000—from sales—$800,000—to get your profit, $200,000. Then you would divide the profit by sales to get your gross profit percentage—in this case, 25 percent.

Companies that have not been in business a year may estimate their gross profit percentage using industry averages.

CASE IN POINT

As the owner of an electronics store, you sell a video cassette recorder priced at $500 to an employee for $350—a 30-percent discount.

But your gross profit percentage is 20 percent.

That means the employee may exclude from income

$100 (20 percent times $500) of the price of the VCR. The remaining $50 is taxable income to the employee.

Admittedly, the IRS isn't likely to know if you or your employees violate these rules. But, as the IRS is fond of reminding us, the law is the law.

If you own more than one business, you may provide nontaxable discounts to employees only on the products that are sold by the company that employs them.

For instance, employees of your sporting goods store may receive discounts on sporting goods but not on the VCRs sold at your electronics store.

One exception to the rule: Employees who provide substantial services for more than one business. Say, for instance, that you employ a bookkeeper to keep the books for both your businesses. That person performs substantial work for both companies; therefore, she would be entitled to employee discounts at both stores.

Another exception to the one-line-of-business rule is made for companies, such as cosmetics manufacturers, that lease floor space from big department stores. The law allows employees of these leased departments to receive discounts on merchandise sold throughout the department store.

Also, the law requires that nontaxable employee discounts be available on a nondiscriminatory basis, which means they must benefit everyone equally.

For instance, it would be discriminatory for you to offer 10 percent discounts to hourly workers and 20 percent discounts to salaried employees.

Discounts may be made available tax-free not only to employees but to their spouses and dependents and to retired and disabled workers. However, reciprocal agreements—where a group of employers agree to provide discounts to each other's employees—are no longer allowed by the rules.

Moreover, certain items are simply not eligible for tax-free discounts. They include real estate, securities, commodities, interests in minerals, and other investment vehicles, such as coins and stamps.

Finally, under the rules, you may be able to arrange discounts for your employees through third parties. Say you manufacture appliances. Under the regulations, an employee of your company may receive a qualified employee discount from a store that sells your appliances.

—————————————— **FYI** ——————————————

Another way to save employees money: Sell damaged or
returned goods to them at the fair market price. You'll get
rid of unwanted items, and your employees will appreciate
the price reductions.

The amount your employees save on these items doesn't
have to be reported as income to them. So there's no
additional paperwork for you.

Frequent-Flier Bonuses
The bad news: Frequent-flier bonuses earned on employer-paid
trips are taxable if they're used for personal trips. The good
news: The IRS hasn't figured out how to calculate the value of
these awards to recipients.

Our advice: Use your frequent-flier bonuses and wait for the
regulations to come out before you worry. No one is likely to
come after you.

No-Additional-Cost Services
Say you, the employer, provide services to your employees, and
these services cost your company nothing. Then, the IRS says,
employees don't have to report the value of the services as
income.

No-additional-cost services are simply unused services—those
a company offers to, but can't sell, to the general public. For example, an airline might offer employees unused standby airline
tickets, or a hotel chain might make available its empty rooms.

These no-additional-cost services qualify as nontaxable fringe
benefits only if they are made available to all employees.

Also, a company engaged in more than one line of business
may provide no-additional-cost services to employees tax free
only in the line of business in which they work. For instance,
a company that owns an airline and a hotel chain may provide
free air travel—but not free hotel rooms—to airline employees.

—————————————— **FYI** ——————————————

Unlike employee discounts, no-additional-cost services may
be expanded to include employees of another company
through a reciprocal agreement.

One sticky point: The companies must be in the same
line of business. For example, two airlines could provide
standby flights to each other's employees. Also, Uncle Sam
demands that the reciprocal agreement be put in writing.

Consider, too, providing no-additional-cost benefits to

spouses and dependents of employees and retired and disabled workers. (These benefits aren't taxable to the recipients.)

Parking

Companies may treat the cost of parking that is provided to a select few executives and owners as nontaxable to them if certain rules are met. Primary among them: The parking must be located near the place of employment (not at a country club or marina some thirty miles away).

TAXTIP

If your company does not own a parking lot, you may rent parking spaces for yourself and employees, and the benefit is deductible by the company but not taxable to recipients.

Alternatively, you and your employees may rent the spaces yourself and report your costs on your expense accounts.

FYI

Why not designate an "employee of the month" and award that person the use of the best parking space in your company lot for the next thirty days?

Vacation Homes

Many businesses purchase ocean- or lakefront cottages and campsites, then rent the property to employees at low rates.

Employees really appreciate the low-cost vacations. Furthermore, the move allows businesses to capture attractive depreciation deductions, since they may treat the cottages and campsites as rental properties.

But be sure the facility is available to all employees.

TAXTRAP

If the property is used primarily by owners and top executives, the IRS may classify it as an entertainment facility.

In such cases, deductions for all expenses related to the purchase, maintenance, and operation of the facility will be disallowed.

Working-Condition Fringe Benefits

These fringes are items, such as protective clothing, that could be deducted by the employee if they weren't provided by the employer. The benefits may be deducted by employers and not reported as income to employees.

────────────────── **TAXTIPS** ──────────────────

A working-condition fringe benefit is another perk that may be provided to business owners and executives on a discriminatory basis.

You may buy magazine subscriptions or special training programs for yourself and your top managers without providing similar benefits to other employees. For example, you could hold lunchtime seminars on everything from computer literacy to stress management and write off the cost.

You may also hire a bodyguard or a chauffeured automobile to take you to and from work—if you need them for security reasons. But, believe me, in the case of an audit, the IRS will ask you to prove that these security arrangements really are necessary.

For businesspeople who frequently travel outside the United States, the IRS will accept as proof a recent history of terrorist activity in the part of the world where you're staying. The IRS also will take as proof threats against you or against people who hold similar positions in your industry.

────────────────── **TAXTRAP** ──────────────────

Writing off the amount you spend on clothes you wear while working is no simple task. Witness these two examples:

Back in 1962, Ozzie and Harriet Nelson were denied a deduction for clothes worn by their two sons on the family's popular television show. Ozzie and Harriet, it seems, failed to prove that their sons, Rick and David, had worn the clothing only during the filming of the TV program.

In 1980, a manager of an Yves St. Laurent shop in Dallas was denied a deduction for clothing she purchased from the designer and wore only at work. The court ruled that even though wearing the designer's clothes was a condition of employment, the articles were acceptable for wear during off hours.

CAFETERIA BENEFIT PLANS

No doubt about it, the hottest fringe-benefit package available nowadays is the cafeteria plan. With this plan, workers get to structure their own benefits package.

Employers give their workers a set amount to spend. Then the employees select the benefits they want from a company-designed menu.

When cafeteria plans were first introduced in the 1970s, employees could receive cash for any benefits they didn't use. However, the 1984 Tax Reform Act prohibited these cash payments.

Moreover, it limited cafeteria plans to benefits that could be deducted by employers and not reported as income to employees—day care, medical insurance, life insurance, and so on. Taxable benefits, such as tuition assistance and reimbursement for the cost of commuting, could no longer be included.

Also, deferred-compensation programs, such as a pension or profit-sharing plan, are no longer eligible for cafeteria programs. However, an exception was made for so-called 401(k) retirement plans. (See chapter 17.)

Enrollment in cafeteria plans is strictly limited to employees. Sole proprietors and partners may not participate.

What's more, cafeteria plans may not discriminate in favor of shareholders and key employees. The law defines a key employee as a person who owns 5 percent or more of the shares in a company or an individual who owns 1 percent or more of a company and earns more than $150,000 a year.

However, participation may be limited by length of employment. For example, it's perfectly legal for you to restrict enrollment in your cafeteria benefit plan to individuals who have worked for you three years or more. Also, you may exclude union workers from the plan if their contracts don't call for participation.

FYI

It's a headache, I know. But employers who maintain cafeteria benefit plans will, for tax years that begin after 1989, be asked to file an information return with the IRS that shows the number of people participating in the plan.

The information return (Form 5500, 5500C, or 5500R) will also reveal the number of people employed by the company, the total cost of the benefit program, and the type of business in which the company is engaged.

CAPITAL PUNISHMENT
Only in the past few years has the IRS required employers to

withhold income taxes on the value of fringe benefits that are reported as income to employees, so there is still enormous confusion on the subject.

Essentially, employers may add the value of a fringe benefit to a single paycheck and withhold taxes on that amount. Or they may spread the value of a fringe over several pay periods in the year, then withhold a small amount each pay period.

If an employer elects the first method, taxes are withheld at a flat 20 percent of the value of the fringe benefit.

If an employer opts for the second method, employers may treat the benefits as part of regular wages and compute withholding taxes on the total, or they may treat the fringes as "supplemental wages" and withhold 20 percent of the value of the benefit.

The rules also include a special provision that permits employers to treat the value of taxable fringe benefits during the last two months of a calendar year—say, you give an employee a company car—as paid to an employee in the following tax year. However, this deferral is available only for benefits actually provided in the last two months of the year.

Any benefits provided during the year must be included on an employee's W-2 Form. The value of the fringe benefits must be included in

- The box labeled "gross income"
- The box numbered "16"

Alternatively, employers may issue a separate W-2 Form for fringe benefits.

TAXTRAP

Have your employees double-check their Social Security numbers. The reason: The IRS may slap a $50 fine on workers who, whether on purpose or by accident, provide employers with an incorrect Social Security number.

TAX STRATEGIES

If your aim is to trim your fringe-benefit bill, consider reducing the number of people you actually employ. Sign on independent contractors instead.

CASE IN POINT

A woman works in your law office as a bookkeeper several days a week. But she's not an employee.

She works as an independent contractor. Legally, she

operates her own business, which consists of providing services not only to you but other businesspeople as well.

As an independent contractor, she is required to report her own income to the IRS by filing a Schedule C with her personal tax return.

All you have to do is report the amount you paid her on a Form 1099—one copy to her and one to the IRS—once a year.

—————————————— **TAXTIP** ——————————————

The IRS has complex rules to determine who is an employee and who is an independent contractor. And Uncle Sam frequently argues with business owners about the status of independent contractors.

Generally, physicians, lawyers, dentists, veterinarians, writers, contractors, subcontractors, public stenographers, auctioneers, and others engaged in a particular profession or trade are independent contractors, not employees.

For the most part, you may call people independent contractors if

- You don't exercise constant control over how they spend their work time.
- You ask them to give you an invoice for each pay period.
- You clearly explain to them what their independent contractor status means.

Also, you should be able to demonstrate to the IRS that your "nonemployee treatment" is consistent with a long-standing, recognized practice in your industry. It helps if independent contractors provide services to a number of clients, not just you.

The IRS summarizes its independent contractor rules as follows:

> Every individual who performs services that are subject to the will and control of an employer, as to both what shall be done and how it shall be done, is an employee.

> It does not matter that the employer allows the employee considerable discretion and freedom of action, so long as the employer has the legal right to control both the method and the result of the services.

FOR MORE INFORMATION
See these IRS publications:

- *Travel, Entertainment, and Gift Expenses* (Number 463)
- *Medical and Dental Expenses* (Number 502)
- *Child and Dependent Care Credit* (Number 503)
- *Educational Expenses* (Number 508)
- *Taxable and Nontaxable Income* (Number 525)
- *Miscellaneous Deductions* (Number 529)
- *Business Expenses* (Number 535)
- *Tax Information for Survivors, Executors, and Administrators* (Number 559)
- *Your Federal Income Tax* (Number 17)
- *Tax Guide for Small Business* (Number 334)
- *Farmers' Tax Guide* (Number 225)
- *Tax Guide for Commercial Fishermen* (Number 595)
- *Tax Information for Direct Sellers* (Number 911)

Try these IRS Tele-Tax tapes:

- *Medical and Dental Expenses* (Number 228)
- *Medical Insurance* (Number 229)
- *Educational Expenses* (Number 238)
- *Child-Care Credit* (Number 306)
- *Social Security Withholding Rates* (Number 406)
- *Form W-2—Where, When, and How to File* (Number 407)
- *Form W-4—Employee's Withholding Allowance Certificate* (Number 408)
- *Paying Taxes on Your Employees* (Number 411)
- *Small Business Tax Workshops—Tax Help for the New Businessperson* (Number 102)

Chapter 16

A HOUSE DIVIDED

Splitting Income to Slash Taxes

Many small business owners and professionals draw upon the talents of their spouses. Husbands, for instance, may help with the bookkeeping; wives may provide marketing advice. Paying spouses for the work they do can save you hundreds of dollars in taxes—more if your marriage partner is not otherwise employed.

_____ **CASE IN POINT** _____

Your wife does not work outside the home, but in the past year she has helped you develop an advertising campaign for your financial-planning business.

For her advice, you pay her a one-time $2,500 consulting fee. These earnings may enable her to open an Individual Retirement Account (IRA).

She contributes $2,000 to the account. As a result, 80 percent of her earnings are sheltered from taxation, and she enjoys the benefits of her own retirement nest egg. (We discuss the rules governing IRAs in the next chapter.)

_____ **TAXTRAPS** _____

If you are audited, the IRS will ask you to prove that your spouse provided a bona fide service, so be sure you can show that he or she did legitimate work.

Also, you must be able to prove that money actually changed hands. If you cannot, the IRS may, on audit, disallow the deduction.

Finally, the law says the money you pay spouses (or any family members) must be theirs to keep. Don't write them a check, have them cash it, then give the money back to you.

FAMILY AFFAIR

You should also pay your children when they do work for your business. This tactic enables you to shift income from a high tax bracket (yours) to a low one (your children's).

Child-labor laws do not apply to youngsters working in family businesses. The government's only criterion is that they be old enough to do "economically useful work."

Exactly what that phrase means is a matter of debate. But the court has accepted as legitimate, salaries paid to children as young as eight years old.

By compensating your offspring for the work they do, you earn a deduction, and they earn spending money or cash to put away for college.

——————— CASE IN POINT ———————

Say you earn more than $100,000 a year as the owner of a small trucking company. You pay your thirteen-year-old son $50 a week—or $2,600 a year—to keep your offices and garage tidy. He spends approximately two hours a day on the job.

On your company tax return, you write off the $2,600 as wages, an allowable business deduction, and report the money as income to your son on a W-2.

The result: You pocket a handsome $2,600 deduction.

——————— TAXTRAP ———————

Say you ask that a portion of your child's earnings be paid back to you as room and board. In this case, you must report that money as rental income.

An attorney recently lost a deduction for the wages he paid his children. His mistake: He made out checks not to them but to their colleges, doctors, and clothing stores.

TAX STRATEGIES

A common device for splitting income among family members is to make your children or other relatives your partners.

Since the passage of the 1986 Tax Reform Act, however, this strategy makes sense only with children who are older than fourteen.

Why? Children under fourteen now have to pay tax on their unearned income of more than $500 at their parents' rate, not their own lower rate.

Also, some special rules apply to family partnerships. Among them: When it comes time to distribute profits, you can't simply divide earnings by the number of family members in the partnership. You must first take into account the services family members provide to the business and compensate them accordingly. (S corporations don't appear to be subject to these rules.)

_____ **CASE IN POINT** _____

A forty-five-year-old father gives his eighteen-year-old son a 50-percent interest in his company. The partnership's net profits total about $100,000 a year.

The father works for the company, but not the son. Under the rules, a value must be assigned to the services the father provides—in this case, the amount decided upon is $40,000. That sum is roughly equal to the amount paid people in comparable jobs in comparable industries.

As a result, the profits are distributed this way: The first $40,000 goes to the father. Then the remaining profits—$60,000—are split equally between father and son. The result: $70,000 goes to the father ($40,000 plus half of the remaining $60,000) and $30,000 to the son.

Also, under the rules, family members must exercise some control over their general partnership interests. That means they must be, in the judgment of the IRS, of sufficient age and mental ability to handle the responsibility a partnership entails.

In the case of minors or people of limited mental ability, general partnership interests must be controlled by a fiduciary and held in trust.

FOR MORE INFORMATION
See these IRS publications:

* *Tax Information on Partnerships* (Number 541)
* *Tax Information on Corporations* (Number 542)
* *Tax Information on S Corporations* (Number 589)
* *Your Federal Income Tax* (Number 17)
* *Tax Guide for Small Business* (Number 334)
* *Farmers' Tax Guide* (Number 225)
* *Tax Guide for Commercial Fishermen* (Number 595)

- *Tax Information for Direct Sellers* (Number 911)

   Try this IRS Tele-Tax tape:

- *Small Business Tax Workshops—Tax Help for the New Businessperson* (Number 102)

Chapter 17

WE'RE IN THE MONEY

Smart Retirement Planning

Some years ago, a young reporter was dispatched by his newspaper to learn how a wealthy old merchant had accumulated his riches.

"Well, it's a long story," the old man began. "And while I tell it, we may as well save the candle."

Then he blew it out.

"Never mind the interview," the young reporter said. "I think I understand your secret."

Nowadays, we don't have to deprive ourselves of such basic necessities as light to accumulate substantial wealth. Indeed, all we have to do is familiarize ourselves with the government's attractive retirement planning rules—and cash in on them.

NEW THINGS ARE MADE FAMILIAR
AND FAMILIAR THINGS ARE MADE NEW

Or so wrote Samuel Johnson back in the eighteenth century. Retirement plans provide one example of Johnson's observation.

Pension plans date to 1759, when a group of Presbyterian ministers adopted a scheme that would provide benefits to their widows and children. But our attitudes toward these plans have changed radically.

In days past, we saw retirement plans simply as a way to salt away money for our golden years. Nowadays, we view them differently—as bona fide wealth-building tools.

This shift in perception came about, in large part, when Congress adopted the 1981 Economic Recovery Tax Act (ERTA). That law mandated the most sweeping reform to date in retirement-planning rules by placing retirement plans for proprietors and partners on a par with corporate plans.

These days, it makes no difference how your business is organized. You're subject to virtually the same rules when it comes to setting up and maintaining retirement and pension plans for yourself and your employees.

In this chapter, we'll provide answers to the most commonly asked questions we hear today about retirement planning. We concentrate on the retirement plan most likely to benefit small business owners and professionals—the Keogh plan.

- Why contribute money to a retirement plan?

The intent of ERTA was simple: Congress wanted us to depend less on government-provided retirement benefits and more on private planning and personal initiative. So we—all of us—were urged to plan ahead for retirement, with some favorable tax regulations as our incentive.

_____ **CASE IN POINT** _____

Say you're in the 33-percent tax bracket and invest $10,000 a year in a mutual fund earning an average return of 10 percent each year. At the end of twenty-five years, you would have accumulated $605,901—after you give Uncle Sam his annual due.

Now, let's say you, as a small business owner, establish a self-funded retirement plan, a Keogh. Through your plan, you deposit the same amount in the same mutual fund.

The fund still earns an average return of 10 percent annually. But, because it's a Keogh, the earnings accumulate tax free. So, at the end of twenty-five years, you would have socked away $983,470. That's a whopping $377,569 difference.

Of course, the money you accumulate in your plan will be taxed when you withdraw it. And your tax bracket at retirement may be no lower than it is today. But you'll be well ahead of the game, since your earnings have had a chance to accumulate tax deferred.

- As a self-employed person, what kind of retirement plan may I fund myself?

A Keogh is the best self-funded retirement strategy. Sometimes called HR-10 plans after the number of the House of Representatives tax bill that created them, Keoghs came into being in 1962. The author of HR-10 was Vincent Keogh, a former New York congressman.

Keogh plans and Individual Retirement Accounts (IRAs) are quite similar: both shelter income from taxes, allowing your cash to build up tax free until age fifty-nine and a half. IRAs, though, were designed for everyone who works; Keogh plans are specifically structured for businesspeople who work for themselves.

The working assumption behind the creation of Keoghs was that the legislators felt that self-employed people should have as good an opportunity to save for retirement as employees who enjoyed the benefits of company-sponsored pension plans.

Keoghs come in two basic forms: defined-benefit plans and defined-contribution plans.

A defined-benefit plan is a type of Keogh account that promises to pay out a preset sum each year when you retire. In 1988, the ceiling on payouts from this type of plan is the lesser of $94,023 or 100 percent of compensation, no matter how your business is organized. (The ceiling may change from year to year with differences in the cost of living.

With a defined-contribution plan, you or your company contribute a specified amount each year until your retirement. Defined-contribution plans come in two types: profit-sharing plans and money-purchase plans. How do they differ?

With a money-purchase plan, you may sock away as much as $30,000 or 25 percent of compensation, whichever is less. With a profit-sharing plan, your contribution is capped at 15 percent or $30,000, again, whichever is less.

But these percentages are a bit misleading. Why? The percentage is applied to your net self-employment income *less* the amount of your Keogh contribution.

So, effectively, you may contribute only 20 percent to a money-purchase plan and 13.043 percent to a profit-sharing plan.

_____ **TAXTIP** _____

A money-purchase plan lets you contribute more toward your retirement nest egg. But it does have one disadvantage.

The law says you must contribute a set percentage to it each year or pay a penalty. Your profit-sharing contribution, on the other hand, is optional. If you need your money for other purposes, you're not obligated to contribute to it.

You may get around this rule, however, by creating what's known as a "paired plan," which consists of both a money-purchase and profit-sharing plan.

Here's the advantage: You may still contribute the full 20 percent, but you put away only 8 percent in the compulsory money-purchase plan. And, while you may contribute up to 12 percent to your profit-sharing plan, these annual contributions are made at your option.

TAXTIP

The law says that the ceiling on contributions to a defined-benefit plan will change each year as the cost of living rises. But the ceiling on contributions to a defined-contribution plan won't change until the ceiling on defined-benefit plans reaches $120,000.

- What's the deadline for setting up a Keogh?

You must set up your Keogh before December 31 or the last day of your taxable year. But you have until the date—including extensions—you file your return to make your contribution.

Another important point: If you're a member of a partnership, the partnership, not you, must set up the Keogh.

- What are my Keogh investment options?

A Keogh plan may include certificates of deposit, stocks, bonds, money market shares, or any other investment vehicle. You may establish a Keogh account with a bank, brokerage house, insurance company, or any other financial institution.

The fund may be managed either by the company that serves as custodian (a bank, for example) or the owner of the account. Most self-employed people, however, prefer to let a professional manager oversee their account.

The money or securities are held in the account tax-free from year to year, and so are any gains or returns on the principal, so long as this income accumulates within the account. (If it is paid out year to year, it is taxed yearly as well.)

Usually, however, all funds are withdrawn at retirement. Then you are taxed on the amount you receive at your ordinary rate.

Remember that the rules on the investment of Keogh funds

are liberal—most financial investments are permitted. However, you may not invest in art objects, antiques, coins, stamps, or other collectibles. (The legislators wanted to keep taxpayers from using their retirement dollars to furnish their homes.) The law does make an exception for silver and gold coins produced by the U.S. treasury—the so-called Eagle coins.

The law even mentions "alcoholic beverages" as one of the prohibited items, since some investors have put money into rare wines and aging Scotch.

What happens if you have a Keogh plan and divert funds into collectibles? The value of the collectibles—as determined by an IRS-approved appraiser, if necessary—is treated as taxable income at your ordinary rates, and 10 percent of that value is tacked on as an added penalty.

- Must employees be covered by my Keogh plan?

If you have employees, you must include your staff members in your Keogh plan. Your contributions in their behalf must be comparable to your own.

If you deposit 15 percent of your income for yourself, you must deposit an amount equal to 15 percent of each employee's salary as well.

Moreover, you may not deduct contributions from your employees' pay. You must make the entire contribution—but the amount is deductible.

- May I borrow money from my Keogh account?

A great temptation to owners of Keogh plans is to dip into the funds to help defray the costs of a trip to Europe, say, or a child's wedding.

But you may not borrow from your own Keogh plan without unpleasant tax consequences. This rule applies to anyone with more than a 10-percent stake in the business.

What happens if you disregard this restriction? As you might expect, the amount of the "loan" will be treated as a "prohibited transaction." And you will be subject to an excise tax on that amount.

If you're wondering how the IRS discovers your borrowing, keep in mind that Keogh plans are not like ordinary bank or investment accounts. They are accounts set up under special rules. One of these regulations requires the custodian or trustee (usually a financial institution) to inform the IRS, if and when you abuse your tax-sheltering privilege.

- **What happens if I contribute more than the allowable amount to my Keogh?**

Another temptation for Keogh plan owners is to pad their accounts. Don't. If you make contributions over the allowable amount, you're subject to a 6-percent penalty on the excess.

The penalty is waived if the excess amount is withdrawn, along with any earnings it generates, before the due date of your tax return.

- **How are Keoghs taxed at retirement?**

Should you decide to withdraw your entire Keogh nest egg at retirement, your withdrawal is covered by special, favorable five-year averaging rules.

When you take out your funds in one lump sum, you average your taxes over five years rather than pay one enormous tax on the full amount.

That's a considerable tax break.

- **What other kind of retirement plans are available to me?**

If you are an employer, you may choose among several types of retirement plans that cover both you and your employees. But you must abide by certain eligibility rules.

For example, businesses used to bar workers under the age of twenty-five from participating in company pension programs, including Keoghs. Present law imposes tough new restrictions on this practice. It cuts from twenty-five to twenty-one the age at which workers must be included in corporate pension programs, and it reduces from twenty-two to eighteen the age at which companies must begin counting employees' years of service for vesting purposes. (Vesting is simply the amount of time workers must stay on the job before they're entitled to any company-contributed pension money that accrues on their behalf.)

Consequently, employers will be paying out more money than ever before to workers who resign or are fired before they retire.

Among the retirement plan options:

- Profit-sharing plans and other corporate pension plans
- Simplified Employee Pension Plans (SEPs are essentially individual retirement accounts set up by employers for employees, including themselves)
- Employee Stock Ownership Plans (with ESOPs the corporate employer contributes a share of its own stock to an ESOP

trust and gets a tax deduction for the value of the contribution)

_____ **TAXTIPS** _____

Profit-sharing plans and ESOPs are complicated and conditions and restrictions abound. Get help from a professional if you decide to put one in place.

Also, if you've missed the deadline for setting up a Keogh, opt for a SEP. The deadline for establishing these plans is April 15.

• What is a 401(k) plan?

The hottest retirement plan today is undoubtedly the 401(k) plan.

The 401(k) is a salary reduction plan established, appropriately enough, under section 401(k) of the Internal Revenue Code. The plan must be sponsored by an employer. The owner of the business may, at his or her option, participate as well.

Here's how a 401(k) works: Employees agree in writing to have their salary reduced by a fixed percentage. The employer may also contribute a fixed percentage of each participant's salary.

This amount is then deposited in a fund. The 401(k) fund is generally managed by a professional money manager and may be invested in a variety of vehicles.

Earnings on the plan accumulate tax-free until retirement. The employees' contribution vests immediately, but distributions are restricted. They may occur only in case of death, disability, retirement, separation from service, at age fifty-nine and a half, or in cases of "hardship." (Uncle Sam, unfortunately, doesn't pinpoint what he regards as a hardship case.)

Meanwhile, the amount of the employee's contribution reduces the amount of his or her salary subject to income tax withholding.

_____ **TAXTIP** _____

Unless you adopt a prototype plan offered by a financial institution or brokerage house, you should obtain professional advice before setting up a 401(k)—or, for that matter, any other retirement plan.

FOR MORE INFORMATION
See these IRS publications:

- *Business Expenses* (Number 535)
- *Employment Taxes and Information Return Requirements— Employees Defined, Income Tax-Withholding, Social Security Taxes, Federal Unemployment Tax, Reporting and Allocating Tips, Information Returns* (Number 539)
- *Tax Benefits for Older Americans* (Number 554)
- *Self-Employed Retirement Plans* (Number 560)
- *U.S. Civil Service Retirement and Disability* (Number 567)
- *Tax-Sheltered Annuity Programs for Employees of Public Schools and Certain Tax-Exempt Organizations* (Number 571)
- *Pension and Annuity Income* (Number 575)
- *Individual Retirement Arrangements* (Number 590)
- *Comprehensive Tax Guide to U.S. Civil Service Retirement Benefits* (Number 721)
- *Your Federal Income Tax* (Number 17)
- *Tax Guide for Small Business* (Number 334)
- *Farmers' Tax Guide* (Number 225)
- *Tax Guide for Commercial Fishermen* (Number 595)
- *Tax Information for Direct Sellers* (Number 911)

Try these IRS Tele-Tax tapes:

- *Pensions and Annuities* (Number 139)
- *Pensions—The General Rule* (Number 140)
- *Lump -Sum Distributions—Profit-Sharing Plans* (Number 141)
- *Social Security Benefit Statement—Form SSA-1099* (Number 210)
- *Individual Retirement Accounts* (Number 218)
- *Ten-Year Averaging for Lump -Sum Distributions* (Number 301)
- *Withholding on Pension and Annuities* (Number 338)
- *Social Security Withholding Rates* (Number 406)
- *Small Business Tax Workshops—Tax Help for the New Businessperson* (Number 102)

Chapter 18

NO FEAR OF FILING

Year-End Tax Planning

Believe me, waiting until year's end to begin your tax planning only makes it more difficult for you to slash your tax liability. That's why it's important to take steps now to trim your tax bill—while there's still time.

When it comes to year-end tax planning, there are two oft-quoted rules of thumb: defer income and accelerate deductions.

By following these tried-and-true prescriptions, you won't avoid taxation but you will, at least, postpone taxes on a portion of your earnings.

The idea, of course, is to keep money in your own pocket—not Uncle Sam's—for as long as possible. Then you can invest the cash or use it in your business.

DEFER INCOME

How you defer income depends, in large measure, on your accounting method. If you're a cash-basis taxpayer (see chapter 7), deferring income is easy. You simply postpone billing clients for a month or even two.

If a client insists on paying you this year—he or she, after all, may want to write off a payment made to you—ask your client to mail the check on the last day of the year.

Checks mailed on December 31 will not reach you until after January 1. The check will be deductible by its sender this tax year, but you won't have to report it as income until next year.

If you're an accrual-basis taxpayer, deferring income is a bit more complicated. One strategy: Put off signing big sales contracts until next year.

_____ **TAXTIP** _____
Not everyone should defer income.

Say your corporation reported earnings of $20,000 in 1988. But business is booming, and you expect your company's income to top $200,000 next year.

Unlike most taxpayers, you should not defer income. You should, if possible, accelerate it. That way, the money will be taxed at your corporation's present lower level.

_____ **TAXTIP** _____

A question we're asked frequently these days: "If rates remain the same from year to year, does it still make sense to defer income?"

The answer is yes, and the reason is simple.

Given the time value of money, it's always better to pay taxes later, rather than sooner. That way you, not the government, have use of your hard-earned dollars.

Even if rates go up, you may prefer to have your money now.

ACCELERATE DEDUCTIONS

It's easier to accelerate deductions than to defer income. The reason is obvious: You control the money you pay out but not the money you take in.

Cash-basis taxpayers should pay all their outstanding bills, including their state taxes, by the end of the year.

Accrual-basis taxpayers should go ahead and purchase in December the supplies, equipment, and so on that they will need in the first few months of the new year. These taxpayers should also review overdue accounts receivable to determine whether they should be written off as bad debts.

Another idea for all taxpayers: Speed up business equipment purchases. Purchase a $10,000 truck on December 30, and you're entitled to realize a depreciation deduction that same year. Wait until January 2 to buy the truck, and you have to wait a full year to reap the first tax benefits. (See chapter 9 for more information about depreciation.)

The law won't allow cash-basis taxpayers to deduct advance payments for rent, interest, and other services, such as utilities and maintenance work. So you can't pay your rent for the next three months and write it off. If you do, and your tax return is audited, the IRS will disallow the deduction.

_____ **TAXTRAP** _____

Avoid investing in tax shelters at the last minute, especially those that promise big tax write-offs on small investments. Chances are, you'll lose your shirt. And even if you don't, the new passive loss rules make investing in tax shelters risky business.

The rules say that you may deduct passive losses only from passive income. If you have no passive income, you're out of luck. You may not deduct your tax shelter losses.

What exactly are passive losses?

In IRS jargon, passive losses refer to losses from a passive activity. A passive activity is any enterprise in which an investor does not "materially participate" in the management. Of course, by definition, limited partners are always engaged in a passive activity.

So if you are a limited partner, you may deduct your losses from the partnership only from profits you receive from other passive investments. The one break: You may carry forward your losses and use them to offset passive income down the road.

ESTIMATED TAXES

Uncle Sam likes to get his money, preferably in advance. So he plays a guessing game with proprietors, partners, and corporations.

Four times each year, these taxpayers must guess what their taxable income will be and deposit a check with Uncle Sam for estimated taxes on that income. If that amount is too high, Uncle Sam will refund the money (after the year-end) with neither a "thank you" nor interest.

If the payment is too small, Uncle Sam will charge a nondeductible penalty. The penalty for underpayment of taxes is adjusted four times a year and is pegged to the prime interest rate. This procedure eliminates any benefit from using the government as a source of "borrowing."

To avoid this nondeductible penalty, proprietors, partners, and corporations usually estimate their taxes within the "safe harbor" rules provided by tax laws:

- They must pay estimated taxes equal to last year's tax, and there will be neither interest nor penalty nor any shortfall. (However, this escape hatch is not available to "large" corporations—those with more than $1 million in taxable income for any of the three preceding years) or
- Sole proprietors and partners must make estimated tax payments of at least 90 percent of the current year's tax

liability to avoid underpayment penalties. Corporations are also required to fork over 90 percent.

In addition, the remaining amount of the tax owed by proprietors and partners is due three and a half months after the end of the taxable year (two and a half months for corporations).

─────────────── **TAXTIP** ───────────────

So, it's been a hard year. Profits are down. Cash is short. Why not reduce estimated tax payments? You can do so at any time. There will be no penalty if your estimated tax payments equal 90 percent of this year's tax liability.

Go ahead. Save some cash.

─────────────── **TAXTRAP** ───────────────

Sometimes you owe the IRS money. Sometimes the IRS owes you money. In either case, interest must be paid. What you may not know: The IRS pays you the prime rate plus two percent on your tax overpayments, but it charges you prime plus *3 percent* on your underpayments.

─────────────── **FYI** ───────────────

Estimated tax payments for individuals are due on April 15, June 15, September 15, and January 15, unless one of those days falls on Saturday, Sunday, or a holiday. In that case, payment is due the next day. Individuals use Form 1040-ES to make their estimated tax payments.

For corporations, estimated payments are due on April 15, June 15, September 15, and December 15, unless the corporation operates on a fiscal year that differs from the calendar year. In that case, estimated payments are due on the fifteenth day of the fourth month of the company's fiscal year, the fifteenth day of the sixth month, the fifteenth day of the ninth month, and the fifteenth day of the twelfth month.

Corporations use Form 1120-W to calculate their tax payments. Then they deposit the payments at their bank using Form 8109.

If you underpay your estimated taxes, fill out Form 2210, "Underpayment of Estimated Tax by Individuals," or Form 2220, "Underpayment of Estimated Tax by Corporations," and attach it to your tax return.

For full details on filing these returns, see our

companion volume, *Laventhol & Horwath Small Business Tax Preparation Book—1989 Edition.*

TAX STRATEGIES

Has your corporation's taxable year just ended or is it about to end? Are your income taxes overpaid for that year? If so, your company can apply for a "quickie" refund.

You must apply after the year has ended and before the tax return is filed, in any event, no later than two and one-half months after the end of the year.

Does it look as if your company is going to have a net operating loss this year? Does it still owe taxes from last year?

If you answer both questions in the affirmative, your company may file to defer payment of last year's tax. The form must be filed within the taxable year of the expected loss. But you must pay interest on the tax you defer.

FOR MORE INFORMATION

See these IRS publications:

* *Your Federal Income Tax* (Number 17)
* *Tax Guide for Small Business* (Number 334)
* *Farmers' Tax Guide* (Number 225)
* *Tax Guide for Commercial Fishermen* (Number 595)
* *Tax Information for Direct Sellers* (Number 911)

Try this IRS Tele-Tax tape:

* *Small Business Tax Workshops—Tax Help for the New Businessperson* (Number 102)

Chapter 19

I SPY

How the IRS Catches Unreported Income

As most school children know, Al Capone was imprisoned not for racketeering or murder but for failing to pay his income taxes. The most notorious criminal of all time eluded the Federal Bureau of Investigation but not the watchful eye of the Internal Revenue Service.

And the IRS didn't even have computers in those days.

Capone was tripped up by the fact that income from every source—except that excluded by law (such as interest on municipal bonds)—is subject to federal taxation. That means money from bank robberies, illegal drug sales, and embezzlements has to be reported in exactly the same manner as wages, salaries, and dividends.

Even money found on the sidewalk is taxable.

Capone, like most other criminals, never reported the money he raked in from his illegal activities. The IRS was able to prove he hadn't owned up to receiving massive amounts of income and nailed him for tax evasion.

Of course, big-time crooks make up only a small fraction of the people who run afoul of the IRS. The majority are average individuals—the neighborhood grocer, druggist, car dealer, retailer, doctor, architect, dentist, lawyer, or banker—who try to trim their tax bills by not reporting a portion of their income.

Most of these people don't end up in jail. The IRS is usually more interested in collecting back taxes and penalties than in throwing people in the slammer. But there are enough exceptions to make cheating a risky business.

Everyone should know how the IRS uncovers unreported income, if for no other reason than to reinforce the point that cheating is a bad idea.

OH, TEMPTATION!

"There is untold wealth in America," a friend of mine likes to say, "especially at income tax time." No doubt, the IRS agrees.

The fact is, many self-employed people, especially those who deal mainly in cash, are tempted to reduce the amount of income they report. All they have to do is skim a portion of their daily receipts from the cash register and stash it in their pockets.

No one will ever know, they think.

Even business owners who receive most of their money in the form of checks play the skimming game by failing to report the few cash payments they do receive.

What is worse and perhaps even more dangerous is that they urge customers or clients to keep quiet about those cash payments or they brag about their actions to friends or associates.

GIMME A BREAK

"George Washington never told a lie," quips a writer for a Salt Lake City newspaper, "but then he never had to fill out a 1040 Form, either."

Though people joke about sidestepping the requirements of the Internal Revenue Code, actual cheating is serious business.

As a business owner or professional in private practice, you already benefit from some deductions that employees cannot take. And the government doesn't care if you take every single one of them. In fact, the IRS encourages you to claim all write-offs to which you are entitled. Minimizing your taxes is just good common sense.

Evading taxes is another matter. You're looking for real trouble if you neglect to report earnings or fabricate deductions.

People who are found guilty of criminal fraud—meaning they deliberately cheated the government—face enormous penalties. Specifically, they may be slapped with a $100,000 fine—$500,000 for corporations—and sent to prison for as long as five years.

UNCLE SAM WANTS YOU

The IRS wields enormous power. Under the law, it may

- Comb through your bank statements without your permission
- Pay people who report their friends or associates for tax evasion

- Put the burden of proof on you to show that you are innocent of any wrongdoing

This guilty-until-proven-innocent posture is contrary to our whole system of justice. That's why many people, myself among them, believe the IRS has more authority than the Constitution ever intended to grant a government agency. But these convictions do us no good. The IRS has the authority. And it uses that power to keep us all in line.

IF JAMES OTIS THOUGHT TAXATION WITHOUT REPRESENTATION WAS BAD, HE SHOULD SEE TAXATION WITH REPRESENTATION

Once the IRS has found evidence of sloppy recordkeeping, it can win a case against you in nothing flat. How?

The law requires you to keep records as proof of your income and deductions. If your records are inadequate, the IRS places the burden of proof on you.

Uncle Sam will demand that you present evidence that your tax return is accurate. If you can't furnish proof, you lose—automatically.

KISS AND TELL

Once in a while, a story appears in the newspaper about a thief who was arrested on an anonymous tip. The informant either saw the crime take place or was told about it by the criminal.

This is the same unseemly method the IRS often uses to snare business owners and professionals. A disgruntled employee or an angry family member turns the person in—to Uncle Sam.

With the help of an informant, the IRS usually has no trouble showing that a person's tax return was, at best, in error and, at worst, fraudulent.

A dentist, for example, was nailed when an assistant he fired told the IRS that fees were recorded with codes that indicated whether the amount should be reported or not.

The assistant, of course, could decipher the codes.

Many business owners think that no one will object to their cheating ways. Some people, in fact, boast about how they rip off the IRS.

But others take a different view. They see a self-employed man or woman who pays less tax than they do, and they resent it. If they have another reason to dislike that particular individual, well, they have nothing to lose by ringing up the IRS.

They may even profit. The IRS pays informants as much as 10 percent of the extra taxes it collects as a result of the information the tipster provides.

YOU CAN BANK ON IT

Just about any accountant can examine your bank statements and tax return and tell you an enormous amount about your lifestyle.

He or she can also tell if you are living within your means, if you are well organized—and if you've neglected to report certain deposits as income.

Many people still cling to the notion that these revealing bank account statements are confidential and available only to the bank and the depositor.

Wrong.

IRS agents may examine them. Also, the law requires your bank to report cash transactions of $10,000 or more to the agency. Uncle Sam assumes that if you can't prove that a questionable bank deposit was a gift or loan or some other nontaxable sum, it is income.

As we've seen, though federal law presumes that you're innocent until proven guilty, the IRS often operates on just the opposite assumption.

TAXTRAP

It happens all the time. People who make frequent bank deposits without noting the source of their funds end up paying tax on income that isn't income at all.

So always jot down the source of money you are depositing—either in your check register or on your deposit slips. The extra few minutes it takes is time well spent.

THE GOOD LORD GIVETH
AND UNCLE SAM TAKETH AWAY

The IRS also has the legal right to examine all kinds of financial records during an investigation—stock purchases, real estate sales, and so on.

Even if you deposit money in a foreign bank account or buy stock on a foreign exchange, the IRS has ways to track those transactions.

Consequently, Uncle Sam often ferrets out unreported income by discovering unexplained increases in your net worth. If you pay cash for a big-ticket item—a house, say, or a new car—and you haven't reported enough income to cover the expenditure, the IRS will probably get you.

Chances are, the IRS knows more than you think. Its research has produced mountains of data on average income, profits, and deductions. And it uses this information to its advantage.

_____ **CASE IN POINT** _____

Say you operate a car wash. You receive almost all of your income in cash, and you're tempted to leave a portion of your revenues off your return.

Don't. The government can figure out if you underreported your income simply from toting up the amount of water and soap you used.

For example, the IRS will have reason to be suspicious if you use twice as much water as an average car wash to produce each dollar of sales.

_____ **FYI** _____

The IRS takes its work seriously. When it audited the tax return of a Nevada brothel, it derived an income figure by analyzing the number of towels used.

No group or industry is too small for IRS scrutiny. Back in the 1950s, for example, the agency singled out the nation's bagel bakeries for special investigation.

Bagel makers across the country ended up with egg on their faces. Among them: D & H Bagel Bakery in Queens, New York. D & H had understated its income for two straight years. In the third year, it had filed no income tax return at all.

The IRS had no trouble determining that D & H had failed to file a return. But how did the agency know that the company had not reported sales of nearly $20,000 a year?

Simple. IRS agents employed a General Mills formula that showed exactly how many bagels could be produced from a 100-pound bag of flour. Agents added up the amount of flour the bakery purchased during the three years in question. With that information in hand, calculating D & H's revenues was a piece of cake.

The agents multiplied the number of bagels produced by the average bagel price. And—voila!—they had a reasonably accurate estimate of sales.

Confronted with the goods, the bakery's owner confessed that he had fudged on his revenues. But, he insisted, "I have a good excuse."

The unreported amounts, he argued, were "expended for legitimate, deductible business expenses." It was common practice in the bagel industry, he explained, to pay employees partially by check and partially in cash. The cash payments were popular, because they eliminated withholding on a portion of the employee's wages.

The amounts he didn't report, he said, were exactly equal to the "legitimate business deductions" that he failed to claim. Since his unreported income didn't exceed his unreported expenses, he argued, he shouldn't be hit with a penalty. The IRS didn't buy it.

For starters, the agency said, the bagel maker provided no evidence to support his claim. What's more, the only employee questioned denied ever receiving payment in cash. (Of course, an employee is unlikely to admit receiving cash payments, since he or she probably didn't report the income in the first place.)

Moreover, the owner acknowledged that he kept his books incorrectly and intentionally understated his sales for two years. He also conceded that he filed no return in the third year.

"We think that the natural inferences that flow from these admissions and facts," the judge wrote, "point clearly to fraud." The owner does not "avoid these inferences simply by an ingenious excuse which is not corroborated."

The result: The baker had to pay back taxes plus a hefty fraud penalty.

FOOL'S GOLD

Flaunting money you didn't report on your return is another way to get caught, especially if you spend more than you earn.

Say your neighbor pays himself a salary of $50,000 a year. But the amount he shells out for personal expenses—house payments, vacations, clothes, entertainment—adds up to $75,000. If he is audited, the IRS will want to know where the extra $25,000 came from.

TAXTRAP

Even if the money is never deposited in the bank, the IRS

may be able to track amounts he's spread around at his favorite stores and restaurants.

FOR MORE INFORMATION
See these IRS publications:

- *Examination of Returns, Appeal Rights, and Claims for Refund* (Number 556)
- *The Collection Process—Income Tax Accounts* (Number 586A)
- *Your Federal Income Tax* (Number 17)
- *Tax Guide for Small Business* (Number 334)
- *Farmers' Tax Guide* (Number 225)
- *Tax Guide for Commercial Fishermen* (Number 595)
- *Tax Information for Direct Sellers* (Number 911)

Try these IRS Tele-Tax tapes:

- *Notice of Under-Reported Income—CP 2000* (Number 342)
- *Small Business Tax Workshops—Tax Help for the New Businessperson* (Number 102)

Chapter 20

INFERNAL REVENUE SERVICE

Surviving an Audit

The place where you file your tax return—one of 10 regional IRS service centers—not only looks like a factory, it operates like a factory.

Envelopes move in and out of these service centers with the same speed and efficiency with which materials flow in and out of any well-managed industrial plant.

You send a check to a service center. IRS employees deposit the money.

You ask for a refund. Service-center personnel send you one—provided your math checks out and the computers aren't on the blink.

Unfortunately, the willingness of these service-center employees to quickly cash your check or slowly forward you a refund is no guarantee that trouble won't crop up later.

The law allows the IRS to audit your return within three years of its due date or the date it is filed, whichever is later. (This restriction disappears if the IRS uncovers evidence of wrongdoing.)

You say you've never been audited? Chances are, you will be. And, chances are, you'll be a nervous wreck by the time the appointed hour rolls around.

The very thought of IRS agents terrifies most people. For some, their fears are well-grounded. If you've cheated in any way, there's a better than even chance that the IRS will discover your dishonesty. Then it will audit your returns from past years, too.

But if you have reported your income honestly and claimed only those deductions that are rightfully yours, you have nothing to worry about. Honest mistakes may cost you a few hundred dollars, but you aren't likely to be slapped with huge penalties for negligence or tax avoidance.

Also, you may find that your mistakes worked against you, not for you. You may even escape the audit with a refund in hand.

THE ONLY THING THAT HURTS MORE THAN PAYING AN INCOME TAX IS NOT HAVING TO PAY AN INCOME TAX

You've suspected that the IRS singles out entire professions, even entire industries, for examination. You're right.

The IRS targets doctors. It targets small business owners. It even goes so far as to read Las Vegas and Atlantic City newspapers for articles about people who have scored big at the gaming tables. (It wants to be sure they report their winnings.)

NO VOLUNTEERS—HOW THE IRS SELECTS RETURNS TO AUDIT

When your tax form arrives at an IRS service center, a clerk types the numbers from your return into a computer. Then the machine goes to work. It examines your return, comparing your deductions with amounts written off by millions of other people in your tax bracket and profession.

If the computer spots an item or a group of items on your return that is out of line—such as extraordinarily large travel and entertainment expenses—it recommends you for an audit.

Then the return goes to an IRS agent. He or she will go over your form and decide whether to proceed with a full-blown audit.

So far, no one has been able to persuade the IRS to reveal the amounts the computer regards as "too high" for each category of deductions. But we know from experience that your chances of being audited depend on your answers to five key questions. Here they are:

1. What is your income?

Your odds of being audited increase with your earnings.

For example, the IRS examines 0.48 percent of returns with gross income of less than $10,000 to $25,000 but 2.8 percent of returns with gross income of $50,000 or more.

2. Are you an itemizer?

People who itemize—a group that includes most small business owners and professionals—are almost twice as likely to be audited as individuals who file a short form.

3. Do you work for yourself?

If you suspect that people who are in business for themselves are audited more frequently than those who work for someone else, you're right.

The reason, I'm sorry to say, is that the IRS has found that people who own their own companies are more likely to cheat on their income tax returns.

4. Do you claim big travel and entertainment expenses?

The IRS scrutinizes these write-offs carefully—and for good reason. Taxpayers frequently pad their T&E deductions.

5. Do you invest in tax shelters?

The IRS targets for examination people who invest in tax shelters. If you put your money in these investment vehicles, your chances of an audit increase dramatically.

Often, the IRS earmarks your return for audit after it has examined—and found problems with—the return of the company from which you purchased your tax shelter.

What's more, the IRS chooses more than 50,000 returns randomly each year for audits as part of its so-called Taxpayer Compliance Measurement Program. These returns are selected with regard to income but without regard to deductions, occupation, or evidence of tax avoidance. Their owners are required to justify, line by line, every item on their returns.

The idea is to keep all of us on our toes—and on our most upright behavior—and to help the IRS determine how well taxpayers are complying with the law.

But like any other government agency, the IRS must live within a budget. Its goal is to promote honesty without spending too much money, so it is limited in the number of audits it performs. It examines only about 1.2 million returns annually out of a total of more than 95.5 million.

That comes to a paltry 1.1 percent of all returns filed. So, when it comes right down to it, the odds are actually heavily against your being audited.

The bottom line: Don't avoid taking deductions that are legitimate just because you fear an examination. Many factors go into identifying a return for audit. You can't control all of them.

--------------------- **TAXTIP** ---------------------

As we've seen, the IRS may examine your return within three years from the date it is filed. You should save your tax forms, plus the materials necessary to substantiate your deductions, for at least that long.

Also, be aware that your state's statute of limitations may exceed the federal statute. In California, for example, the statute of limitations is four years. We advise our clients to wait until both the federal and state statutes of limitations expire before they pitch their old tax returns.

Ask your accountant for the limitation in your state.

_____ **TAXTRAP** _____

Here's something you may not know but should. When Uncle Sam asks—and you agree—to extend the federal statute of limitations on your return, the state statute of limitations may be automatically extended as well.

SPECIAL DELIVERY—WHEN THE IRS SENDS YOU A BILL

As a rule, the IRS sends out two kinds of notices.

One is a letter informing you that the IRS believes you have made a mistake and requesting more money. The other is an audit notice.

If you receive one of these notices, don't panic. And don't send money until you have checked to make sure the agency is correct.

The request for an increased payment is usually produced by a computer. The machine may have found an error. But it may be an error you made copying a number onto your return. Or the machine may have even made a mistake. Or it may be that you simply need to fill out an additional income tax form.

_____ **CASE IN POINT** _____

Say you went into business for yourself early this year. You calculated your quarterly estimated tax payments on your actual income—as you earned it—not on the amount you made last year when you were working for someone else. You received little income in the first and second quarters.

So you sent Uncle Sam virtually no money. When you filed your tax return, the IRS slapped you with a penalty for underpaying estimated taxes.

Here's what happened: You or your accountant failed to file Form 2210, "Underpayment of Estimated Tax by Individuals," to explain your actions.

The IRS computer, in its simple-minded way, automatically assumes that you had no reason for paying your estimated taxes in the way that you did. In this case, you don't owe the IRS a penalty for underpaying your taxes in the first two quarters. You owe it a form.

The first step, then, in responding to a demand for money from the IRS is to check your return. Or ask your tax preparer to do the work for you.

If you disagree with the IRS assessment, write a letter explaining your position. Don't forget to include the reference number on the letter you received.

Better yet, enclose a copy of the letter the IRS sent you. That way, the IRS representative doesn't have to search for your file.

If you are unable to determine why the computer is dunning you, write the IRS and ask for additional information. But, whatever you do, never ignore an IRS notice.

SCARLET LETTER

Should you face an actual audit, you will receive a letter from the IRS saying that it wants to verify the accuracy of your return and asking to meet with you. (The IRS never uses the word "audit.")

Take this letter seriously.

Generally speaking, examinations come in two varieties—the office audit and the field audit. For an office examination, you are asked to meet with the IRS auditor at his or her place of business. The letter you receive asks you to bring records to back up specific deductions, such as travel and entertainment expenses.

For a field audit, the IRS comes to visit you. This examination is more complicated—and more dangerous—than an office audit. And it is conducted by more experienced agents.

Chances are, the IRS wants to visit you, because it wants to scrutinize so many of your records that it would not be practical for you to bring the documents to the IRS office.

FYI

If the IRS sets a date for an audit that is inconvenient for you, immediately call the IRS office and request a change. In most cases, the agency will cooperate.

YOU MAY FIRE WHEN YOU ARE READY, GRIDLEY

Get organized well before the day of your audit. Pull together all the information the IRS asks to see, but don't provide more data than it requests.

If it wants to see proof of your travel expenses, provide proof of your travel expenses. Do not bring receipts that back up your home office deductions.

If your tax return was prepared by a professional, ask that person to help you decide which records you should take with you.

I GET BY WITH A LITTLE HELP FROM MY FRIENDS— WHO SHOULD GO TO THE AUDIT?

If you and your spouse signed a joint return, either of you may attend the audit. Or you may stay home and send your attorney or accountant as your representative.

CPAs and attorneys are automatically entitled to represent you not only at audits but at all official IRS proceedings. Other tax preparers qualify as "enrolled agents" only if they pass a special IRS examination. As a rule, though, you may send just about anyone to represent you at your audit.

The list of "authorized" representatives includes:

- Officers of your company
- Your full-time employees
- Members of your immediate family (spouses, parents, brothers, sisters, children, and so on)
- Trustees of your estate

If, however, you send someone to represent you, you must sign an authorization form (Form 2848D) or grant that person power of attorney (Form 2848).

_____ **TAXTIP** _____

You, your attorney, and your CPA may all go to your audit, but we wouldn't advise it. If too many people show up, the IRS may suspect you have something to hide.

Having good tax counsel at an audit can prevent you from making mistakes and save you money. On the other hand, your adviser will charge you for the time he or she spends.

Our advice: If your letter from the IRS covers only a few areas, and you have the records to back up your deductions, you probably can safely handle the matter yourself. However, if you feel unsure of yourself or if your tax situation is complicated, consider asking your tax adviser to accompany you to the examination.

ON THE FIRING LINE

Office auditors concentrate on only a few selected portions of your return. These items are outlined in the letter you received from the IRS.

However, don't be surprised if the IRS representative asks a few routine questions about the sources of your earnings. He or she will try to uncover unreported income.

For the most part, though, omissions—such as the $20 you won at the race track—won't necessarily be uncovered. And even if they are, the IRS wants your money, not your hide. Only a tiny fraction of people—the most flagrant tax cheats—go to prison for tax evasion.

If the audit is at the IRS office, leave early so you will arrive on time. Dress in your usual style. Don't, as a lot of people do, try to look down-and-out. It won't help. Also, don't try to impress the auditor with who you know, even if the auditor's boss is your best friend.

During the examination, whether it's an office or field audit, do not let your guard down. But don't pick a fight. Speak only when you are asked a question, and provide only the information requested.

Respond. Then stop talking. If you say more than you need to, you may leave yourself open for questions about other items.

Also, do not discuss politics. And do not launch into a diatribe about the unfairness of the tax system or discuss what your neighbor gets away with. Revealing your neighbor's sins won't make the auditor leave you alone. It will simply encourage him or her to audit your neighbor.

Finally, stay calm, and do not hurry the examiner. The IRS, not you and not your tax preparer, will decide when an audit is finished.

I AM NOT A CROOK

Be especially careful if an IRS agent tells you that the examination of your return is anything other than routine.

Also, beware if your auditor turns out to be an IRS special agent or is accompanied by someone who identifies himself or herself as a special agent. Our advice: Terminate the interview on the spot, and get legal help fast.

Special agents are employed by the criminal division of the IRS. Their participation in your audit means you are under investigation for criminal wrongdoing.

The law requires the IRS to tell you before your audit begins that it is not routine, but an agent will probably do so in such a calm manner that you may not realize what is happening.

APPEALING TO A HIGHER AUTHORITY

The law does not require you to accept an IRS agent's findings. You may appeal IRS assessments through the agency's appeals division to the courts.

The first step, if you disagree with your auditor's findings, is to request a meeting with his or her supervisor.

If you still object to the results of your audit, you may request a conference with a representative of the Office of the Regional Director of Appeals.

If an agreement is not reached with the Office of the Regional Director, you may, at any time in these proceedings, take your case to court.

_____ **TAXTIP** _____

Weigh attorney's fees against the amount the IRS is requesting. You may be better off ignoring your principles and paying the government.

Your Odds of Victory in Court

Court	Taxpayer Wins	IRS Wins	Split Decision
Tax Court	6.3%	62.0%	31.7%
District Court	33.8	55.7	10.4
Claims Court	46.3	46.3	7.4
Appeals Court	10.6	82.8	6.6
Supreme Court	42.9	57.1	—

BOTTOM LINE

One point should be kept clearly in mind about IRS audits: the best time to prepare for an audit is before it happens. You must maintain records throughout the year to substantiate your income and deductions. And a good time to get your records in order is tax-preparation time.

FOR MORE INFORMATION

For additional information on the appeals process, write the U.S. Tax Court, 400 Second St., N.W., Washington, D.C. 20217. See these IRS publications:

- *Examination of Returns, Appeal Rights, and Claims for Refund* (Number 556)
- *The Collection Process—Income Tax Accounts* (Number 586A)
- *Your Federal Income Tax* (Number 17)
- *Tax Guide for Small Business* (Number 334)

- *Farmers' Tax Guide* (Number 225)
- *Tax Guide for Commercial Fishermen* (Number 595)
- *Tax Information for Direct Sellers* (Number 911)

Try these IRS Tele-Tax tapes:

- *Problem Resolution Program—Special Help for Problem Situations* (Number 103)
- *Examination Procedures and How to Prepare for an Audit* (Number 105)
- *The Collection Process* (Number 106)
- *Penalty and Interest Charges* (Number 326)
- *IRS Notices and Bills—How to Pay* (Number 327)
- *Penalty for Underpayment of Estimated Tax—Form 2210* (Number 329)
- *Audit Appeal Rights* (Number 332)
- *Second Request for Information About Your Tax Form* (Number 340)
- *Notice of Intent to Levy* (Number 341)
- *Notice of Under-Reported Income—CP 2000* (Number 342)
- *Small Business Tax Workshops—Tax Help for the New Businessperson* (Number 102)

COMPLETE CHECKLIST OF OFFICIAL IRS TAX INFORMATION

Fact: A young accountant starting out in business today needs a shelf more than thirty-three feet long just to hold the regulations essential to his or her practice.

Fortunately, most businesspeople can get by with a much smaller library for tax-planning purposes. Indeed, this book tells you just about everything you need to know.

Should you, however, find yourself wanting to read the official IRS line on a tax topic, rest assured. The government probably publishes a pamphlet on the subject.

Here for your convenience and easy reference is a guide to the extensive—and free—IRS services and publications. In this section, you will learn:

- Where to obtain IRS booklets
- What publications are available
- How to use the Tele-Tax telephone service
- What information is available on Tele-Tax tape

The information in this section is adapted from the *Taxpayer's Guide to IRS Information, Assistance, and Publications* (Number 910).

WHERE TO OBTAIN IRS PUBLICATIONS

Copies of IRS booklets are easy to come by. All you have to do is write the IRS Forms Distribution Center for your state at the address shown in the following table. You don't even have to send a stamped self-addressed envelope. (Use these same addresses to obtain tax forms.)

IRS Forms Distribution Centers

State	Address
Alabama	Caller No. 848 Atlanta, GA 30370
Alaska	P.O. Box 12626 Fresno, CA 93778
Arizona	P.O. Box 12626 Fresno, CA 93778
Arkansas	P.O. Box 2924 Austin, TX 78769
California	P.O. Box 12626 Fresno, CA 93778
Colorado	P.O. Box 2924 Austin, TX 78769
Connecticut	P.O. Box 1040 Methuen, MA 01844
Delaware	P.O. Box 25866 Richmond, VA 23260
District of Columbia	P.O. Box 25866 Richmond, VA 23260
Florida	Caller No. 848 Atlanta, GA 30370
Georgia	Caller No. 848 Atlanta, GA 30370
Hawaii	P.O. Box 12626 Fresno, CA 93778
Idaho	P.O. Box 12626 Fresno, CA 93778
Illinois	P.O. Box 338 Kansas City, MO 64141
Indiana	P.O. Box 6900 Florence, KY 41042
Iowa	P.O. Box 338 Kansas City, MO 64141
Kansas	P.O. Box 2924 Austin, TX 78769

State	Address
Kentucky	P.O. Box 6900 Florence, KY 41042
Louisiana	P.O. Box 2924 Austin, TX 78769
Maine	P.O. Box 1040 Methuen, MA 01844
Maryland	P.O. Box 25866 Richmond, VA 23260
Massachusetts	P.O. Box 1040 Methuen, MA 01844
Michigan	P.O. Box 6900 Florence, KY 41042
Minnesota	P.O. Box 338 Kansas City, MO 64161
Mississippi	Caller No. 848 Atlanta, GA 30370
Missouri	P.O. Box 338 Kansas City, MO 64161
Montana	P.O. Box 12626 Fresno, CA 93778
Nebraska	P.O. Box 338 Kansas City, MO 64141
Nevada	P.O. Box 12626 Fresno, CA 93778
New Hampshire	P.O. Box 1040 Methuen, MA 01844
New Jersey	P.O. Box 25866 Richmond, VA 23260
New Mexico	P.O. Box 2924 Austin, TX 78769
New York Western New York	 P.O. Box 260 Buffalo, NY 14201
Eastern New York	P.O. Box 1040 Methuen, MA 01844
North Carolina	Caller No. 848 Atlanta, GA 30370
North Dakota	P.O. Box 338 Kansas City, MO 64141

State	Address
Ohio	P.O. Box 6900 Florence, KY 41042
Oklahoma	P.O. Box 2429 Austin, TX 78769
Oregon	P.O. Box 12626 Fresno, CA 93778
Pennsylvania	P.O. Box 25866 Richmond, VA 23260
Rhode Island	P.O. Box 1040 Methuen, MA 01844
South Carolina	Caller No. 848 Atlanta, GA 30370
South Dakota	P.O. Box 338 Kansas City, MO 64141
Tennessee	Caller No. 848 Atlanta, GA 30370
Texas	P.O. Box 2924 Austin, TX 78769
Utah	P.O. Box 12626 Fresno, CA 93778
Vermont	P.O. Box 1040 Methuen, MA 01844
Virginia	P.O. Box 25866 Richmond, VA 23260
Washington	P.O. Box 12626 Fresno, CA 93778
West Virginia	P.O. Box 6900 Florence, KY 41042
Wisconsin	P.O. Box 338 Kansas City, MO 64141
Wyoming	P.O. Box 2924 Austin, TX 78769

Taxpayers with foreign mailing addresses should write the IRS Distribution Center, P.O. Box 25866, Richmond, VA 23260.

Taxpayers in Puerto Rico and the Virgin Islands should contact representatives of the IRS stationed in those territories. In Puerto Rico, write the Director's Representative, U.S.

Internal Revenue Service, Federal Office Building, Chardon St., Hato Rey, PR 00918. In the Virgin Islands, write the Department of Finance, Tax Division, Charlotte Amalie, St. Thomas, VI 00801.

LIST OF IRS PUBLICATIONS

The IRS publishes a host of free tax guides. Here's a list of the most useful ones. When ordering copies, remember to specify both the titles and publication numbers.

• *Your Federal Income Tax* (Number 17)

Guides you through the 1040 return and explains the tax laws that cover salaries, interest, dividends, deductions, and so on. Examples illustrate typical solutions to typical problems. Filled-in sample forms and schedules show how to report income and deductions.

• *Tax Guide for Small Business* (Number 334)

Explains in general terms the federal tax laws that apply to businesses. Also describes the four major forms of business organization and the tax implications of each.

The first section contains general information on business organization and accounting practices. Part 2 discusses depreciation.

Parts 3 and 4 explain how to calculate business income for tax purposes. They describe the kinds of income you must report and the different types of business deductions you may take.

The fifth part discusses the rules that apply when you sell or exchange business assets or investment property. Included are chapters on the treatment of capital gains.

Part 6 explains the tax rules governing sole proprietorships, partnerships, corporations and S corporations.

Part 7 looks at some of the credits you can claim to reduce your income tax and some of the other taxes you may have to pay in addition to income tax.

The last part shows how to fill out the main business tax forms—Schedule C, Schedule F, and so on.

• *Farmers' Tax Guide* (Number 225)

Describes how the federal tax laws apply to farming. Gives examples of typical, one-family farming situations. Also discusses the kinds of farm income you must report and the different deductions you may take.

- *Tax Guide for Commercial Fishermen* (Number 595)

Does for fishermen what Number 225 does for farmers. Familiarizes you with the federal tax laws as they apply to the fishing business and is intended for sole proprietors who use Schedule C to report profit or loss from fishing. The guide does not cover corporations or partnerships.

- *Employer's Tax Guide* (Number 15), *Agriculture Employer's Tax Guide* (Number 51), *Federal Tax Guide for Employers in the Virgin Islands, Guam, and America Samoa* (Number 80), *Federal Tax Guide for Employers in Puerto Rico* (Number 179)

Every employer (people with an employer identification number) automatically receives the employer's tax guide, which covers payroll taxes, each year when it is revised. Copies of the more specialized guides are available upon request.

- *Tax Guide for U.S. Citizens and Resident Aliens Abroad* (Number 54)

Discusses the tax situations of Americans and resident aliens who live and work abroad or who have income from foreign countries. In particular, explains the rules for excluding income and excluding and deducting certain housing costs. Answers are provided to frequently asked questions.

- *Federal Highway Use Tax on Trucks, Truck Tractors, and Buses* (Number 349)

Explains what types of trucks and buses are subject to the federal highway motor vehicle use tax, a source of funds for the national highway construction program. The tax is paid by the owner of the truck. The publication shows these owners how to figure the tax due.

- *Fuel Tax Credits* (Number 378)

Describes fuel tax credits available to businesses, such as manufacturers, that buy fuel in large quantities.

- *Federal Estate and Gift Taxes* (Number 448)

Explains U.S. estate and gift taxes.

- *Travel, Entertainment, and Gift Expenses* (Number 463)

Summarizes what expenses you may deduct for business travel, transportation, entertainment, and gifts. The publication summarizes the deduction and substantiation rules for employees and employers.

- *Exemptions* (Number 501)

Describes when you can take exemptions. Each exemption you have lowers your taxable income. Besides your personal exemption, you may be able to take additional exemptions for your spouse's age or blindness. You may also qualify for an exemption for each person who qualifies as your dependent.

- *Medical and Dental Expenses* (Number 502)

Tells you how to figure your deduction for medical and dental expenses. Provides examples to help you calculate medical expense deductions, which you may take only if you itemize. Tax tips remind you of items you may have overlooked.

- *Child and Dependent Care Credit, Employment Taxes for Household Employees* (Number 503)

Explains the credit you may be able to take if you pay someone to care for your dependent who is under fifteen, for your disabled dependent, or for your disabled spouse. Tax law defines "disabled" to mean a person who is physically or mentally unable to care for himself or herself.

- *Tax Information for Divorced or Separated Individuals* (Number 504)

Describes tax rules of interest to divorced or separated individuals. Covers filing status, dependency exemptions, and treatment of alimony and property settlements.

- *Tax Withholding and Estimated Tax* (Number 505)

Explains the two methods for paying taxes on your earnings:

Your company withholds income tax from your pay. You can have more or less money withheld, depending on the number of dependents you choose to claim.

If you do not pay your tax through withholding or do not pay enough tax, you might have to pay estimated tax.

- *Educational Expenses* (Number 508)

Explains how you may write off educational expenses in business. You deduct some of these expenses as adjustments to income, and you write off others as itemized deductions.

- *Tax Calendars for 1989* (Number 509)

Lists due dates for tax returns and payments.

- *Excise Taxes for 1989* (Number 510)

Describes business excise taxes.

- *Tax Information for Visitors to the United States*
  (Number 513)

Familiarizes people with the general requirements of U.S. income tax laws for foreign visitors.

- *Foreign Tax Credit for U.S. Citizens and Resident Aliens*
  (Number 514)

Explains what foreign taxes qualify for the foreign tax credit. If you paid foreign income tax, you may be able to take the foreign tax credit to avoid the burden of double taxation.

- *Foreign Workers, Scholars, and Exchange Visitors*
  (Number 518)

Gives federal tax information for foreign visitors who are in the United States on an "F," "J," "H," "L," or "M" visa. Also provides information about tax-treaty provisions that apply to various kinds of earned income from U.S. sources.

- *U.S. Tax Guide for Aliens* (Number 519)

Gives guidelines on how to determine your U.S. tax status and figure your U.S. tax. Resident aliens, like American citizens, generally are taxed on income from all sources—that is, income earned both inside and outside the United States.

- *Scholarships and Fellowships* (Number 520)

Explains U.S. tax laws that apply to citizens who study, teach, or conduct research in the United States or abroad under scholarship and fellowship grants.

- *Moving Expenses* (Number 521)

Shows how, if you changed job locations this year, you may be able to deduct your moving expenses. You may qualify for a deduction whether you are an employee or self-employed, but the expenses must be connected with starting work at a new job location.

You must also meet a distance and time test. You may deduct your allowable moving expenses even if you do not itemize deductions.

• *Tax Information on Selling Your Home* (Number 523)

Explains what is the basis of a home, how you may postpone the tax on part or all of the gain on the sale of your home, and how you may exclude part or all of the gain from your gross income if you are fifty-five or older.

• *Credit for the Elderly and the Permanently and Totally Disabled* (Number 524)

Describes how to figure the credit. You may be able to claim this credit either if you are sixty-five or older or younger than sixty-five, have retired on disability, and were permanently and totally disabled when you retired.

• *Taxable and Nontaxable Income* (Number 525)

Discusses wages, salaries, and other compensation received for services rendered. Also addresses the subject of miscellaneous taxable and nontaxable income.

• *Charitable Contributions* (Number 526)

Explains how the charitable contribution deduction is taken by taxpayers who itemize their deductions.

• *Rental Property* (Number 527)

Defines rental income, discusses rental expenses, and explains how to report them both on your return. Also covers casualty losses on rental property and the sale of rental property.

• *Miscellaneous Deductions* (Number 529)

Discusses expenses you generally may take as miscellaneous deductions, such as employee business expenses.

• *Tax Information for Owners of Homes, Condominiums, and Cooperative Apartments* (Number 530)

Gives information about home ownership and federal taxes. Explains how to determine basis, how to treat settlement and closing costs, and how to calculate the value of repairs and improvements you make. Also discusses itemized deductions for mortgage interest, real estate taxes, and casualty and theft losses.

• *Reporting Income from Tips* (Number 531)

Gives advice about keeping track of cash and charge tips. Also explains the new rules about the expanded information that employers must report to the IRS for their employees' tip income.

- *Self-Employment Tax* (Number 533)

Explains the self-employment tax, a Social Security tax for people who work for themselves.

- *Depreciation* (Number 534)

Discusses the various methods of depreciation. Also covers what can be depreciated and how to depreciate assets placed in service after 1980.

- *Business Expenses* (Number 535)

Provides information about such business expenses as salary for employees, interest, taxes, insurance, and education. Also outlines the choice to capitalize certain business expenses and discusses complex amortization and depletion rules.

- *Net Operating Losses and At-Risk Limits* (Number 536)

Explains limits on claiming business losses.

- *Installment Sales* (Number 537)

Discusses sales arrangements—installment sales—that provide for part or all of the selling price to be paid in a later year.

Gain from an installment sale is reported only as the payments are actually received, whether you use the cash or accrual method of accounting. You are taxed only on the part of each payment that represents your profit on the sale.

- *Accounting Periods and Methods* (Number 538)

Explains what accounting periods and methods may be used for figuring your federal taxes and how to apply for approval to change from one period or method to another.

- *Employment Taxes and Information Return Requirements— Employees Defined, Income Tax Withholding, Social Security Taxes, Federal Unemployment Tax, Reporting and Allocating Tips, Information Returns* (Number 539)

Explains your responsibility, if you have employees, to withhold federal income tax from their wages. You also have to pay Social Security taxes (FICA) and federal unemployment tax (FUTA). This publication discusses the rules for filing information returns when you make payments to people who are not employees and for reporting and allocating tips.

- *Tax Information on Partnerships* (Number 541)

Describes the tax rules that apply to partnerships.

- *Tax Information on Corporations* (Number 542)

Explains the tax rules that apply to corporations.

- *Sales and Other Dispositions of Assets* (Number 544)

Shows how to figure gains and losses on various transactions, such as trading or selling stock or real estate. Also explains the tax results of different kinds of gains and losses. Not all gains are taxed in the same way.

- *Interest Expense* (Number 545)

Points out what items may and may not be deducted as interest. Where on the return you deduct interest depends on whether you borrowed money for personal use, for rental or royalty property, or for your business.

- *Nonbusiness Disasters, Casualties, and Thefts* (Number 547)

Explains when you can deduct the uninsured part of a casualty or theft. Casualties are events such as hurricanes, earthquakes, tornadoes, fires, floods, vandalism, and car accidents. Also shows how to treat the sum you receive from insurance or other sources.

- *Deductions for Bad Debts* (Number 548)

If someone owes you money and you cannot collect on the debt, you may be able to claim a deduction for a worthless or bad debt. This brochure shows you how.

For a bad debt to qualify for the deduction, there must be a true creditor–debtor relationship between you and the person or organization that owes you the money. There must be a legal obligation to pay you a fixed sum of money, and you must realize a loss because of your inability to collect the money owed to you.

- *Condemnations and Business Casualties and Thefts*
  (Number 549)

Helps you figure your gain or loss if you have property that is condemned or if you sell or exchange it under threat of "imminence of condemnation." Also explains deductions for casualties (earthquakes, hurricanes, fires, and so on) and thefts to business property.

- *Investment Income and Expenses* (Number 550)

Explains what types of investment income are and are not taxable, when the income is taxed, and how to report it on your return. Also discusses investment-related expenses and explains how to figure your gain or loss when you sell or trade your investment property.

- *Basis of Assets* (Number 551)

Explains how to determine the basis of property. Usually the basis of property you buy is its cost. If, however, you received property in some other way, such as by gift or inheritance, you normally must use a basis other than cost.

- *Tax Benefits for Older Americans* (Number 554)

Provides tax information of special interest to older Americans. Explains such items as the sale of a home and pension and annuity income. Also includes some filled-in forms and schedules to show how these and other items are reported.

- *Community Property and the Federal Income Tax* (Number 555)

Written for married taxpayers who live in one of the following community property states: Arizona, California, Idaho, Louisiana, Nevada, New Mexico, Texas, or Washington.

- *Examination of Returns, Appeal Rights, and Claims for Refund* (Number 556)

Explains the procedures for the examination of items of partnership income, deduction, gain, loss, and credit. Information is given on how to file a claim for refund, the time for filing a claim for refund, and the limit on the amount of refund. This publication is particularly helpful if your return is examined by the IRS.

- *Tax Information for Sponsors of Contests and Sporting Events* (Number 558)

A handy guide to tax laws that affect sponsors of sporting events.

- *Tax Information for Survivors, Executors, and Administrators* (Number 559)

Helps you report and pay the proper federal income and estate taxes if you have the responsibility for settling an estate.

- *Self-Employed Retirement Plans* (Number 560)

Discusses retirement plans—Keoghs and HR-10s—for self-employed persons and certain partners in partnerships.

If you set up a retirement plan that meets specific legal requirements, you may be able to deduct your payments to the plan. In addition, income earned by the plan (interest, dividends, and so on) will be tax free until it is distributed.

- *Determining the Value of Donated Property* (Number 561)

Helps donors and appraisers determine the value of property (other than cash) that is given to qualified organizations. Explains what kind of information you need to support a charitable deduction that you claim on your personal return.

- *Mutual Fund Distributions* (Number 564)

Discusses the federal income tax treatment of distributions paid or allocated to you as an individual shareholder.

- *Tax Guide for U.S. Citizens Employed in U.S. Possessions* (Number 570)

Written for people who make their homes in Puerto Rico, Guam, American Samoa, and other U.S. possessions.

- *Tax-Sheltered Annuity Programs for Employees of Public Schools and Certain Tax-Exempt Organizations* (Number 571)

Tells you about the exclusion allowance, the limit on employer contributions, and the tax benefits of qualified annuity plans.

- *Pension and Annuity Income* (Number 575)

Explains how to report pension and annuity income on your federal tax return. Also explains the special tax treatment for lump-sum distributions from pensions, stock-bonus plans, and profit-sharing plans.

- *Information for Business Taxpayers—Business Taxes, Identification Numbers, Recordkeeping* (Number 583)

Shows sample records that a small business can use if it operates as a sole proprietorship. Records like these help you complete accurate tax returns and ensure that you pay only the tax you owe.

The law does not require any special kind of records. You may choose any system that suits your business and shows your income clearly. Your permanent books must show not only your gross income, but also your deductions.

- *Disaster and Casualty Loss Workbook* (Number 584)

Helps you figure your loss from a disaster or casualty. It will help you most if you use it now to establish the value of your property before any losses occur.

- *The Collection Process—Income Tax Accounts* (Number 586A)

Explains your legal rights if you owe the government money.

- *Business Use of Your Home* (Number 587)

Helps you decide if you qualify to deduct certain expenses for using part of your home in your business. You must meet specific tests, and your deduction is limited. The worksheet at the end of the publication helps you calculate your deduction.

- *Tax Information for Homeowners' Associations* (Number 588)

Gives tax information on homeowners' associations. Discusses which associations may elect to be tax-exempt, how to make the election, and what tax obligations there are for organizations that are not exempt. Also provides a sample filled-in return for homeowners' associations.

- *Tax Information on S Corporations* (Number 589)

Covers the fundamentals of doing business as an S corporation.

- *Individual Retirement Arrangements* (Number 590)

Explains the benefits of having an individual retirement arrangement (IRA) and points out what to look for when setting one up. Topics covered include eligibility, the amount you may deduct, types of IRAs, and the tax treatment of distributions and rollovers.

- *Income Tax Benefits for U.S. Citizens Who Go Overseas* (Number 593)

Briefly reviews various U.S. tax provisions that apply to U.S. citizens or resident aliens who live or work abroad.

- *The Collection Process—Employment Tax Accounts* (Number 594)

Explains your rights and duties as an employer.

- *Tax Information on Unemployment Compensation*
  (Number 905)

Explains unemployment compensation rules from the employer's perspective.

- *Jobs and Research Credits* (Number 906)

Discusses two credits that may be available to businesses. The first, the targeted jobs credit, is based on a percentage of wages to qualified employees. The second, the research credit, is based on the amount a business spends for research and experimentation.

- *Tax Information for Handicapped and Disabled Individuals*
  (Number 907)

Explains tax rules of interest to handicapped and disabled people and to taxpayers with disabled dependents. For example, a tax credit is available for certain disability payments. Also, medical expenses may be deducted, and a credit is available for expenses incurred caring for disabled dependents.

- *Bankruptcy* (Number 908)

Runs through the income tax consequences of bankruptcy and discharge of debt for individuals and small businesses.

- *Alternative Minimum Tax* (Number 909)

Discusses the alternative minimum tax, which applies to individuals, trusts, and estates with large amounts of passive income—interest, rents, royalties, and so on.

- *Tax Information for Direct Sellers* (Number 911)

Provides help for direct sellers, people who sell consumer products, such as Avon cosmetics, to others on a person-to-person basis.

- *Tax Information on Social Security Benefits* (Number 915)

Explains when you have to include part of your Social Security income on your federal income tax return.

- *Identification Numbers Under ERISA* (Number 1004)

Lists the types of identification numbers employers must obtain.

- *Filing Requirements for Employee Benefit Plans*
  (Number 1048)

Explains paperwork requirements for setting up employee-benefit plans.

• *List of Original Issue Discount Obligations* (Number 1212)

Explains the tax treatment of original issue discount (OID) obligations. Describes how brokers and other middlemen, who may hold the obligations as nominees for the owners, should report OID to the IRS.

• *Employee's Daily Record of Tips and Employee's Report of Tips to Employer* (Number 1244)

Explains how you must report if you are an employee who receives tips. Copies of the monthly tip report you must give your employer are included, as well as a daily list you can use for your own records.

EASY LISTENING: HOW TO USE TELE-TAX
Tele-Tax is a telephone service of the IRS that provides taped information on about 150 tax-related subjects. The tapes, which run about two to three minutes each, give pertinent data and advice on such topics as preparing for an audit and filing estimated taxes.

For taxpayers using a push-button phone, Tele-Tax is in operation twenty-four hours a day, seven days a week. Those with a rotary or dial telephone can access the service during normal business hours (9 A.M. to 5 P.M.) Monday through Friday.

To use Tele-Tax, follow these instructions:

• Select by number the tape you want to hear. (A complete list of tapes and numbers follows.) You can listen to up to three tapes on each call you make.
• Have a piece of paper handy to take notes.
• Dial the Tele-Tax number for your area.
• Follow the recorded operator's instructions.

Telephone numbers for Tele-Tax are listed in the following table. Numbers listed are for use with push-button telephones. Those numbers that can be used with either push-button or rotary (dial) telephones are marked with an (R). Also, keep in mind that if you call from outside the local area, you'll have to pay a long-distance charge.

Tele-Tax Numbers

Location		Number
Alabama		
Birmingham		(205) 251-9454
	(R)	(205) 251-3881
Huntsville		(205) 534-5203
Mobile		(205) 433-6993
Montgomery		(205) 262-8304
Alaska		
Anchorage		(907) 279-0653
	(R)	(907) 279-8689
Arizona		
Phoenix		(602) 261-3560
	(R)	(602) 261-3560
Tucson		(602) 624-9042
Arkansas		
Little Rock		(501) 372-3891
	(R)	(501) 374-3117
California		
Bakersfield		(805) 861-4105
Carson		(213) 632-3555
El Monte		(213) 571-6902
Fresno		(209) 268-5395
Los Angeles		(213) 617-3177
	(R)	(213) 617-3177
Laguna Niguel	(R)	(714) 831-4246
Oakland		(415) 839-4245
	(R)	(415) 839-4245
Oxnard		(805) 485-7236
Riverside		(714) 351-6769
Sacramento		(916) 448-4367
	(R)	(916) 448-4556
San Diego		(619) 293-5020
San Francisco		(415) 863-4039
San Jose		(408) 293-5606
	(R)	(408) 287-4631
Santa Ana		(714) 836-2974
Santa Maria		(805) 928-7503
Stockton		(209) 463-6005
Van Nuys		(213) 904-6393
Visalia		(209) 733-8194

Location		Number
Colorado		
Colorado Springs		(303) 597-6344
Denver		(303) 592-1118
	(R)	(303) 592-1118
Fort Collins		(303) 223-0688
Connecticut		
Bridgeport		(203) 335-0700
Hartford		(203) 547-0015
	(R)	(203) 247-5500
New Haven		(203) 777-4594
Waterbury		(203) 754-4235
Delaware		
Dover		(302) 674-1118
Wilmington		(302) 652-0272
	(R)	(302) 571-1097
District of Columbia		(202) 628-2929
	(R)	(202) 628-2929
Florida		
Daytona Beach		(904) 253-0669
Ft. Lauderdale		(305) 523-3100
Jacksonville		(904) 353-9579
	(R)	(904) 353-9579
Miami		(305) 374-5144
	(R)	(305) 372-0397
Orlando		(305) 422-0592
	(R)	(305) 843-0762
St. Petersburg		(305) 578-0424
Tallahasee		(904) 222-0807
Tampa		(813) 229-0815
West Palm Beach		(305) 655-1996
Georgia		
Albany		(912) 435-1415
Atlanta		(404) 221-6572
	(R)	(404) 221-6572
Augusta		(404) 722-9068
Columbus		(404) 327-0298
Macon		(912) 745-2890
Savannah		(912) 355-9632

Location		Number
Hawaii		
Honolulu		(808) 546-7162
	(R)	(808) 546-3700
Idaho		
Boise		(208) 383-0034
	(R)	(208) 344-8628
Illinois		
Aurora		(312) 851-2718
Bloomington		(309) 828-6116
Champaign		(217) 398-1779
Chicago		(312) 886-9614
	(R)	(312) 886-9614
East St. Louis		(618) 875-4050
Ottawa		(815) 433-1568
Peoria		(309) 637-9305
Quad Cities		(319) 326-1720
Rockford		(815) 987-4280
Springfield		(217) 789-0489
	(R)	(217) 753-0316
Indiana		
Evansville		(812) 422-1026
Gary		(219) 884-4465
Indianapolis		(317) 634-1550
	(R)	(317) 634-1550
South Bend		(219) 232-5459
Iowa		
Cedar Rapids		(319) 399-2210
Des Moines		(515) 284-6117
	(R)	(515) 284-4050
Quad Cities		(319) 326-1720
Waterloo		(319) 234-0817
Kansas		
Wichita		(316) 264-3147
	(R)	(316) 262-4454
Kentucky		
Erlanger		(606) 727-3338
Lexington		(606) 233-2889
Louisville		(502) 582-5599
	(R)	(502) 582-6372

Location		Number
Louisiana		
New Orleans		(504) 529-2854
	(R)	(504) 589-4620
Maine		
Augusta	(R)	(207) 623-3854
Portland		(207) 775-0465
Maryland		
Baltimore		(301) 244-7306
	(R)	(301) 244-7306
Cumberland		(301) 722-5331
Frederick		(301) 663-5798
Hagerstown		(301) 733-6815
Salisbury		(301) 742-9458
Massachusetts		
Boston		(617) 523-8602
	(R)	(617) 523-8602
Springfield		(413) 739-6624
Michigan		
Ann Arbor		(313) 665-4544
Detroit		(313) 961-4282
	(R)	(313) 961-4282
Flint		(313) 238-4599
Grand Rapids		(616) 451-2034
Kalamazoo		(616) 343-0255
Lansing		(517) 372-2454
Mt. Clemens		(313) 463-9550
Pontiac		(313) 858-2336
Saginaw		(517) 753-9911
Minnesota		
Duluth		(218) 722-5494
Rochester		(507) 288-5595
St. Paul		(612) 224-4288
	(R)	(612) 224-4288
Mississippi		
Gulfport		(601) 863-3302
Jackson		(601) 960-4168
	(R)	(601) 960-4808
Missouri		
Jefferson City		(314) 636-8312
Kansas City		(816) 421-3741

Location		Number
St. Louis		(314) 241-4700
	(R)	(314) 241-4700
Springfield		(417) 883-3419
Montana		
Billings		(406) 656-1422
Great Falls		(406) 727-4902
Helena		(406) 443-7034
	(R)	(406) 443-0600
Nebraska		
Lincoln		(402) 471-5450
Omaha		(402) 221-3324
	(R)	(402) 221-3326
Nevada		
Las Vegas		(702) 385-1778
	(R)	(702) 382-1189
New Hampshire		
Manchester		(603) 623-5778
Portsmouth	(R)	(603) 431-0780
New Jersey		
Atlantic City		(609) 348-2636
Camden		(609) 966-3412
Hackensack		(201) 487-1817
Newark		(201) 624-1223
	(R)	(201) 624-1223
Paterson		(201) 278-5442
Trenton		(609) 599-2150
New Mexico		
Albuquerque		(505) 766-1102
	(R)	(505) 243-4557
New York		
Albany		(518) 465-8318
	(R)	(518) 465-3566
Binghamton		(607) 722-8426
Brooklyn		(718) 858-4461
	(R)	(718) 858-4461
Buffalo		(716) 856-9320
	(R)	(716) 856-9320
Manhattan		(212) 406-4080
	(R)	(212) 406-4080
Mineola		(516) 248-6790

Location		Number
Poughkeepsie		(914) 452-1877
Rochester		(716) 454-3330
Smithtown		(516) 979-0720
Syracuse		(315) 471-1630
White Plains		(914) 683-0134
North Carolina		
Asheville		(704) 254-3044
Charlotte		(704) 567-9885
Durham		(919) 541-5283
Fayetteville		(919) 483-0735
Greensboro		(919) 378-1572
	(R)	(919) 379-1168
Raleigh		(919) 755-1498
Winston-Salem		(919) 725-3013
North Dakota		
Bismarck		(701) 258-8210
Fargo		(701) 232-9360
	(R)	(701) 232-1070
Grand Forks		(701) 746-0324
Minot		(701) 838-1234
Ohio		
Akron		(216) 253-1170
Canton		(216) 455-6061
Cincinnati		(513) 684-3531
	(R)	(513) 684-3531
Cleveland		(216) 522-3037
	(R)	(216) 522-3037
Columbus		(614) 469-2266
Dayton		(513) 225-7237
Lima		(419) 224-0341
Mansfield		(419) 525-3474
Toledo		(419) 255-3743
Youngstown		(216) 744-4200
Oklahoma		
Oklahoma City		(405) 235-3434
	(R)	(405) 235-4907
Tulsa		(918) 599-0555
Oregon		
Eugene		(503) 687-6737
Portland		(503) 294-5363
	(R)	(503) 294-5363
Salem		(503) 399-5784

Location		Number
Pennsylvania		
Bethlehem		(215) 861-0325
Erie		(814) 459-7419
Harrisburg		(717) 236-1356
Jenkintown		(215) 887-1261
Lancaster		(717) 392-0980
Norristown		(215) 275-0242
Philadelphia		(215) 592-8946
	(R)	(215) 592-8946
Pittsburgh		(412) 281-3120
	(R)	(412) 281-3138
Reading		(215) 373-4568
Scranton		(717) 961-0325
Wilkes-Barre		(717) 823-9552
Williamsport		(717) 323-4242
Rhode Island		
Providence		(401) 861-5220
	(R)	(401) 521-6440
South Carolina		
Charleston		(803) 722-0369
Columbia		(803) 254-4749
	(R)	(803) 799-8169
Greenville		(803) 235-8093
South Dakota		
Aberdeen	(R)	(605) 229-6856
Brookings		(605) 692-4507
Rapid City		(605) 348-3454
Sioux Falls		(605) 335-7081
Watertown		(605) 882-4979
Tennessee		
Chattanooga		(615) 892-5577
Jackson		(901) 664-1858
Johnson City		(615) 282-1917
Knoxville		(615) 521-7478
Memphis		(901) 525-2611
Nashville		(615) 242-1541
	(R)	(615) 242-1541
Texas		
Austin		(512) 479-0391
	(R)	(512) 478-6422

Location	Number
Dallas	(214) 767-1792
(R)	(214) 767-1792
El Paso	(915) 778-9907
Ft. Worth	(817) 334-3888
Houston	(713) 850-8801
(R)	(713) 850-8801
San Antonio	(512) 680-9591
Utah	
Salt Lake City	(801) 355-9328
(R)	(801) 359-9218
Vermont	
Burlington	(802) 658-0007
	(802) 658-1149
Virginia	
Bailey's Crossroads	(703) 557-0034
Bristol	(703) 669-0565
Danville	(804) 797-2223
Norfolk	(804) 441-3623
Richmond	(804) 771-2369
(R)	(804) 771-2165
Roanoke	(703) 982-6062
Washington	
Seattle	(206) 343-7221
(R)	(206) 343-7221
Spokane	(509) 455-9213
Tacoma	(206) 383-4668
West Virginia	
Charleston	(304) 343-3597
Huntington	(304) 523-0104
Parkersburg (R)	(304) 422-4011
Wisconsin	
Green Bay	(414) 433-3884
Madison	(608) 264-5349
Milwaukee	(414) 291-1783
(R)	(414) 291-1783
Racine	(414) 886-1615
Wyoming	
Cheyenne	(307) 634-1198
(R)	(307) 638-6109

WHAT YOU WILL LEARN FROM TELE-TAX

Below is a list of subjects you'll find on Tele-Tax tapes plus the tape numbers. Again, remember, the telephone company will bill you for long-distance charges if you dial a number that is not a local call for you.

Tele-Tax Titles and Tape Numbers

Tape Number	Title
IRS Procedures and Services	
100	*IRS Help Available—Volunteer Tax Assistance Programs, Toll-Free Telephone, Walk-In Assistance, and Outreach Program*
101	*Tax Assistance for the Handicapped and Deaf*
102	*Small Business Tax Workshops—Tax Help for the New Businessperson*
103	*Problem Resolution Program—Special Help for Problem Situations*
104	*Public Libraries—Tax Information Tapes and Reproducible Tax Forms*
105	*Examination Procedures and How to Prepare for an Audit*
106	*The Collection Process*
107	*Tax Fraud—How to Report*
108	*Special Enrollment Examination to Practice Before IRS*
109	*Organizations—How to Apply for Exempt Status*
Filing Requirements, Filing Status, Exemptions	
110	*Who Must File?*
111	*Which Form—1040, 1040A, or 1040EZ?*
112	*When, Where, and How to File*
113	*Filing Requirements for a Dependent Child*
114	*Filing as a Single*
115	*Filing Joint or Separate*
116	*Filing as Head of Household*
117	*Filing as a Qualifying Widow/Widower*
118	*Filing Status for Separated Individuals*
119	*Exemptions for Age and Blindness*
120	*Dependent—Who Can Be Claimed?*

Tape Number	Title
121	*Dependent Child—Divorced or Separated Parents*
122	*Dependent—Items to Include in Determining Support*
126	*Estimated Tax*
127	*Amended Returns*
128	*Decedents*

Types of Income

130	*Wages and Salaries*
131	*Tips*
132	*Interest Received*
133	*Dividends and Dividend Exclusion*
134	*Refund of State and Local Taxes*
135	*Alimony Received*
136	*Business Income*
137	*Sole Proprietorship Income*
138	*Capital Gains and Losses*
139	*Pensions and Annuities*
140	*Pensions—The General Rule*
141	*Lump-Sum Distributions—Profit-Sharing Plans*
143	*Rental Income and Expenses*
200	*Renting Vacation Property, Renting to Relatives*
201	*Royalties*
202	*Farming and Fishing Income*
204	*Unemployment Compensation*
205	*Gambling Income and Expenses*
206	*Bartering Income*
207	*Scholarships, Fellowships, Grants*
208	*Nontaxable Income*
209	*Social Security and Tier 1 Railroad Retirement Taxability*
210	*Social Security Benefit Statement—Form SSA-1099*

Adjustments to Income

212	*Deduction for Married Couples When Both Work*
213	*Moving Expenses*
214	*Employee Business Expenses*
215	*Business Use of Car*

Tape Number	Title
216	*Business Travel Expenses*
217	*Business Entertainment Expenses*
218	*Individual Retirement Accounts*
219	*Alimony Paid*
225	*Bad Debt Deduction*
226	*Tax Shelters*

Itemized Deductions

227	*Should I Itemize?*
228	*Medical and Dental Expenses*
229	*Medical Insurance*
231	*Property Taxes*
232	*Sales Tax*
233	*Interest Expense*
234	*Contributions*
235	*Casualty Losses*
236	*Miscellaneous Expenses*
237	*Office-in-the-Home Expenses*
238	*Educational Expenses*

Tax Computation

240	*Tax Table*
241	*Tax-Rate Schedules*
243	*Tax and Credits Figured by the IRS*
244	*Income Averaging*
300	*Self-Employment Tax*
301	*Ten-Year Averaging for Lump-Sum Distributions*
303	*Alternative Minimum Tax*
304	*Gift Tax*
305	*Estate Tax*

Tax Credits

306	*Child-Care Credit*
307	*Earned-Income Credit*
308	*Residential-Energy Credit*
309	*Credit for the Elderly*
310	*Tax Credit for Contributions to Candidates for Public Office*
312	*Qualified Royalty Owners' Exemption (windfall profit tax)*

General Information

316	*Refunds—How Long They Should Take*

Tape Number	Title
317	*Copy of Your Tax Return—How to Get One*
319	*Tax-Shelter Registration*
320	*Extensions for Time to File Your Tax Return*
325	*Form W-2—What to Do If Not Received*
326	*Penalty and Interest Charges*
327	*IRS Notices and Bills—How to Pay*
329	*Penalty for Underpayment of Estimated Tax—Form 2210*
330	*Recordkeeping*
331	*How to Choose a Tax Preparer*
332	*Audit Appeal Rights*
333	*Failure to Pay Child/Spousal Support*
335	*Withholding on Interest and Dividends*
336	*Highway Use Tax*
337	*Checklist, Common Errors When Preparing Your Tax Returns*
338	*Withholding on Pension and Annuities*
339	*Your Tax Form Is Overdue—Let Us Hear From You*
340	*Second Request for Information About Your Tax Form*
341	*Notice of Intent to Levy*
342	*Notice of Underreported Income—CP 2000*

Basis of Assets, Depreciation, Sale of Assets

343	*Sale of Personal Residence—General*
344	*Sale of Personal Residence—How to Report Gain*
400	*Sale of Personal Residence—Exclusion of Gain, Age 55 and Older*
401	*Basis of Assets*
402	*Depreciation—General*
403	*Depreciation—Accelerated Cost Recovery System*
404	*Installment Sales*

Employer Tax Information

406	*Social Security Withholding Rates*
407	*Form W-2—Where, When, and How to File*
408	*Form W-4—Employee's Withholding Allowance Certificate*
409	*Federal Tax Deposits—General*

Tape Number	Title
410	*Employer Identification Number—How to Apply*
411	*Paying Taxes on Your Employees*
412	*Form 942—Employer's Quarterly Tax Return for Household Employees*
413	*Form 941—Deposit Requirements*
414	*Form 941—Employer's Quarterly Federal Tax Return*
415	*Form 940—Deposit Requirements*
416	*Form 940—Employer's Annual Federal Unemployment Tax Return*
417	*Targeted Jobs Credit*
418	*Tips—Withholding and Reporting*

Tax Information for Aliens and Citizens Living Abroad

420	*Resident and Nonresident Aliens*
425	*Dual Status Alien*
426	*Alien Tax Clearance*
428	*Foreign Earned-Income Exclusion—General*
429	*Foreign Earned-Income Exclusion—Who Qualifies*
430	*Foreign Earned-Income Exclusion—What Income Qualifies*
431	*Foreign Tax Credit*

SUBJECT-MATTER INDEX

The following subject-matter index should make it easier for you to find the booklets you need. (The number entries are publication numbers.)

A

Accelerated cost-recovery system, 527, 534, 587
Accident insurance, medical expenses, 502, 907
Accounting periods and methods, 538
Accrual method, 538
ACRS recovery tables, 534
ACTION volunteers, 525
Actuarial tables, 575
Acupuncture, 502
Adjustments to income:
  Alimony paid, 504
  Employee business expenses, 463
  IRS (or SEP-IRA), payments to, 590
  Keogh plan, payments to, 535, 560
  Moving expenses, 521
  Penalty for early withdrawal of savings, 550
Administrators of estates, 448, 559
Adoption expenses:
  Deductible, 529
  Medical expenses, preadoption, 502
Advance payments:
  Earned income credit, 505, 539
  Future sales, 538
Advertising expenses, 535
Age 65 or over, 501, 524, 554

Alcohol fuel credit, 378
Aliens, 513, 518, 519
Alimony, 504
All-savers certificates, 550
Alternate ACRS method, 534
Alternative minimum tax, 909
Alternative tax on capital gains, 542
Amended returns:
  Claims for refunds, 556
  U.S. citizens abroad, 54
Amortization, 535
Annuities, 554, 560, 575
  Estate and gift taxes, 448
  Joint and survivor, 575
  Loans from employer plans, 560, 571, 575
  Tax-sheltered, 571
  Variable, 575
  Withholding on, 505, 539, 575
Apartments, condominiums, cooperatives:
  Owner's deductions, 530
  Sale of, 523
Appeal rights and claims for refunds, 556
Appreciation in value of property:
  Charitable donation, 556, 561
  Sale of assets, 544
Assessments for local improvements, 527, 530, 535

Associations:
  Homeowners, 588
  Investment clubs, 550
Attorney fees:
  As business expense, 535
  Deductible, 529
  Divorce, 504
  Investment expense, 550
  Personal expense, 529
Averaging income, 506
Aviation fuel, noncommercial,
  excise tax, 510
Awards and prizes, 525

B
Babysitters, 503, 907
Bad debts, 548
Bankruptcy, 908
Bar examination fees, 529
Bargain purchases, 550
Barter income, 525
Basis, 550, 551
  Adjusted, 534
  Bonds, 550
  Condemnation, 549
  Cost, 551
  Gifts, 551
  Home, 530
  Inherited property, 551, 559
  Intangible property, 551
  Liquidation, property
    received in, 542
  Mutual funds, 550, 564
  Other than cost, 551
  S corporation stock, 589
  Stocks, 550
Beneficiaries:
  Annuity, 575
  Estate, 559
  Inheritance, 525, 559
  IRA, 590
Blindness:
  Exemption for, 501, 907
  Guide dogs, 502, 907
  Medical deductions, 502, 907

Blood donations, 526
Bonds:
  Amortization of premium,
    535
  Basis, 550, 551
  Convertible, 544
  Coupon, 550
  Discounted, 550
  Industrial development
    bonds, 550
  Marketable, 550
  Original issue discount, 1212
  State, 550
  Treasury, 550
  U.S. Savings, 550
Bonuses:
  Employee, 525
  Employer's deduction, 535
  Employment taxes, 539
Books and records, business,
  583
Boycotts, international, 514
Bribes and kickbacks, 535
Brokerage fees, 550
Buildings:
  Demolition, 534
  Depreciation, 534
  Historic, 535
  Sale, 544
Burglary, 547
Business:
  Bad debt, 548
  Energy investment credit,
    572
  Expenses, 463, 535
  Sale of interest, 544
  Start-up costs, 535
  Taxes, 583
  Use of home, 529, 530, 587

C
Campaign contributions:
  Business expense, 535
Cancellation of debt:
  Bankruptcy, 908

Business debt, 908
Personal debt, 525, 908
Cancellation of lease, 521,
535, 544
Capital contributions:
Corporation, 542
Partnership, 541
Capital expenditures:
Basis, 534
Business, 535
Medical expense, 502, 907
Capital-gains distributions,
550, 564
Capitalizing expenses, 535
Car expenses:
Business, 463
Car pool, 463, 525
Charitable, 526
Medical, 502, 907
Moving, 521
Carrybacks and carryovers:
Capital loss, 463
Charitable contributions, 526
Credits, alternative
minimum tax, 909
Foreign-tax credit, 514
Investment credit, 572
Jobs credit, 906
Net-operating loss, 536, 909
Research credit, 906
Termination of estate, 559
Carrying charges:
Capitalizing, 535
Personal expense, 545
Straddles, 550
Cash method, 538
Casualty losses, 547
Workbook, 584
Cemetery, contribution for,
526
Certified historic structures,
535
Child, exemption for, 501
Child-care credit, 503, 907
Child-support payments, 504

Christian Science
practitioners, 502
Circulation expenses, 535
Citizens abroad, 54, 593
Civil defense volunteers, 526
Civil service annuities, 567
Claim procedures, 594
Cleaning and laundry
expenses:
Business expense, 463
Work clothes, 529
Closing costs, 530
Clothes, work, 529
Club dues, 463
Collection of income, expenses
of, 529, 550
Commissions, 525
Commitment fees, 535
Communications excise tax,
510
Community income and
property, 504, 555
Commuting, 463, 529
Compensation, 525, 535, 590
Damages, 525, 547, 549
Unemployment, 525, 905
Compete, agreement not to,
535, 544
Condemnations, 523, 549
Condominiums, 530
Contracts, long-term, 538
Contributions:
Appreciated property, 526,
561
Business organizations,
donations to, 535
Capital, 542
Charitable:
Corporation, 542
Estates, 448, 559
Individuals, 526
Employee plans, 535, 560
Partnership, 541
Valuation, 561
Convention expenses, 463

Conversion to rental property, 523, 527

Cooperatives:
 Apartments, 530
 Interest payments, 545

Copyrights:
 Depreciation, 534, 535
 Sale of, 544

Corporations, 542

Corporations, S, 589

Corporations, small-business stock losses, 544, 550

Cost, annuity, 575

Cost depletion, 535

Cost-of-living allowance, 525

Coupons, qualified discount, 538

Courts, appeal to after examination, 556

Credits:
 Alcohol fuel, 378
 Business energy investment, 572
 Child and disabled dependent care, 503, 907
 Diesel fuel, 378
 Disability, permanent and total, 524
 Elderly, for, 524, 554
 Foreign tax, 514
 Gasoline tax, 378
 Investment, 572
 Jobs, 906, 907
 New home buyers, repayment of, 523
 Partnership items, 541
 Rehabilitated building investment, 572
 Research expenses, 906
 Social Security tax, overpaid, 505
 Special motor fuels, 378, 510
 Unified, estate and gift taxes, 448
 Withholding tax, 505

Crops, unharvested, 544

Cruise ship, conventions, 463

Custodian fees, 529, 550

D

Damaged property, 547, 549

Damages:
 Antitrust, 535
 Compensation for, 525
 Severance, 549

Day care facilities, 587

Dealers:
 Mortgages, 535
 Securities, 535, 538

Death benefits, 525

Death-benefit exclusion, 525, 559, 575

Debt-financed income or property, 598

Debts:
 Assumption of, 544
 Bad debts, 548
 Cancelled, 525, 908
 Interest on, 545

Decedents, 448, 559

Decedents' medical expenses, 502, 559

Declining balance depreciation, 534

Deductions:
 Adoption expenses, 529
 Amortization, 535
 Bad debts, 548
 Business use of home, 529, 530, 587
 Car expenses, 463
 Casualty losses, 547, 549
 Charitable contributions, 526
 Convention expenses, 463
 Dental expenses, 502, 907
 Depletion, 535
 Depreciation, 534
 Dividends received, 542
 Education expenses, 508, 529
 Employees, 463, 529

Entertainment expenses, 463
Estate tax, 559, 575
Expenses of producing
  income, 529, 550
Final income tax return of
  decedent, 559
Fines:
  Business, 535
  Personal, 529
Foreign housing costs, 54
Foreign income taxes, 514
Gambling losses, 525, 529
Gift expenses, 463
Income, expenses of
  producing, 529, 550
Interest expenses, 535, 545
Investment expenses, 550
IRA payments, 590
Legal expenses:
  Business, 535
  Personal, 529
Married couple when both
  work, 17
Medical expenses, 502, 907
Miscellaneous, 529
Moving expenses, 521
Partnerships, 541
Pension plan, payments to,
  535, 560, 571, 575, 590
Personal exemptions, 501
Rental expenses, 527
Taxes, 535
Thefts, 547
Travel, transportation, 463
Demolitions, 534
Demonstrator cars, sale of,
  544
Dental expenses, 502, 907
Departing aliens, 513, 518,
  519
Dependent care assistance
  paid by employer, 525
Dependents, 501, 504
  Medical expenses of, 502
Depletion, 535

Deposits:
  Due dates, 509
  Employment taxes, 539
  Excise taxes, 510
Depreciation of property:
  Accelerated Cost Recovery
    System, 527, 534, 587
  Asset depreciation range
    system, 534
  Basis, 534, 551
  Car, 463
  Home, business use, 587
  Home, rental use, 527
  Methods, 534
  Recapture, 544
  Sale of, 544
Destruction of property, 547
Determination letters,
  employee-benefit plans, 560
Development expenses for oil,
  gas, and geothermal wells,
  535
Direct sellers, 911
Directors' fees, 525
Disability:
  Income, 525
  Payments, 907
  Pensions and annuities, 907
  Permanent and total, tax
    credit for, 524
Disabled dependent care, 503,
  907
Disaster area losses, 547, 549
  Workbook, 584
Disclosure statement, IRA,
  590
Discount, original issue, 1212
Dispositions:
  Depreciable property, 544
  Installment obligations, 537
  Partner's interest, 541
Distributions:
  Corporate, 542, 550
  Estates, 559

Individual retirement
  arrangements (IRAs), 590
Keogh plans, 560
Mutual funds, 564
Partnerships, 541
S corporations, 589
Dividends, 542, 550
  Estate, 559
  Exclusion, 550
  Mutual fund, 564
  Received, deduction for
    corporations, 542
  Reinvestment plan, 550, 564
  S corporations, 589
Divorced taxpayers, 504
  Exemptions, 501, 504
  Individual retirement
    arrangement (IRAs), 590
Doctors, medical, 502, 907
Domestic help, 503, 539, 907
Drilling expenses, 535
Drug expenses, 502, 907
Dual-status tax year, 519
Due dates, 509
Dues, 529, 535

E
Earned income:
  Foreign, 54
  Tax credit, advance payment,
    505, 539
Earnings and profits, 542
Easements on property, 544
Education:
  Expenses, 508, 535
  Foreign scholars, 518
  Scholarships and fellowships,
    520
Elderly persons:
  Sale of home, 523, 554
  Tax credit for, 524, 554
Embezzlement, 547
Employee-benefit plans, 535,
  560
  Filing requirements, 1048

Employee expenses, 463, 529,
  535
Employees, defined, 539, 560
Employees' pay, 535
Employer-paid education or
  dependent care, 525
Employer identification
  number, 583
Employment abroad:
  U.S. citizens, 54
  U.S. possessions, 570
Employment agency fees, 529
Employment interview, 463,
  529
Employment taxes:
  Employer information, 15,
    539
  Household employees, 503,
    539, 907
  Social-Security taxes (FICA),
    503, 539, 907
  Unemployment tax (FUTA),
    503, 539, 907
Endowment insurance
  proceeds, 525
Energy credit, business,
  investment credit for, 572
Entertainment expenses, 463
Environmental excise taxes,
  510
ERISA, identification numbers
  under, 1004
Estate and gift taxes, 448
  Annual exclusion, 448
  Basis, 559
  Disclaimers, 448
  Filing requirements, 448,
    559
  Marital deduction, 448, 559
  Unified rate schedule, 448
  Valuation methods, 448
Estates and trusts, income
  from, 525, 559
Estimated tax:
  Corporation, 542

Individual, 505, 554
Nonresident aliens, 519
Examination of return, 556
Excess accumulations, IRA,
  590
Excess payments:
 IRA, 590
 Keogh plan, 560
Excise taxes, 510
Exclusion of income earned
  abroad, 54, 593
 U.S. possessions, 570
Executors of estates, 448, 559
Exemption from withholding,
  505, 539
Exemptions, 501, 554
Expenses:
 Advance payment, 538
 Business, 535
 Condemnation award,
  securing, 549
 Decedent, 559
 Exploration, mineral
  deposits, 535
 Foreign housing costs, 54
 Income-producing, 529, 550
 Personal, 529
 Recovery of, 525
 Rental, 527
 Securing condemnation
  award, 549
Extension of time to file tax
  return:
 Estate, 448
 Fiduciary, 559
 Gift, 448
 Personal, 17

F
Fair-market value:
 Charitable contributions,
  526, 561
 Defined, 537, 544, 551, 561
 Valuation, 561

Family:
 Employees, 539
 Partnerships, 541
Farmers and farming, 225
 Estimated tax, 505
 Farming syndicates, 536
Fees:
 Check-writing, 529
 Club membership, 463
 Commitment, 535
 Custodian, 529, 550
 Directors', 525
 Finders', 535
 Legal, 535
 License and regulation, 535
 Personal services, 525
 Service broker, 529
Fellowships, 518, 520
Fiduciaries, 559
Filing requirements:
 Age 65 or older, 554
 Corporations, 542
 Employee benefit plans, 1048
 Estates, 448
 Gift taxes, 448
 IRA, 590
 Partnerships, 541
 S corporations, 589
Final return, individual, 559
Finance charges, 545
Finance leases, 535
Fines, 529, 535
Fire losses, 547, 549
First-in, first-out (FIFO)
  inventory, 538
Fishing business, 595
 Estimated tax, 505
Fixing-up expenses, home, 523
Flood losses, 547, 549
Foreign convention expenses,
  463
Foreign earned income, 54
Foreign employer, 525
Foreign income taxes, 514

Foreign moving expenses, 54, 521
Foreign scholars, 518
Foreign tax credit, 514
Foreign visitors to the U.S., 513, 519
Foster child, exemption, 501
Franchises, 544
Fraternal societies, contributions to, 526
Fuel tax credit or refund, 378
Funeral expenses:
  Estates, 448, 559
  Individuals, 502, 529

G
Gains and losses, 544
  Basis, 551
  Capital-gain distributions, 550
  Casualty losses, 547, 549
  Condemnation, 549
  Corporations, 542
  Depreciable property, 544
  Employee stock options, 525
  Estate, 559
  Investment property, 550
  Liquidating dividends, 542, 550
  Mutual funds, 564
  Nonresident aliens, 519
  Partner's interest, 541
  S corporations, 589
  Sale of assets, 544, 550
  Stock options, 550
  Thefts, 547, 549
Gambling winnings and losses, 525, 539
  Reporting requirements, winnings, 539
  Withholding requirements, winnings, 539
Gas and oil property, sale of, 544

Gasohol, 510
Gasoline tax, credit or refund, 378
Gift expenses, 463
Gift taxes, 504
Gifts, bequests, and inheritances, 448
  Basis, 551, 559
  Business, 463
  Debts, canceled or forgiven, 908
  Depreciable property, 544
  Exclusion from income, 525
  Home, 523
  Mutual funds, 564
  Partnership interest, 541
  Property received as, 559
  Survivor annuities, 559, 575
Goodwill:
  Depreciation, 534
  Partnership, 541
  Sale of, 544
Graduate students, 520
Grants, 518, 520
Gross estate, 448, 559
Gross income test, dependents, 501
Gross profit percentage, 537
Group-term life insurance, 525, 535
Guaranteed wage, 525
Guaranteed payments to partners, 541
Guide dogs for blind and deaf, 502, 907

H
Handicapped persons, 502, 907
Health insurance, 502, 907
Hearing aids, 502, 907
Heat, light, and power, 535
Highway motor vehicle use tax, 349

Historic structures, 535, 572
Holding period for
  investments, 523, 544, 550
Home:
  Business use of, 529, 530,
    587
  Changed to rental, 527
  Construction, 523
  Owner's deductions, 530
  Purchase, 523
  Repairs and improvements,
    530
  Sale of, 523
  Sale of, age 55 or older, 523,
    554
Homeowners' associations,
  588
Hospitalization, 502, 907
Housekeeper, child care, 503,
  907
Housing allowances, 525
HR-10 plans, 560

I

Identification numbers:
  Employer, 503, 583
  ERISA, 1004
Illegal payments, business,
  535
Improvements and repairs:
  Assessments for, 527, 530
  Business property, 535
  Depreciation, 534
  Home, 530
  Rental property, 527
  Selling a home, 523
Income, 525
  Accrual of, 538
  Advance payments, 538
  Constructive receipt, 525,
    538
  Corporate, 542
  Decedent, 559

  Disability, 525
  Effectively connected, 518,
    519
  Foreign source, 54
  Investment, 550
  Mutual-fund distributions,
    564
  Nontaxable, 525
  Other than cash, 525
  Partnership, 541
  Rental, 527
  S corporations, 589
  Social Security benefits, 525,
    915
  Taxable, 525
  Tips, 531, 1244
  Unemployment
    compensation, 525, 905
Income-producing property,
  550
Incorporating a business, 542
Individual retirement
  arrangements (IRAs), 535,
  590
Information returns, 539
Inherited property, basis, 551
Installment buying, 545
Installment obligations,
  disposition of, 537
Installment payments, estate
  tax, 448
Installment sales, 537
Insurance:
  Beneficiaries, 559
  Borrowing on policy, 545
  Business, deductible and
    nondeductible premiums,
    535
  Casualty losses, 547, 549
  Employer-financed, 525
  Estate tax, 448
  Exchange of policy, 544
  Foreign insurer, excise tax,
    510

Group-term, 535
Home, 529
Interest on policy, 550
Keogh plans, 560
Life, 525, 529, 535
Malpractice, 529
Medical, 502, 907
Proceeds, life, 525
Thefts, 547, 549
Interest:
Below-market loans, 448, 525
Income, 550
Original-issue discount, 1212
Interest expense, 545
Construction period, 535
Deduction, 545
Limit on investment interest, 545, 550
Money-market certificates, to buy, 545
Prepaid interest, 535
Refunded, 545
Rule of 78's, 538, 545
Shared appreciation mortgage, 545
Unstated, 537
International air travel facilities, excise tax, 510
International boycott, 514
Interview expenses:
Business, 535
Reimbursed, 525
Inventions, sale of, 544
Inventories, 538
Investment clubs, 550
Investment counsel fees, 550
Investment credit, 572
Investment in annuity contract, 575
Investment income and expenses, 550, 564
Investment interest, 545, 550
Investment property, 550
Involuntary conversions, 549

J
Job:
Expenses of looking for a new job, 529
Interview, 535
Moving expenses, 521
Travel expenses, 463
Jobs credit, 906, 907
Joint and survivor annuities, 575
Joint interests, gross estate, 448
Joint return:
Decedent and surviving spouse, 559
Nonresident aliens, 519
Joint ventures, 541
Jury-duty fees, 525

K
Keogh plans, 535, 560
Key-person insurance, 535
Kickbacks, 535

L
Labor costs, 535
Last-in, first-out (LIFO) inventory, 538
Leases, 535
Cancellation, 521
Legal separation, 504
Letters, memorandums, 544
Leveraged lease, 535
Liabilities:
Assumptions of, 544
Partnership, 541
Contested, 535, 538
License fees, 529
Liquidation:
Corporation, 542
Distributions in, 550
Partner's interest, 541
Livestock, raised, 551

Loan-origination fees (points), 530, 535, 545
Loan-placement fees (points), 530, 535, 545
Loans from pensions or annuities, 560, 571, 575
Loans, interest on:
  Below market, 448, 525
  Business expenses, 535
  Personal expenses, 545
Lobbying expenses, 535
Lockout and strike benefits, 525
Long-term contracts, 538
Losses:
  Abandonment, 534
  At-risk limits, 536
  Bad debt, 548
  Business expenses, 535
  Business property, 544
  Condemnations, 549
  Disasters, casualties, 547, 549
    Workbook, 584
  Estate, 559
  Exchange of property, 544
  Gambling, 529
  Home, sale of, 523
  Involuntary conversions, 549
  Net operating, 536
  Not recognized, 544
  Options, 544
  Partnerships, 541
  Recovery in later year, 548
  Rental, 527
  Reporting, 544, 547, 549
  S corporations, 589
  Sales and other dispositions, 544
  Small-business stock, 544
  Thefts, 547, 549
  Worthless securities, 550
Lost property, 547

Lots, sale of, 544
Low-income housing rehabilitation, 535
Lump-sum payments:
  Beneficiaries, 559
  Employees' plan, 575
  Retirement annuities, 575
  Rollovers, tax-free, 590
  Special 10-year averaging, 575
  Wages, 525

M
Maintenance of household, 501, 504
Malpractice insurance, 529
Management of property, 550
Manufacturing:
  Excise taxes, 510
  Inventories, 538
Marital deduction, estate and gift taxes, 448
Market discount, 550
Married couple when both work, deduction, 17
Meals and lodging:
  Business travel, 463
  Medical expenses, 502, 907
  Moving expenses, 521
  Standard meal allowance, 463
  Taxability of, 525
Medical-expense reimbursement plans, 535
Medical expenses, 502, 907
  Decedent, 559
  Reimbursement, 502, 907
  Schools, special, 502
Medicare, 502, 907
Memberships, club dues, 463
Mileage allowances:
  Business car, 463
  Charitable contributions, 526

Medical expenses, 502, 907
Moving expenses, 521
Standard rate, 463
Mines, 535
Minimum tax, 542
Miscellaneous deductions, 529
Model custodial account, 590
Model trust, 590
Money-market certificates, 545
Mortgaged property, sale of, 544
Mortgages:
Interest expense, 545
Property exchanged, effect on, 544
Motor fuels excise tax, 510
Moving expenses, 521
Foreign move, 54, 521
Multiple-support declaration, 501
Municipal bonds, 550
Musical compositions, 544
Mutual funds, 550, 564

N
Net operating loss, 536
New home:
Construction, 523
Purchase, 523
New job:
Moving expenses, 521
Travel expenses, 463, 529
Noncommercial aviation fuel, excise tax, 510
Nonresident aliens, 513, 518, 519
Estates, 448, 559
Joint return, 519
Nonresident U.S. citizens, 593
Nontaxable exchanges, 544, 550
Nontaxable income, 525

Notes, payments received on, 550
Nursing services, 502, 907

O
Obsolescence, 534
Office expenses, 535
Office in home, 529, 530, 587
Oil and gas property:
Depletion, 535
Drilling and development expenses, 535
Old-age benefits, 554
Operating loss, net, 536
Options, 525, 544, 550
Employee stock, 525
Stock, 550
Original-issue discount, 550, 1212
Out-of-pocket expenses, contributions, 526
Outside salesperson, 463
Overseas, tax information for U.S. citizens, 54

P
Paid-in capital, 542
Parking fees and tolls, 463
Partners and partnerships, 541
Patents, depreciation, 534
Payments:
Beneficiaries to, 559
Employee plans, 535, 560, 590
In kind, 539
Installment, 537
Payroll taxes, 503, 539
Penalties:
100 percent, 594
Deductibility, 535
Deposits not made, 594
Early withdrawal of savings, 550

Estimated tax, 505
Filing late, 594
Nondeductibility, 545
Paying late, 594
Pensions:
Loans from employer plans,
560, 571, 575
Self-employed retirement
plans, 560
Simplified employee, 535,
590
Taxation of, 554, 575
Withholding on, 505, 539,
575
Percentage depletion, 535
Percentage method of
withholding, 539
Per-diem allowances, 463
Periodic payments, alimony,
504
Permanent and total
disability, defined, 907
Personal exemption, 501
Personal injury, damages, 525
Personal loans, interest on,
545
Personal property:
Changed to business use, 544
Depreciation, 534
Installment sales, 537
Sale of, 544
Section 1245, 544
Physical presence test for
residency, 54
Points, 530, 535, 545
Political contributions, 535
Pollution-control facilities, 535
Possessions, U.S., exclusion
for citizens employed, 570
Power of attorney, 556
Premature distributions:
IRA, 590
Keogh plan, 560
Tax-sheltered annuity, 571

Premiums, bond amortization,
535, 550
Prepaid expenses, 535, 538
Prepaid income, 538
Prepaid interest, 535, 545
Prepaid medical insurance,
502
Present value, annuity, 575
Prizes and awards, 525
Professional expenses, 529,
535
Profit-sharing plans,
distributions, 575
Prohibited transactions, 560,
590
Promissory notes, 544
Prompt assessment, request
for, 559
Property:
Abandoned, 534
Appreciation in value, 544
Assessments, 535
Basis, 551
Business, 544
Business use, partial, 463,
587
Capital assets, 544
Casualty losses, 547, 549
Charitable contributions,
526, 561
Community, 555
Condemned, 549
Depletion allowance for
mineral deposits, 535
Depreciable, 534
Estate, 448, 559
Exchanges, 544
Exchanges, investment
property, 550
Inherited, 544, 559
Installment sales, 537
Intangible, 534, 544
Investment, 550
Involuntary conversion, 549

Leased, 534, 535
Levy, exempt from, 594
Like-kind, 544, 549
Recovery property,
  percentage tables, 534
Rental, 527
Repossessed, 537
Sales and exchanges, 544
Section 1231, 544, 549
Section 1245, 544
Section 1250, 544
Settlements, 504
Taxes, 535
Thefts, 547, 549
Protective clothing, 529
Protest, written after
  examination, 556
Psychiatric care, 502, 907

R
Raffles, income from, 525
Real estate taxes, 523, 530,
  535
Real property:
  Basis, 551
  Depreciable, 534, 544
  Foreign investment in U.S.,
    519
  Installment sales, 537
  Rental, 527
  Repossessed, 537
  Sale, 544
  Subdivision, 544
  Trade or business, 544
  Valuation, estate, 448, 559
Reallocation of income and
  deductions, 535
Recapture of depreciation, 544
Recapture of investment
  credit, 572
Records and recordkeeping
  requirements:
  Car expenses, 463

Employee's and employer's
  expenses, 463
Employment taxes, 503, 539
Entertainment, 463
Gifts, business, 463
Small business, 583
Travel, 463
Recoveries:
  Bad debt, 525, 548
  Losses, 547, 549
  Taxes, 525, 535
Recovery property, 534
  Disposition of, 544
  Investment credit, 572
Reforestation expenditures,
  535
  Investment credit for, 572
Refund feature, annuities, 575
Refunds:
  Claim for, 556
  Decedents, 559
  Excise taxes, 378
  Interest, 545
  Net operating loss, 536
  State income tax, 525
Rehabilitated building
  investment, credit for, 572
Rehabilitation, low-income
  housing, 535
Reimbursements and
  allowances:
  Casualty or theft losses, 547,
    549
  Employee's expenses, 463
  Involuntary conversions, 549
  Medical expenses, 502
  Moving expenses, 521
  Outside salesperson, 463
  Travel, transportation, 463
Reinvested dividends, 550,
  564
Related taxpayers:
  Dependents, 501
  Employee's expenses, 463

Gains and losses on
  transactions, 544, 550
Religious organizations,
  contributions to, 526
Relocation payments, 521
Rental:
  Advance rent, 527, 535
  Business expenses, 535
  Home, use of, 527
  Property, 527
  Sale of property, 527, 544
  Temporary, sale of home, 523
Rents and royalties, effect of
  depletion, 535
Repayment of items
  previously reported as
  income, 525, 538
Replacement period, 523, 547,
  549
Replacements:
  Home, 523
  Involuntary conversions, 549
Reporting requirements:
  Charitable contributions, 526
  Employee benefit plans, 1048
  Withholding taxes, 539
Repossessions, 537
Research and experimentation
  expenses, 535
Research credit, 906
Reserves:
  Anticipated liabilities, 535
  Bad debts, 548
  Depreciation, 534
Residence test, bona fide, 54
Resident aliens, 518, 519
Retail and use taxes, 510
Retained earnings, 542
Retirement arrangements,
  individual, 590
Retirement income, 554
Retirement of bonds, 550
Retirement plans for self-
  employed individuals, 560

Returns:
  Corporation, 542
  Decedent, separate, 559
  Due dates, 509
  Employment, 539
  Estate, 448
  Estimated tax, 505
  Excise, 510
  Fiduciary, 559
  Gift, 448
  Individual, final, 559
  Nonresident alien, 519
  Partnership, 541
  S corporations, 589
Returns of magazines,
  paperbacks, and records,
  538
Rollovers to an IRA, 571, 575,
  590
Royalty income, 525
Rule of 78s, 538, 545

S
S corporations, 550, 589
Salaries, 525, 535
Salary-reduction agreement,
  571
Sales and exchanges:
  Basis, 551
  Business property, 544
  Depreciable property, 544
  Holding period, 544
  Home, 523
    Age 65 or older, 523, 554
  How to report, 544
  Installment, 537
  Investment property, 550
  Mutual funds, 564
  Nonresident aliens, 518, 519
  Nontaxable exchanges, 544
  Partnership interests, 541
  Patents and copyrights, 544
  Rental property, 527
  Reporting, 544

Sales tax, 535
Salespersons, outside, 463
Salvage value, 534
Savings account interest, 550
Savings bonds, U.S., 550, 559
Scrip dividends, 550
Section 179 deduction, 534
Section 911 exclusion, 54
Section 1231 gains and losses, 544
Section 1244 stock, 544, 550
Section 1245 property, 544
Section 1250 real property, 527, 544
Securities, worthless, 548
Self-employed retirement plans, 535, 560, 590
Self-employment income and tax, 533
Selling expenses:
  Business, 535
  Home, sale of, 523
Separated spouses, 504
  Community property states, 555
Separate maintenance decree, 504
Separation agreement, alimony, 504
Series E, EE, H, and HH bonds, 550
Service charges, 545
Settlement costs, 530
Severance damages, 549
Severance pay, 525
Shared appreciation mortgage, 545
Shareholder, S corporation, 550, 589
Short sale of stock, 544, 550
Short tax year, 538
  ACRS, 534
Short-term gains and losses, 544

Sick pay, tax withholding on, 505, 539
Simplified employee pensions:
  Treatment by employee, 590
  Treatment by employer, 535
Small business, 334, 589
Small business investment company stock, 544, 550
Small business, recordkeeping for, 583
Small business stock, 544
Social Security:
  Benefits, 525, 915
  Household workers, 503, 907
  Taxable benefits, 525, 915
  Withholding requirements, 503, 539
Solar energy grants, 525
Sole proprietorships, sale of, 544
Spouse:
  Child and dependent care credit, 503
  Exemption for, 501, 504
  Expenses for, 463
  IRA for a nonworking, 590
  Medical expenses of, 502
  Surviving, 559
Start-up costs, amortization, 535
State bonds, interest, 550
State income tax refunds, 525
State or local income taxes, 535
Stock:
  Basis, 550, 551
  Charitable donation of, 561
  Distribution of, 542
  Dividends, 550
  Employee options, 525
  Exchange of, 544, 550
  Identifying, 544
  Investment income and expense, 550

Mutual funds, 564
Options, 550
Redemptions, 542
Sale of, 544, 550
Short sales, 544, 550
Small business, 544, 550, 589
Splits, 544, 550
Wash sales, 544, 550
Worthless, 544, 550
Stockholders:
  Contribution by, 542
  Distributions of property, 542
  Investments, 550
  S corporations, 589
  Transactions with
    corporations, 542
Stolen or embezzled property,
  547, 549
Storm damage, 547, 549
Straddles, 550
Straight-line depreciation, 534
Strike and lockout benefits,
  525
Students:
  Charitable contribution for
    expenses, 526
  Exemptions, dependency, 501
  Expenses, 508
  Scholarships, 518, 520
Subscriptions to professional
  journals, deductibility, 529
Substantiation:
  Appraisals:
    Donated property, 561
    Home, 523
    Investment property, 550
  Casualty or theft losses, 547,
    549
  Entertainment expenses, 463
  Gift expenses, 463
  Travel, transportation, 463
Supplemental unemployment
  benefits, 525, 905
Supplies and materials, 535

Support, decree of, 504
Support of dependents, 501,
  504
Surviving spouse, 559
Survivor annuities, 559, 575

T
Tangible property,
  depreciation of, 534
Tax benefits for older
  Americans, 554
Tax calendars, 509
Tax counsel fees, 504, 529
Tax court, 556
Tax credit for the elderly and
  the disabled, 524, 554
Tax-exempt interest, 550
Tax-free exchanges, 544
Tax penalties, estimated tax,
  505
Tax preference items, 542, 909
Tax-sheltered annuities, 571
Tax shelters, 536, 550
Tax treaties, 54, 518
Tax year, 538
Taxable estate, 448
Taxable gift, 448
Taxable income, defined, 525
Taxable income, estate, 559
Taxes:
  Business, 583
  Deductibility, 530, 535
  Employment, 503, 539
  Estimated, 505
  Excise, 510
  Foreign, 514
  Income averaging to
    compute, 506
  Investments, 550
  S corporations, 589
  Transactions with
    corporations, 542
Teachers, education expenses,
  508

Temporary assignment, 463
Ten-year averaging rules, 575
Termination, estate, 559
Termite damage, 547
Theft losses, 547, 549
Threat of condemnation, 549
Three-year rule, annuities, 575
Timber, coal, and iron ore:
  Depletion, 535
  Sale of, 544
Tips, 531, 539, 1244
  Income, 525
  Report of, for employees, 1244
  Reporting rules for employers, 531, 539
  Tax withholding, 505, 539
Tools, 529, 535
Trademarks and trade names, 534, 535, 544
Trades, nontaxable, 550
Trading stamps, 538
Transfer, moving expenses, 521
Transient workers, 463
Transportation and travel expenses:
  Business, 463
  Educational, 508
  Employee, 463
  Medical, 502, 907
  Moving, 521
Transportation by air, excise tax, 510
Treasury bills, bonds, and notes, interest, 550, 559
Treasury stock, sale of, 550
Treaties, tax, 54, 518
Tuition reduction, 520

U
Unadjusted basis, depreciation, 534

Undistributed capital gains, 564
Unemployed spouse, IRA for, 590
Unemployment compensation, 525, 905
Unemployment tax (FUTA), 539
Uniforms, 529
Union:
  Assessments, 529
  Benefits, 525
  Dues, 529
Unpaid expenses, 535
Unpaid salary, 535
Unrealized receivables, partnership, 541
Unstated interest, 537, 545
U.S. Claims Court, 556
U.S. Court of Appeals for the Federal Circuit, 556
U.S. District Court, 556
U.S. Tax Court, 556
Use tax, highway, 349
Useful life, depreciation, 527, 534
Usurious interest, 550
Utilities, 535

V
Vacation allowances, 525, 535
Vacation homes, 527
Vacation pay, accrual, 535
Valuation:
  Casualty or theft losses, 547
  Charitable contributions, 526, 561
  Condemnation, 549
  Estate, 448, 559
  Gifts, 448
  Inventories, 538
Value, fair-market, defined, 544
Vandalism loss, 547

Vehicles, use tax, 349
Veterans' benefits, 525
VISTA, 525

W
Wage bracket method of
  withholding, 539
Wages, 525, 535
Windfall profit tax, 510
Withholding:
  Backup, 505, 539
  Employer information,
    reporting requirements, 539
  Exemption from, 505, 539
  Form W-3, 539
Forms W-2, W-2c, W-2G, W-
    2P, W-4, W-4P, W-4S, or W-
    5, 505, 539
  Gambling winnings, 505, 539
  Methods, 539
  Nonresident aliens, 518, 519
  Pensions and annuities, 505,
    539, 575
  Salaries, 505
  Sick pay, 505, 539
  Tips, 505, 531, 539
  Wages, 505, 539
Work clothes, 529
Worker's compensation
  insurance, 525
Worthless debts, 548

INDEX

Accelerated Cost Recovery System (ACRS), 78
Accelerated method of depreciation, 73
Accelerating deductions, 165–166
Accounting methods (*See also* Accrual accounting; Cash accounting): FIFO, 68–70, 72; and IRS, 64–65; LIFO, 68, 70–72; mixture of, 63; switching, 64–65; and taxes, 64; variation of, 63
Accrual accounting: accelerating deductions in, 165; deferring income in, 164; disadvantages of, 60–61; financial statements in, 60–61; income in, 60; and IRS, 61–62; and taxes, 64
Advance payments, 61–62
Advertising materials, 124
Airplanes, company, 139
Alternative minimum tax (AMT), 23–24, 46
Application to Change an Accounting Method, 72
Application to Use LIFO Inventory Method, 72
Assets: in corporation, 44, 48; intangible, depreciation of, 76–78; in partnerships, 31; in proprietorship, 15–16, 21; in S corporation, 53–54
Athletic facilities, 133–134
At-risk rules, 18–19, 31–32, 43

Auditing: appealing, 183; and criminal wrongdoing, 182; dates for, 180; fear of, 176; handling of, 181–182; letters for, 179–180; odds for, 11; and organizational form, 5, 11; preparing for, 180–181; selections for, 177–178; support people for, 181; targets of, 177; tax planning for, 183; time span for, 176; victory in, 183
Automobiles (*See* Cars)
Awards, 125

Bank accounts, 15, 172
Bankruptcy, 39
Benefits (*See* Fringe benefits)
Bookkeeping, 27
Business gifts: advertising materials, 124; awards, 125; deductions for, 123–124; to employees, 123; grants, 125–126; point-of-purchase sales aids, 124–125; prizes, 125; qualified-plan award, 125; scholarships, 125–126; tax planning for, 126–127
Business meals, 114–116
Business-pleasure trips, 117–119

Cafeteria benefit plans, 148–149
Capital (*See also* Investment): in corporation, 38–39; and organization form, 9; in

(Capital *cont.*)
partnerships, 26–27; in proprietorship, 13; in
S corporation, 50–51
Cars (*See also* Travel and
entertainment): actual costs
of, 99–101; and commuting,
104; company, 99; deduc-
tions for, 100; demonstrator,
141–142; depreciation of,
101, 104; fair market value
of, 102–103; flat amount
costs of, 99–101; and IRS,
104–105; lease value of,
102–103; mileage logs for,
105–106; and parking fees,
100; personal usage of, 101–
102; reimbursed expenses
for, 104; and 70-30 rule,
105; standard milage costs
of, 99–101; tax planning for,
105–106; and tolls, 100
Cash accounting: accelerating
deductions in, 165; advantages of, 59; businesses
using, 58–59; disadvantages
of, 59–60; expense write-offs
in, 59–60; income in, 58–59;
and taxes, 64
Catering, 142
C corporation, 37
Child care centers, 97, 132–
133
Child-labor laws, 153
Clothing, 147–148
Cohan rule, 107
Common stock, 38–39
Commuting, 104
Constructive-receipt rules, 60
Convention, 76, 86
Corporation: advantages of,
47–48; assets in, 44, 48; at-
risk rules in, 43; C, 37; capi-
tal in, 38–39; complexity of,
39; control of, 39–40; con-

version of, to S corporation,
52–53; costs of, 40; dividends in, 7; estimated taxes
for, 167; fiscal year in, 47;
flexibility of, 40–41; income
from converting to, 48;
insurance in, 135–136;
insurance write-offs in, 44;
under law, 35; liabilities in,
7, 41–43; life of, 43; losses
on, 43; number of, 8; ownership in, 43–44; perks in, 44;
personal-service, 37–38; privacy in, 44; regular, 37;
salaries in, 7, 41, 45; sales
from, 8; selling, 20; Social
Security tax in, 46; state
laws on, 47; stock in, 38–39;
surtax for, 47; taxes in, 36–
38, 44–47; various proce-
dures for forming, 7
Costs (*See* specific types of)
Country club dues, 116–117
Criminal wrongdoing, 182
Cruise ships, 119

Day care centers, 97, 132–133
Death benefits: dependent-care
plans, 132–133; life insurance, 130–131; survivor
benefits, 130
Debts, bad, 62–63
Defensive driving courses, 139
Deferring income, 164–165
De minimis fringe benefits,
139–141
Demonstrator automobiles,
141–142
Dependent care plans, 132–
133
Depreciation: accelerated
method of, 73–75; of cars,
101, 104; definition of, 73; of
equipment, 65, 73, 79; of
home office property, 95; of

intangible assets, 76–78; items qualifying for, 73; of real estate, 85–87; recovery periods of, 78–79; reforms in, 4; straight-line method of, 73–74; tables for, 80–82; and taxes, 75, 75, 79

Dining facilities, 142

Disability insurance, 134–135

Discounts, employee, 143–145

Dividends, 7, 44 (*See also* Income)

Dues, club, 116–117

Economic Recovery Tax Act (ERTA) of 1981, 78, 87, 156–157

Education programs, 142–143

Employee discounts, 143–145

Employee Stock Ownership Plans (ESOPs), 161–162

Entertainment (*See* Travel and entertainment)

Entertainment log, 108–110

Entrepreneurship (*See* Proprietorship)

Equipment: depreciation of, 65, 73, 79

Estimated taxes, 166–167

Exercise classes, 135

Expanding costs, 65

Expense allowance, 79

Expenses, 59–60 (*See also* specific types of)

Family employees, 153–154

Family partnerships, 32

FIFO (First In First Out): description of, 68; and higher prices, 71; switch from, 72; and taxes, 72; use of, 69–70

Financial statements, 21, 60–61, 172–173

First In First Out (*See* FIFO)

Fiscal year: in corporation, 47; and organizational form, 10–11; in partnership, 34; in proprietorship, 24–25; in S corporations, 57; and Tax Reform Act of 1986, 34

Food (*See* Meals)

Form 401(k) plan, 162

Form 970, 72

Form 1040-ES, 167

Form 2210, 167

Form 2220, 167

Form 2553, 52–53

Form 3115, 64, 72

Form 4562, 75

Frequent-flier bonuses, 145

Fringe benefits: airplanes, company, 139; death benefits, 130–133; defensive driving courses, 139; *de minimis*, 139–141; demonstrator cars, 141–142; dining facilities, 142; disability insurance, 134–135; discrimination in, 130; education programs, 142–143; employee discounts, 143–145; exercise classes, 135; frequent-flier bonuses, 145; health plans, 133–134; and IRS, 129; *maximus*, 140; medical insurance, 135–138; mental health insurance, 135; no-additional-cost services, 145–146; parking, 146; retirement plans, 139; stop-smoking programs, 138; stress-management programs, 138; tax planning for, 150–151; vacation homes, 146–147; weight-loss programs, 138; working-condition fringe benefits, 147–150

General partnerships, 6, 30
(*See also* Partnership)
Gifts (*See* Business gifts)
Grants, 125–126
Gross profit percentage, 143
Guaranteed payments, 29–30

Health plans: athletic facilities, 133–134; disability
insurance, 134–135; exercise
classes, 135; medical insurance, 135–137; medical-
reimbursement plans, 137–
138; mental health services,
135; stop-smoking programs,
138; stress-management programs, 138; weight-loss
programs, 138
Hobbies, 16–19
Hobby-loss rules, 17
Home office: and day care centers, 97; deductions for, 95–
96; depreciation of property
of, 95; and IRS, 90–91; leasing, 94; as meeting place for
clients, 94; as principle
place of business, 91–94; in
rental house, 96; requirements for, 91; as separate
building, 94–95; and taxes,
93
HR-10 plans (*See* Keogh plans)

Income (*See also* Unreported
income): in accrual accounting, 60; advance, 62; in cash
accounting, 58–59; and constructive-receipt rules, 60;
from conversion to corporation, 48; deferring, 164–165;
rental, 85–86; splitting,
152–154
Incorporation (*See also* Corporation; S corporation):

benefits of, 46–47; costs of,
15, 40, 46; and privacy, 21
Installment sales, 65–67
Insurance: in corporation, 44;
disability, 134; life, 130–
131; medical, 135–138; in
partnership, 32–33; in proprietorship, 20
Interest, 85, 96, 167
Internal Revenue Code, 17–19
Internal Revenue Service (*See*
IRS)
Inventory (*See also* FIFO;
LIFO): definition of, 68–69;
selecting method of, 68–70;
switching methods of, 72
Investment, 18–19, 84–85 (*See
also* Capital):
Investment seminars, 120
IRAs (Individual Retirement
Accounts), 152, 158
IRS (Internal Revenue Service) (*See also* Auditing):
and accrual accounting, 61–
62; and car deductions, 104–
105; and depreciation items,
73; and employee discounts,
144; fear of, 1, 176; and
financial statements, 172–
173; and fringe benefits,
129; and home-cooked
meals, 116; and home office,
90–91; and insurance, 135–
136; and inventory, 68–69;
jargon of, 2; and life insurance, 131; and losses, 16–19;
notices sent out by, 179;
operation of, 176; overpay-
ment to, 167; and
partnership, 6; power of,
170–172; and proprietor-
ship, 5; and rehabilitation
credit, 87–88; seriousness of,
173–174; and start-up costs,

65; and survivor benefits, 130; targets of, 177; and travel and entertainment, 107–108; underpayment to, 167; and unreported income, 169

Keogh plans: borrowing policies of, 160; deadline for setting up, 159; defined-benefit plans, 158–159; defined-contribution plans, 158–159; employee coverage in, 160; and IRAs, 158; more than allowable amounts to, 161; options of, 159–160; origin of, 158; in proprietorship, 20–21; as self-funded strategy, 157; taxes on, 159, 161

Last In First Out (*See* LIFO)
Laventhol & Horwath, 2–3
Leasing, home office, 94
Liabilities: in corporation, 7, 41–43; and organizational form, 9; in partnership, 6, 30; in proprietorship, 5, 15; in S corporation, 8, 53
Life insurance, 130–131
LIFO (Last In First Out): description of, 68; and higher prices, 71–72; switch from, 72; use of, 70–71
Limited partnerships, 6, 30, 34 (*See also* Partnership)
Loans, 62–63
Loss carryback, 16, 31
Loss carryforward, 16, 31
Losses: beyond control, 18; in corporation, 43; in hobbies, 16–19; and IRS, 16–19; and organizational form, 10; in partnerships, 31–32; in proprietorship, 16–19; rebounds

from, 19; in S corporation, 54

Malpractice, 41
Maximus fringe benefits, 140
Meals: business, 114–116; cafeteria, 148–149; in dining facility, 142; home-cooked, 116
Medical insurance, 135–138
Medical-reimbursement plans, 137–138
Mental health services, 135
Merchandise (*See* Inventory)
Midmonth convention, 86
Midquarter convention, 76
Midyear convention, 76
Mileage logs, 106
Modified Accelerated Cost Recovery System (MACRS), 73
Mortgage payments, 84–85, 96

No-additional-cost services, 145–146

Office (*See* Home office)
Office of the Regional Director of Appeals, 183
150-percent-declining-balance method, 74
One-line-of-business rule, 143–144
Oral log, 109
Organizations, business: and auditing by IRS, 11; corporations, 7–8; mixture of, 8; partnerships, 6–7; proprietorships, 5–6; S corporations, 8; selecting, 8–11
Ownership (*See also* Organizations): in corporation, 43–44; in partnerships, 32; in pro-

(Ownership *cont.*)
prietorship, 19–20; in
S corporation, 55

Parking fees, 100, 146
Partnership: advantages of,
34; agreement of, written,
28; assets in, 31; at-risk
rules in, 31–32; bookkeeping in, 27; capital in, 26–27;
complexity of, 27–28; control in, 28; cost of, 29;
definition of, 6; estimated
taxes for, 167; failure of, 7;
family, 32; fiscal year in, 34;
flexibility of, 29–30; general, 6; guaranteed pay-
ments in, 29–30; industries
formed in, 27; insurance in,
32–33, 135; and IRS, 6; liabilities in, 6, 30; life of, 30–
31; limited, 6; losses in, 31–
32; number of, 7; ownership
in, 32; perks in, 32–33; privacy in, 33; sales from, 7;
and Schedule K-1, 27–28;
selling, 20, 29; shelter in,
33; Social Security tax in,
33; taxes in, 26, 33
Party, 115
Payments (*See* specific types
of)
Pension plans, 156, 161 (*See
also* Retirement plans)
Perks: airplanes, company,
139; in corporation, 44;
defensive driving courses,
139; *de minimis* fringe benefits, 139–141; discrimination
in, 130; and organizational
form, 10; in partnership,
32–33; in proprietorship,
20–21; in S corporation, 55

Personal-service corporations,
37–38
Personal tax returns, 43, 55–
56
Planes, company, 139
Point-of-purchase sales aids,
124–125
Preferred stock, 38–39
Prizes, 125
Profit-sharing plans, 21, 162
Property (*See* Real estate)
Proprietorship: advantages of,
25; assets in, 15–16, 21;
bank accounts in, 15; capital in, 13; complexity of, 13–
14; control in, 14; cost of,
14–15; estimated taxes for,
167; expense allowance in,
79; failure of, 6; financial
statements in, 21; fiscal
year in, 24–25; flexibility of,
15; insurance in, 20, 135;
and IRS, 5; liabilities in, 5–
6, 15; life of, 15–16; losses
in, 16–18; number of, 6;
ownership in, 19–20; perks
in, 20–21; privacy in, 21;
profit-sharing plans in, 21;
profits in, 16–19; retirement
plans in, 20–21; sales from,
6; selling, 19–20; shelter in,
21; Social Security tax in,
33; spouses in, 20; taxes in,
22–24
Publications, 143

Qualified-plan award, 125

Real estate: deductions for,
84–85, 87; depreciation of,
85–87; for entertainment,
117; investment in, 84–85;
rehabilitation credit on, 87–
88; as reward, 125; taxes on,
85; for vacation, 146–147

Recapture rules, 79
Regular corporation, 37
Rehabilitation credit, 87–88
Rental residences, 117
Retirement plans: deductions
for, 139; ESOPs, 161–162;
Four 401(k) plan, 162;
Keogh plans, 157–161; mon-
ey-purchase plan, 158–159;
paired plan, 159; in past,
156; in present, 157; in pro-
prietorship, 20–21; SEPs,
161; shift in, 156–157
Revenue Act of 1987, 65

Salaries, 7, 41, 45, 162 (*See
also* Income):
Schedule K-1, 27–28
Scholarships, 125–126
S corporation: advantages of,
57; assets in, 53–54; built-in
capital gains from converting to, 51–52; capital in,
50–51; complexity of, 51–52;
control in, 52; conversion to,
from corporation, 52–53;
cost of, 52–53; fiscal year in,
57; flexibility of, 53; under
law, 50; liabilities in, 8, 53;
life of, 53–54; losses in, 54–
55; number of, 8; ownership
in, 55; perks in, 55; privacy
in, 55; restrictions on, 51,
55; sales from, 8; selling, 20;
shelter in, 55; Social Security tax in, 56; state
recognition of, 56; stock in,
50–51; taxes in, 50, 55–57
Section 183, 17–19
Seminars, investment, 120
70-30 rule, 105
Shelter, tax (*See also* Real
estate): cautions on, 165–
166; in corporation, 44; and

organizational form, 10; in
partnership, 33; in propri-
etorship, 21; in S corpora-
tion, 55
Simplified Employee Pension
Plans (SEPs), 161
Small business (*See* S corpora-
tion)
Social club dues, 116–117
Social Security number, 149
Social Security tax: in corpo-
ration, 46; number for, 149;
in partnership, 33; in pro-
prietorship, 33; in S
corporation, 56
Splitting income, 152–154
Spouses, 120–121, 152–154
Start-up costs, 65
Stock, 38–39, 50–51
Stop-smoking programs, 138
Straight-line method of depre-
ciation: for cars, 104;
creation of, 73; for home
office property, 95; for real
estate, 86–87
Stress-management programs,
138
Subchapter S (*See* S corpora-
tion)
Subchapter S Revision Act of
1982, 50, 54
Subscriptions, 143
Surtax, 47
Survivor benefits, 130

Taxes (*See also* Social Security
tax; Tax planning): and
accrual accounting, 64; and
advanced income, 61–62;
AMT, 23–24, 46; at-risk
rules, 18–19, 31–32, 43; bad
debts, 62–63; bounced
checks, 60; and cash
accounting, 64; constructive-

(Taxes *cont.*)

receipt rules, 60; in corporation, 36–38, 44–47; day care
centers, 97; deferring payment of last year's, 168; and
depreciation, 75, 79; difficulty in understanding, 2;
estimated, 166–167; evad-
ing, 170; expanding costs,
65; expense allowance, 79;
fear of paying, 1; and FIFO,
72; and home office, 93; on
income from converting to
corporation, 48; incorporation costs, 40, 46;
installment sales, 65–67;
insurances, 20–21; on
Keogh plans, 159, 161;
learning about, 4; and
LIFO, 72; midquarter con-
vention, 76; and
organizational form, 10; in
partnership, 26, 33; personal returns, 43, 55–56;
personal-service corporation,
37–38; planning for paying,
1–2; in proprietorship, 22–
24; on real estate, 85; recapture rules, 79;
S corporation, 50, 55–57; and
S corporation, conversion to,
52; spouses in proprietorships, 20; start-up costs, 65;
surtax, 47; TMT, 24; withholding, 149–150
Tax-free discounts, 144–145
Tax planning: accrual
accounting, 60–63; for auditing, 183; for business gifts,
126–127; for cars, 105–106;
cash accounting, 58–60; and
changes in tax system, 4;
for corporation, 7–8; for
fringe benefits, 150–151;

goal of, 58; by Laventhol &
Horwath, 2–3; and organizational form of business, 5,
8–11; for partnership, 6–7;
for proprietorship, 5–6; reasons for, 1–2, 4; for
S corporation, 8; for splitting income, 153–154; year-
end, 164–168
Tax Reform Act of 1984, 129,
141, 148
Tax Reform Act of 1986, 34,
65, 73
T & E (*See* Travel and entertainment)
Tentative minimum tax
(TMT), 24
Tickets, sporting and theatrical, 114
Tolls, 100
Travel and entertainment
(T & E): abroad trips, 119–
120; associated, 112–114;
business meals, 114–116;
business-pleasure trips,
117–119; country club dues,
116–117; cruise ships, 119;
deductions for, 107, 112–
114; directly related, 112;
extravagant, 111–112; goodwill, 114; home-cooked
meals, 115–116; hotel costs
versus meal costs, 117;
investment seminars, 119–
120; and IRS, 107–108; logs
for, 108–110; lunch alone,
115; oral log of, 109; party,
115; in past, 107; penalty
for falsely deducting, 107–
108; in present, 107; property for entertainment, 117;
receipts for, 108; reciprocal
rules, 115; rental resi-
dences, 117; social club

dues, 116–117; spouse's
accompaniment, 120–121;
substantiation of, 107, 109–
110; tickets, sporting and
theatrical, 114
200-percent-declining-balance
method, 74

Underpayment of Estimated
Tax by Corporations, 167
Unreported income: and bank
accounts, 172; informants
of, 171–172; and IRS, 169–
171; penalty for, 170; and

recordkeeping, 171; temptation of, 170

Vacation homes, 146–147
Vesting, 161 (*See also* Retirement plans)

Weight-loss programs, 138
Withheld income taxes as
fringe benefit, 149–150
Working-condition benefits:
cafeteria benefits, 148–149;
clothing, 147–148; withheld
income taxes, 149–150

Comprehensive information to save time and money!

LAVENTHOL & HORWATH

SMALL BUSINESS TAX PREPARATION BOOK

THE TAX PREPARATION BOOK
NO SMALL BUSINESS
CAN AFFORD TO BE WITHOUT

**From One Of America's Leading Accounting Firms
For Small And Medium-sized Businesses**

LH Laventhol & Horwath
Certified Public Accountants

**AVAILABLE FROM AVON BOOKS—
ORDER YOUR COPY NOW!**
75617-X/$14.95 US/$18.95 Can